Raymond Williams at 100

Raymond Williams at 100

Edited by Paul Stasi

ROWMAN & LITTLEFIELD
Lanham • Boulder • New York • London

Published by Rowman & Littlefield
An imprint of The Rowman & Littlefield Publishing Group, Inc.
4501 Forbes Boulevard, Suite 200, Lanham, Maryland 20706
https://rowman.com

6 Tinworth Street, London SE11 5AL, United Kingdom

British Library Cataloguing in Publication Information Available

Library of Congress Cataloging-in-Publication Data

Names: Stasi, Paul, 1972- editor.
Title: Raymond Williams at 100 / edited by Paul Stasi.
Description: Lanham : Rowman & Littlefield, [2021] | Includes
    bibliographical references and index.
Identifiers: LCCN 2020056599 (print) | LCCN 2020056600 (ebook) | ISBN
    9781538145074 (cloth) | ISBN 9781538154311 (pbk) | ISBN 9781538145081 (epub)
Subjects: LCSH: Williams, Raymond--Criticism and interpretation.
Classification: LCC PR6073.I4329 Z867 2021 (print) | LCC PR6073.I4329
    (ebook) | DDC 828/.91409--dc23
LC record available at https://lccn.loc.gov/2020056599
LC ebook record available at https://lccn.loc.gov/2020056600

Contents

List of Figures

Acknowledgments

I would like to thank the authors for their fine contributions and patience with my occasionally heavy hand as an editor; Sarah Brouillette, for her assistance in thinking about the project; Daniel Hartley, for his help with the initial proposal; Jennifer Greiman and Omaar Hena for inviting me to talk about Williams at Wake Forest; Tim Butters for sharing his photos of *Secret Abergavenny* and Janet Herrod of the Abergavenny Museum for the photo used on the cover; and Bret Benjamin, for his always-astute readings of my contributions as well as his correct, if predictable, suggestion that they include more Marx. Many thanks too to Gurdeep Mattu, Dhara Snowden, Scarlet Furness, Chris Fischer, and all those at Rowman & Littlefield who helped see the volume through to press.

Abbreviations of Works by Raymond Williams

"BSS"	"Base and Superstructure in Marxist Cultural Theory"
BC	*Border Country*
C	*Communications*
CC	*The Country and the City*
CM	*Culture and Materialism: Selected Essays*
CS	*Culture and Society: 1780–1950*
D	*Drama from Ibsen to Brecht*
EN	*The English Novel from Dickens to Lawrence*
"FM"	"The Future of Marxism"
"IC"	"The Idea of Culture"
K	*Keywords: A Vocabulary of Culture and Society*
"LR"	"A Lecture on Realism"
LR	*The Long Revolution*
ML	*Marxism and Literature*
MT	*Modern Tragedy*
PL	*Politics and Letters: Interviews with "New Left Review"*
PM	*Politics of Modernism: Against the New Conformists*
PF	*Preface to Film*
PMC	*Problems in Materialism and Culture*

"RCN"	"Realism in the Contemporary Novel"
RWT	*Raymond Williams on Television: Selected Writings*
RH	*Resources of Hope: Culture, Democracy, Socialism*
SC	*The Sociology of Culture*
TV	*Television: Technology and Cultural Form*
TI	*Tenses of the Imagination*
T	*Towards 2000*
W	*What I Came to Say*
WS	*Writing in Society*

Introduction

The Meaning of Solidarity:
Raymond Williams at 100

Paul Stasi

The November/December 2018 issue of the *New Left Review* featured a little-known text by Raymond Williams titled "The Future of Marxism." Ostensibly a review of George Lichtheim's *Marxism: An Historical and Critical Study*, which argued that Marxism had, more or less, failed, its ideas hardened into dogmas that revealed their "transcendental and unrealizable, nature," "The Future of Marxism" contains some of Williams's most familiar themes (qtd. in "FM" 54). But despite his characteristic defense of the "human" dimension "in which, because of living pressures, men try to understand their world and improve it," as against the fixed points of robotic dogma, Williams takes issue with Lichtheim's thesis and, in doing so, engages more directly than in much of his more famous work with a world economic system and the pressures that empire asserts on the United Kingdom. How is it possible to argue that Marxism has failed, Williams asks, when "Marxism-Leninism is now the official doctrine of about a third of the world" ("FM" 55)? Williams goes on to reject two related claims. The first reads communism and fascism as equal systems of terror; the second argues that the Soviet Union and the United States "are growing visibly more alike" ("FM" 57). "It seems to me to be a very common error, in judging societies" Williams says, with respect to both of these arguments, "to abstract one element which they share, and then go on to assume that as whole societies they are identical" ("FM" 56). "Much more important" than surface similarities "is that the kind of society each elite is aiming at is quite different" ("FM" 57). "If you want to make a true judgment of the society," Williams concludes, "you have to look at all the forces active in it" ("FM" 56). Among these "active forces" is an international dimension—in this case the Cold War—that Williams's other work often seemed to ignore:

> The shape of Western society is itself being primarily determined by this international struggle, to which the open welfare state seems merely a marginal accompaniment. Indeed, the continuation in Britain of this sense of an easy, improving society seems to me to depend on ignoring the fact of international military struggle, which is changing us deeply from inside, and also on ignoring the facts about the changing nature of the world economy, which will hardly leave us to go comfortably on as we are. ("FM" 64)[1]

If Williams makes clear his retention of "national and political loyalties"—to lose them, he confesses, "would be to lose everything"—he nevertheless understands that these only exist in conjunction with larger world historical forces ("FM" 64). Any true reckoning with British society will need to engage with its place in a world economic system that is never, simply, outside, but is, in fact, altering the very fabric of the nation itself.

This Williams is a very different figure from the one who appears in Joseph North's 2017 text *Literary Criticism: A Concise Political History*, for here Williams is seen to inaugurate a turn away from an engaged form of literary criticism to a quietist practice of cultural analysis, one that has renounced its desire to impact the culture at large. As Francis Mulhern notes, this is a "familiar presence here made strange."[2] North's main argument is easily summarized: Criticism, understood as a "programmatic commitment to using works of literature for the cultivation of aesthetic sensibility, with the goal of more general cultural and political change," has been overtaken by scholarship, which has "tended to treat literary texts chiefly as opportunities for cultural and historical analysis."[3] Echoing Marx's famous aphorism, North declares that "literary scholars on the left have tried merely to interpret the world," whereas the point had once been to change it.[4] To that end, North wishes to re-center criticism on a more materialist footing and, in doing so, reverse the historical/contextual turn he lays squarely at Williams's feet. It is worth looking at this argument a bit more closely, as well as at the debate it occasioned in the pages of the *New Left Review*, for doing so will help clarify some central aspects of Williams's career, including the importance of the category of experience and the precise critique of the aesthetic he launched. Far from the neutral analyst of culture for its own sake, Williams is, quite obviously, practicing precisely the kind of materialist aesthetics for which North seems to long. By replicating the blind spots of the early Williams, North ends up drastically misreading his later work.

North's story is told through three historical moments. In the first, I. A. Richards, a figure North believes we have consistently misread, developed an "incipiently materialist account of the aesthetic" alongside the tools of close reading and practical criticism.[5] Within North's text, this materialism remains perpetually incipient. Never defined directly, it seems to consist simply of refusing to see the aesthetic as a "self-sufficient category insulated from the rest of life."[6] More often it is described as the cultivation of taste, the "attempt to enrich the culture directly by cultivating new ranges of sensibility, new modes of subjectivity, new capacities for experience—using works of literature as a means."[7] The next period is dominated by F. R. Leavis, who redirects the tools of criticism "so that their emphasis lay not on cultivating the aesthetic capabilities of readers, but on the cultivation of aesthetic judgment."[8] Aesthetics are here returned to their more familiar idealist ground.[9] What interests us is the third period, whose surprising authority is Williams. Having inherited Leavis's misreading of Richards, Williams rejects the very idea of the aesthetic, when he should, instead, have been reimagining it on materialist footing. The upshot of the story is that what seems like progress is actually reaction:

> though the turn to the historicist/contextualist paradigm has generally been understood as a local victory for the left over the elitisms of mid-century criticism, this has been largely an error. In fact, it is better to say that the opposite is true: in its most salient aspects, the turn to the current paradigm in the late 1970s and early 1980s was symptomatic of the wider retreat of the left in the neoliberal period and was thus a small part of the more general victory of the right.[10]

North then positions Williams squarely at the root of a rightward turn in literary criticism that persists to this day.

There are numerous problems with this story, most of which are dealt with quite succinctly in a review by Dermot Ryan that appeared in *boundary 2*.[11] What is important for us, here, is North's curious critique of Williams, who would seem, as Mulhern notes, the *best* instance of "the radical intellectual practice North now calls for."[12] Indeed, for Williams, "there was no dissociated 'scholarship' . . . and no habit of burnishing professional activity and calling it politics."[13] Rather, Williams offers us an exemplary instance of a literary critic who refused to separate his criticism from his politics, both of which were dedicated to a lifelong effort to improve the lives of the working class. North's reply to Mulhern acknowledges as much. And it goes some way to reconciling Williams's materialism with North's own hopes for literary criticism. But in doing so, North highlights the contradictions in his own argument, contradictions that help illuminate some of the core values of Williams's work, including his emphasis on what he called the "declaration of situation" and the place of personal experience within the supposedly objective aims of practical criticism (*PL* 342).

What is perhaps most characteristic about North's work—and the place of his sharpest difference with the Williams of, say, *Marxism and Literature*—

is his over-estimation of the political efficacy of aesthetic sensibility. Indeed, his entire argument seems to rest on the notion that cultivating taste is the route to positive social change, a goal that historical/contextualizing criticism has abandoned. The obvious, if nevertheless essential, reply is to note the many atrocities committed by humans with highly developed aesthetic capacities. History provides innumerable examples from which to choose. The cordoning off of aesthetics from worldly affairs is, then, less a category error than a structural fact of bourgeois society, one that allows for precisely the disconnect between aesthetic sensibility and political action that negates North's value-laden claims for the aesthetic's real-world effects. As Karl Marx notes, "because one individual or class of individuals is forced to work more than required for the satisfaction of its need—because *surplus labour* is on one side, therefore not-labour and surplus wealth are posited on the other." By "not-labour" Marx refers, simultaneously, to surplus population—the reserve army of the poor—as well as cultural achievements. "The creation of *disposable time*," Marx concludes, "is then also creation of time for the production of science, art, etc."[14] This fact cannot simply be wished away by claiming "materialism" for the banal insight that aesthetics are tied to the world.

This point is not an idle one, for North, more or less, re-creates the argument of *Culture and Society* in a context that has radically changed. *Culture and Society*, of course, outlined the ways in which a particular discourse of culture separated itself out from a rapidly industrializing society, becoming the vantage point from which to critique that society's alienating effects. Perhaps its most damaging absence was its lack of engagement with the manifestly reactionary statements of many of its key figures. For *Culture and Society* was organized around a constitutive paradox: cordoning off the aesthetic from the political, while, simultaneously, claiming that autonomous aesthetic realm as the place from which to launch a critique of politics, a paradox exactly replicated in North's book. But the situation in which Williams wrote was quite distinct from our own. Williams was working within—but most powerfully against—a Leavisite tradition, in a context memorably described by E. P. Thompson in his critique of *The Long Revolution*: "With a compromised tradition at his back, and with a broken vocabulary in his hands, he did the only thing that was left to him: he took over the vocabulary of his opponents, followed them into the heart of their own arguments, and fought them to a standstill in their own terms."[15] North, in contrast, writing from within the heart of neoliberalism, takes aim at critical movements with whose goals he is in manifest sympathy. In doing so, his book, unwittingly, and despite many protests to the contrary, can only serve conservative ends.

But Williams did not stop there. Rather, he continued to refine and deepen the political implications of his literary criticism, and surprisingly enough it is to these later works—*The Country and the City*, in particular—to which North turns in his reply to Mulhern. Here North argues that Williams "did not in fact reject the category of the aesthetic entirely" but "in his better moments posited his critique of idealist aesthetics as a clearing operation," a position that finds ample support, for instance, in the interviews in *Politics and Letters*.[16] Indeed, North draws on Williams's comments on aesthetic autonomy from those interviews, alongside his critique of the English country house, to articulate "a new aesthetic sensibility" through which we might be "struck by the *value* of experiences, in the full sense of value, which includes the moral, the social, the political, the historical."[17] Looking at the country house, Williams invites us to also look at what surrounds it. In guiding our attention to "what your eyes are quite aware of when you're looking at it,"—a direct quotation from *The Country and the City*—Williams offers a way of seeing in which "the 'social impulses' are right there in the senses themselves."[18]

North's sensitive reading of these two passages suggests something essential to Williams's thought: the ways in which our habits of perception are always immediately also social. But in doing so, North also makes, as Lola Seaton observes, a category mistake. "Perhaps the first thing to note about the excerpt," Seaton writes, "is that it is not obviously suitable for North's purposes: we are seeking a model for *literary* criticism, yet here Williams is discussing country houses—not, for example, country-house poems."[19] As it turns out, this mistake is crucial. For in describing Williams's reading of a country house as an aesthetic, North actually illustrates precisely why Williams came to reject the notion of aesthetics as a separate sphere. Reversing the movement of *Culture and Society*, Williams here, first, suggests the ways in which all of our social perceptions are, in some measure, aesthetic, while, then, simultaneously illustrating how the aesthetic is, itself, immediately also social. And he does so through his characteristic emphasis on experience, which here becomes, in Seaton's words, a way of both "personalizing a general history" but also, and crucially, "'sociologizing' himself."[20] Aesthetics are thus returned to their basis in sense perception, but a sense perception newly understood as social rather than individual.[21] Far from simply creating "new modes of subjectivity, new capacities for experience," the cultivation of aesthetic sensibility, in Williams's hands, is guided toward quite specific social aims.

Here is the passage in question:

> It is fashionable to admire these extraordinarily numerous houses: the extended manors, the neo-classical mansions, that lie so close in rural Britain. People still pass from village to village, guidebook in hand, to see the next and yet the next example, to look at the stones and the furniture. But stand at any point and look at that land. Look at what those fields, those streams, those woods even today produce. Think it through as labour and see how long and systematic the exploitation and seizure must have been to rear that many

houses, on that scale. See by contrast what any ancient isolated farm, in un-
counted generations of labour, has managed to become, by the efforts of any
single real family, however prolonged. And then turn and look at what these
other "families", these systematic owners, have accumulated and arrogantly
declared. It isn't only that you know, looking at the land and then at the house,
how much robbery and fraud there must have been, for so long, to produce that
degree of disparity, that barbarous disproportion of scale. The working farms
and cottages are so small beside them: what men really raise, by their own
efforts or by such portion as is left to them, in the ordinary scale of human
achievement. What these "great" houses do is to break that scale, by an act of
will corresponding to their real and systematic exploitation of others. (*CC*
105–6)

Seaton's gloss on this passage is crucial:

> In a rudimentary sense Williams is enjoining his readers to compare the coun-
> try houses with the ancient farms, to look from one to the other and back
> again . . . But Williams is also exhorting us to attempt a more complex and
> ambitious comparison: to juxtapose not just different features of the landscape,
> but different ways of seeing it. Telling us to stand still and look up, Williams is
> encouraging us to weigh the vision of the landscape, ascribed in our guide-
> books—which we might think of as society's "official" way of seeing—with
> our own experience of the landscape, with what we actually see before our
> eyes.[22]

The two ways of seeing, here—what Seaton refers to as the difference between "society's 'official'" view and what we can observe with our own
eyes—might also plausibly be called the aesthetic and the historical/contex-
tual. In one view, the country house is simply beautiful, a monument shorn of
context, both of its own making and of its particular location. And what this
aesthetic view does is "break that scale," creating habits of perception that
prevent us from seeing these origins. In this way, the country house establishes its acontextual beauty as *the* standard by which to judge everything
around it by conditioning our very habits of seeing. Ahistorical aesthetics,
then, are exactly part of an alienated and reified society, one which has
enshrined its particular idea of beauty as *the* idea of beauty. This is why
Williams makes it clear, in *Politics and Letters*, that "most of them are not
beautiful" (*PL* 348). It is not just that this particular notion of beauty obscures its origins; rather, this obfuscation also negates, for Williams, their
beauty itself.

This second view, then, is what I am calling the historical/contextual, but
the first thing to notice about it is that it rests, essentially, on the techniques
of close reading. Look at what's in front of you, Williams enjoins time and
again, and keep looking. Observe what is around you and connect the things
you observe, one to the other. Then build up from these observations until

something like the full social weight of what you are seeing emerges.[23] Williams here offers a textbook example of the two aspects of culture he famously defined in "Culture Is Ordinary": "the known meanings and directions, which its members are trained to; the new observations and meanings, which are offered and tested" (*RH* 4). "The making of a mind" is a two step-process: "first, the slow learning of shapes, purposes and meanings" from the culture at large and, "second, but equal in importance, is the testing of these in experience"—for there is "nowhere else you can test" them (*RH* 4, 4, 13). In this way, Williams refuses to separate out culture as the "best that has been thought and said," from everyday experiences. Indeed, some of his harshest invective are reserved for "this extraordinary decision to call certain things culture and then separate them, as with a park wall, from ordinary people and ordinary work" (*RH* 5). As this quotation makes clear, this separation is one of the key elements of a class-bound society.[24] The polemical assertion is that culture belongs to everyone: it is, "in a real sense a national inheritance" (*RH* 8).

What we observe, with Williams, when we attend closely to the country house, then, is this "extraordinary decision" in action; we see the habit of mind that produces aesthetic autonomy. Two closely related points result from this. The first is that autonomy is socially produced, an argument Williams shares with Adorno. The second is the way in which autonomy is encoded in a particular version of the social order, one that rests on the separation of areas of our social life that are, in fact, constitutive of each other. Thus, in *The Long Revolution*, Williams situates aesthetic production within a broader conception of social organization. "We must see art," Williams maintains, "as an extension of our capacity for organization: a vital faculty which allows particular areas of reality to be described and communicated" (*LR* 54). "The 'creative' act, of any artist," Williams argues, is "the process of making a meaning active, by communicating an organized experience to others" (*LR* 52). And yet when society changes rapidly, the communication of common meanings becomes fraught. "It is in such a period," Williams concludes, "that we develop theories of art which while rightly stressing the individual offering neglect the reality of communication" (*LR* 52). Autonomous aesthetics—with the related emphasis on individual works and artistic genius, over and against the communication of common meanings—develop for socially grounded reasons. Linking art "with our ordinary social life," Williams offers a way of seeing that grounds this seeing in relation to the world from which it emerges.

Which returns us to experience. Terry Eagleton was perhaps the first, if not the last, to take issue with Williams's reliance on experience, a category he tied directly back to *Scrutiny* and Williams's Leavisite training. "To combat ideology," Eagleton remarked, "*Scrutiny* pointed to experience—as though that, precisely, were not ideology's homeland."[25] But Eagleton's essay is also framed as an argument about literary criticism, and so it allows us some insight into the discussion about Williams's place in the larger landscape of twentieth-century literary criticism. "If the task of criticism," Eagleton asks, "is to smooth the troubled passage between text and reader, to elaborate the text so that it may be more easily consumed, how is it to avoid interposing its own ungainly bulk between product and consumer?"[26] By essay's end, this problem turns out to be a false one. "Criticism is not," Eagleton concludes, "a passage between text and reader."[27] Rather,

> Its task is to show the text as it cannot know itself, to manifest those conditions of its making (inscribed in its very letter) about which it is necessarily silent. It is not just that the text knows some things and not others; it is rather that its very self-knowledge is the construction of a self-oblivion. To achieve such a showing, criticism must break with its ideological pre-history, situating itself outside the space of the text on the alternative terrain of scientific knowledge.[28]

Ideology versus science: we are, obviously enough, on Althusserian terrain, and so the polemic against humanism is of a piece with a faith in the ability of scientific knowledge to transcend ideology, itself perhaps the most ideological notion of all. We can also understand why Eagleton is so critical of the intrusion of the personal into Williams's argumentative style, for in revealing how Williams's "unruffled, almost Olympian impersonality" is, in fact, personal defensiveness, Eagleton is showing just how far from scientific objectivity Williams remained.[29]

In doing so, he betrays a fundamental misunderstanding of Williams's recourse to the personal. Indeed, if Williams continually referred to his own experience, he did so strategically; since, as Seaton points out, the external rules of society are "imbricated in the innermost structures of our consciousness, the process of questioning and rejecting them involves not simply an investigation into our shared culture, but an 'extended inquiry' into ourselves."[30] The engagement with a cultural artifact—a country house, say—is never an interaction between a disembodied mind and a neutral object, but rather the process of a situated subject, bringing its own historical and cultural ideas into relation with a particular object, formed out of its own particular history, a process we might say of communication. The scientifically objective critic, in other words, is like the ahistorical country house, shorn of history and context, which is to say reified and alienated. And as we have already seen, Williams refused exactly these separations. Just as a "true judgment of society" requires an engagement with "all the forces active in it," so an accurate reading of the critical situation requires a recognition of those elements actively occluded by the guidebook way of seeing. By acknowledging the subjective situation of the critic, Williams is actually able to "manifest those conditions" about which a text "is necessarily silent."

In this way, Williams presents us with a practical criticism built on the notion that works of art mediate specific historical moments in formally complicated ways. To make this point we can return to *The Country and the City*, one of whose leitmotifs concerns the "necessary and functional links between the social and moral orders" of these two types of social organization "which were so easily and conventionally contrasted" (*CC* 48). "The exploitation of man and of nature, which takes place in the country," Williams argued, "is realized and concentrated in the city" (*CC* 48). "There is no innocence," he continues, in "the idea of a 'traditional' order" for "it is a deep and persistent illusion to suppose that time confers on these familiar processes of acquisition an innocence which can be contrasted with the ruthlessness of subsequent stages of the same essential drives" (*CC* 50). At the same time, the development of the countryside is most often due to "forces within the order itself," which offer an "often brutally vigorous" story of growth (*CC* 39). Williams has, here, a fine sense of the dialectical nature of progress, a dialectic tied directly to class inequity: "Following the fortunes, through these centuries, of the dominant interests, it is a story of growth and achievement, but for the majority of men it was the substitution of one form of domination for another" (*CC* 39). "There is only one real question," Williams concludes: "Where do we stand, with whom do we identify . . . ?" (*CC* 38).

Williams is working here against two related errors. The first considers the countryside to be the place of unchanging rural traditions destroyed by the ravages of capitalist modernity. The second understands the rural world as an impediment to a progressive modernity. What each fails to see is that it was the development of forces active within the rural world which propelled it forward. Modernization did not come from elsewhere but from within the feudal order itself. Indeed, the development of an urban modernity was always entirely related to developments in the countryside, which was never the prehistory of the city but rather contemporaneous with its emergence. In both cases, then, Williams offers images of interrelation and process where we tend to project independence and stasis. That is to say, Williams replaces a reified vision of history with a living one.

Which brings us, at long last, to the country house poem and, in particular, Williams's reading of Marvell's "Upon Appleton House." "Marvell's poem," Williams argues, "is truly transitional" (*CC* 58). "The origin of the house is no longer mystified," but rather acknowledged, even as it is accompanied "by an increased willingness and ability to look at the immediate environment" (*CC* 55, 56):

> Yet the most remarkable and beautiful part of the poem (and that it is a composition of different ways of seeing, different essential directions and interests, is itself significant) is the look and walk into the fields and woods

> beyond. The magical country, yielding of itself, is now seen as a working
> landscape filled with figures . . . . All these are seen, but in a figure: the
> conscious look at a passing scene: the explicit detached view of landscape.
> (*CC* 56).

"The tension within this remarkable poem," Williams concludes, is "of a
different order from anything that preceded it" (*CC* 57).

Several things are striking about this argument. The first is that Williams
considers the poem remarkable and beautiful—aesthetic judgments he insists
upon—but what makes it so is the way it mediates a set of social contradictions. Williams's analysis is less concerned to unmask the poem—a task
Eagleton recommends and North deplores—than it is to use historical context
to illuminate the precise intervention the poem makes in its historical moment. This intervention is constitutive of the poem *as* an aesthetic object. As
with the country house itself, then, careful attention to the poem reveals the
process of its own making. And if the poem is transitional, what that teaches
us is "the critical folly of assimilating all country-house poems to a single
tradition, as if their occupants were some kind of unbroken line" (*CC* 58).
Just as the social order itself is varied, laced with contradictory forces—what
Williams will later name residual, emergent, and dominant—so is the poem
and the larger tradition to which it belongs.

But alongside this cultivation of a particular way of reading is a statement
of interest. With whom do you identify? Williams elaborates on precisely
this moment in *Politics and Letters*:

> I think there are two stages in the argument . . . . The first is that the very
> process of restoring produced literature to its conditions of production reveals
> that conventions have social roots, that they are not simply formal devices of
> writing. The second is that historical identification of a convention is not a
> mere neutral registration, which is incompatible with judging it. Indeed, so far
> as literary evaluation proper is concerned . . . the crucial evaluative function is
> the judgment of conventions themselves, from a deliberate and declared posi-
> tion of interest. . . . But what is much more important than that distinction
> [between poems better written than others] is the distinction of the convention:
> the capacity to see what the form was produced from and was producing. (*PL*
> 306)

Pressed a bit further, Williams put an even finer point on his argument: "If
you don't feel offence at this profoundly conventional mystification, in the
strictest sense, then what is the meaning of solidarity?" (*PL* 307).

Reading attentively, situating the conventions of literature within their
historical moment, allows one to understand their historical purchase. The
way of seeing Williams offers us is an aesthetic that combines historical and
social forces into the cultivation of a particular aesthetic sensibility. The very
thing North argues for is what Williams himself was doing—not as a realiza-

tion of the aesthetic argument, but as its refutation. Refusing the bourgeois separation of areas of our social life, Williams was a thinker who manifestly understood that the point of critique was not merely to interpret the world, but to try to change it.

"The relation between systems of thought," Williams argues in "The Future of Marxism," "and actual history is both complex and surprising" ("FM" 55). As I write this introduction, it is July of 2020. I have been more or less quarantined in my house for the last four months due to a virus that has killed, at latest count, some 500,000 people across the world. Forty million citizens of the United States of America are unemployed, while demonstrations rock the country and an ignorant and evil fool of colossal proportions tweets himself and some 40 percent of the electorate into an increasingly racist corner. Right-wing demagogues rule over many of the world's countries, blithely ignoring or exacerbating a climate crisis increasingly visible in our daily lives. It is a deeply uncertain and contradictory moment, one in which the forces of reaction and progress find themselves face-to-face with another. Williams's long revolution has never, at least in my conscious political life, seemed simultaneously so far and so near.

In some ways, our moment can seem an odd one to return to Williams. Years of neoliberal austerity have eroded the social basis that was the grounds of Williams's faith in the people. "If one's representativeness," Seaton asks, "relies on the continued existence of certain shared experiences, can it withstand the disappearance of the sociological conditions of those experiences?"[31] And yet if we take the long view—as Mark Allison argues we should—perhaps there are lessons in Williams's career that transcend our immediate circumstances. The "international military struggle," is still central to national politics, in both the United States and the United Kingdom, as murderous domestic police forces inherit weapons and tactics from a ramped-up war on terror, while dreams of imperial power, past and present, fuel xenophobic racism. Those of us working in the neoliberal university, which can only articulate the importance of education in terms of returns on investment, will recognize Williams's observation that since "education is tied to social advancement in a class society . . . it is difficult to hold both to education and to social solidarity" (*CC* 202). Meanwhile a surprisingly robust socialist revival—originating, in part, in a generation free from Cold War propaganda—has enlivened national debate in the Anglophone world. But more than these particular points, what Williams offers is a career guided by commitment—a life work that took place in multiple spheres at once and whose thinking never hardened into dogma. As I corresponded with the writers of this volume, I found that most of us were actively involved in labor struggles, whether through college unions or in our local communities. As academics, we historicize the work that we read and the categories through which we read them, articulating new understandings of aesthetics or utopia or modern media culture that break through inherited and reified terms. Or we analyze the various real-world paths through which these objects reach us. Or we use the tools Williams gave us—structures of feeling, mediation, utopia, distance—and test them in our own experience. Running through all of these essays, then—direct in some, implicit in others—is the attempt to use Williams's thought to press against the many impasses of our moment.

The volume is divided into two sections. The first, called Keywords, focuses on Williams's conceptual vocabulary. Anna Kornbluh sets Williams's understanding of mediation against the current scholarly fetish for immediacy, while Mark Allison suggests that Williams's understanding of what he calls "long politics"—developed through a rereading of *Culture & Society*—can help us see beyond the immediate squabbles of our moment. Similarly, Mathias Nilges finds in Williams's idea of utopia a disappointment that avoids disillusionment, one that presses us to rethink our own intellectual commitments in the face of new historical developments. This section closes with Thomas Laughlin's reading of perhaps Williams's most important, if challenging, concept: "structures of feeling." For Laughlin, "structures of feeling" must be situated squarely within the Marxist tradition about which Williams, at times, appeared skeptical. "Structures of feeling," Laughlin suggests, is a fundamental rethinking of the notion of base/superstructure, one that acknowledges the importance of cultural production precisely by recognizing its material determinations.

The second section, Knowable Communities, develops readings of the kind Williams always insisted upon, ones that trace the formal and real-world means by which cultural objects define and delimit notions of community. Daniel Hartley explores how Williams's attempt to overcome distance through a truly democratic understanding of cultural literacy sheds a cold light on the failings of our own neoliberal universities. Madhu Krishnan traces the local networks through which African literature makes its way to the United Kingdom. My essay takes up Williams's defense of Dickensian sentiment to analyze Arundhati Roy's *The Ministry of Utmost Happiness* and its understanding of a literature committed to political struggle. Finally, Daniel Worden analyzes Williams's work on television, showing us how *The Wire* incorporates elements of its own technological production into a narrative that both crosses and reinforces class divides.

"Perhaps . . . the future of Marxism," Williams wrote, "depends on a recovery of something like its whole tradition." But in doing so we should not be caught up in "the struggle over the inheritance." "The only thing that matters," Williams concludes, "is the reality of socialism" ("FM" 65). Our volume takes up Williams's thought, then, partly as a project of recovery, but more importantly as one guided by a present understood as a site of perpetual struggle and contradiction, which requires our active intervention so that a socialist future might, one day, emerge.

NOTES

1. This point is particularly striking since the idea of an "easy, improving society" is often considered one of the liabilities of *The Long Revolution*. As Perry Anderson remarks, though it is tempting, "The Future of Marxism" "cannot be read as if were simply an unknown complement to *The Long Revolution*. At points the two are effectively not compatible." See Perry Anderson, "The Missing Text: Introduction to 'the Future of Marxism,'" *New Left Review* 1, no. 114 (2018): 49.

2. Francis Mulhern, "Critical Revolutions," *New Left Review*, no. 110 (2018): 42.

3. Joseph North, *Literary Criticism: A Concise Political History* (Cambridge, MA: Harvard University Press, 2017), 3, 2.

4. Ibid., 20.

5. Ibid., 14.

6. Ibid., 30.

7. Ibid., 6.

8. Ibid., 15.

9. It is worth noting that North continually misreads Kant—his main instance of idealist aesthetics—for whom *The Critique of Judgment* was never about aesthetic objects, but was primarily an attempt to understand how one could connect the realms of freedom and necessity—ought and is—through a faculty rooted in the senses and yet somehow conversant with the universals Kant felt were a requirement for sociality as such, which is why he located judgment in the *sensus communis*. To be sure, there are idealist elements in all of this, but to suggest that Kant removed aesthetics from materiality in a cordoned-off area of experience confined to works of art is simply wrong.

10. North, *Literary Criticism*, 3.

11. For instance, North dramatically underestimates the real-world ambitions and, indeed, impact of the sea changes in literary scholarship introduced by feminism, race studies, queer theory, and postcolonialism—all of which, in their best incarnations, seek both to cultivate new modes of aesthetic attention and then, crucially for North's argument, use them to alter the culture at large. He also seems, quite damagingly, to misunderstand the work of contextualization that is his nemesis, work that, again in its best form, helps us to better understand the power and depth of a literary text's engagement with the cultural situation from which it emerges. And though he critiques historical contextualization, his work relies on its premises, even as its reading of the historical context conditioning literary studies is quite thin, resting on a relatively unexamined and direct relationship between an ill-defined neoliberal base and a superstructural criticism that entirely bypasses the institutional structures mediating the two. Each of these criticisms is dealt with quite well in Dermot Ryan, "Review of Joseph North's *Literary Criticism: A Concise Political History*," *boundary 2*, January 29, 2018.

12. Mulhern, "Critical Revolutions," 49.

13. Ibid.

14. See Karl Marx, *Grundrisse*, trans. Martin Nicolaus (New York: Penguin Books, 1973), 401.

15. E. P. Thompson, "The Long Revolution Part I," *New Left Review* 1, no. 9 (1961): 27.

16. Joseph North, "Two Paragraphs in Raymond Williams: A Reply to Francis Mulhern," *New Left Review*, no. 116/117 (2019): 169. In *Politics and Letters*, Williams says, "What I would hope will happen is that after the ground has been cleared of the received idea of literature, it will be possible to find certain new concepts which would allow for special emphases" (*PL* 325).

17. North, "Two Paragraphs," 181, 182.

18. Ibid., 175.

19. Lola Seaton, "Ends of Criticism," *New Left Review*, no. 119 (2019): 112.

20. Ibid., 124.

21. Curiously enough Williams thus provides the very link, grounded in the senses, between individual and society that Kant sought from *The Critique of Judgment*.

22. Seaton, "Ends of Criticism," 115.

23. In this way, Williams fulfills Marx's famous methodological point in the introduction to the *Grundrisse*. "The concrete is concrete because it is the concentration of many determinations," Marx writes. Therefore, "the method of rising from the abstract to the concrete" is how one proceeds from isolated facts—abstract in their immediacy—to concrete wholes. Marx, *Grundrisse*, 101.

24. And as Seaton makes clear, the echoes of the country house in this line are not accidental. Referring to this passage, as well as a comment about George Eliot's "country-house England," Seaton suggests that "country houses are here a kind of shorthand for exclusionary cultural elitism." Seaton, "Ends of Criticism," 115.

25. Terry Eagleton, "Criticism and Politics: The Work of Raymond Williams," *New Left Review* 1, no. 95 (1976): 6. A series of charges follow from this point. Misunderstanding ideology, Williams held to an organicist conception of society and a nostalgic overvaluing of ordinary people, values characteristic of the "petty-bourgeois liberal humanism" animating Williams's "residual populism" (5, 15). In each case, Williams overestimates the subjective element in culture, failing to recognize its irredeemably ideological character. Indeed, ideology is a kind of master term for the essay; ideology and its cognates appear some forty times in a scant twenty-one pages.

26. Ibid., 3.

27. Ibid., 23.

28. Ibid.

29. Ibid., 8. The irony is that, in spending so much time on personalized attacks on Williams, Eagleton makes the same error, absent the sociologizing.

30. Seaton, "Ends of Criticism," 122.

31. Ibid., 124.

Part I

Keywords

Chapter One

Mediation Metabolized

Anna Kornbluh

In the hyper-mediatized late capitalism of the first world, the means of production and circulation of images rests in the hands of many an individual consumer, while the ideology of human capital and dismantling of public welfare responsibilizes individuals for their own self-optimization. Colluding together, these two techno-ideological and political-economic conditions result in a fraught conflation of self-expression with economic growth. Toddlers of YouTube self-monetizing, mompreneurs pumping brands, hillbilly elegy-ing all the way to the highest office in the land: we are all sole proprietors bootstrapping across dystopia. Everyone lives their best life, everyone wants to be mirrored, everything is under surveillance, everything feeds the rapid-uptake algorithm. Across platforms, this conflation compresses representation; media become prized for their expressiveness, immersiveness, instantaneity, hashtag "nofilter." Grotesquely privatized hyper-mediatized late capitalism thus paradoxically propels a fetish of immediacy.

If Marxism has a readymade way to explain this fetish of immediacy ("The ideas of the ruling class are in every epoch the ruling ideas"[1]), less obvious is what Marxism offers by way of positive counter. What are the prospects for *mediacy* that contravene the industry of immediacy? Can critique of the technological and political substrate of immediacies dispel the fetishistic lure? Can collective action somehow challenge the illusion of self-expression, lend images nuance, once again thicken the symbolic? Can a real movement to abolish the present state of affairs reconfigure value, including the currency of immediacy?

Establishing a political alternative to the immediacies of the human capital regime cannot be accomplished in the pages on an academic essay collection. But framing a conceptual alternative, an account of the density, contradictions, and overdetermination of mediacy—an account that can foment actions—is within an essay's warrant. Such an alternative is also, luckily for this collection's contributors, already largely under construction in Raymond Williams's towering body of work. The theory of *mediation* is a central and unsung feat in his career, and we do well to celebrate his one-hundredth birthday by revisiting that leitmotif. Although incomplete, Williams's theory nonetheless remains the most substantive in the Marxist aesthetic tradition, outlining mediation as *the complex social activity of representation*. An indispensable basis for any counter to the cult of immediacy, Williams's theory tethers images to the capitalist mode of production, while simultaneously appraising the resonant meaning within concrete situations and practices; it beholds the struggle for sense at the heart of everyday desires and it ramifies that struggle into collective emancipation.

Mediation is thus in broadest terms the sense making and sensuous rendering of the mode of production, a vocation for representation to render "relatable" and thinkable the abstract, systemic conditions of social life. These broad terms can be balanced by the simplest terms Williams eventually formulates: mediation is the "necessary processes of composition in a specific medium" (*SC* 24). "Medium," of course, encompasses the material, mode, and/or technology of representation, but for Williams it importantly also means "writing," including both communicative/informative genres and the noninstrumental, para-communicative creative language we know as literature. Throughout his career, Williams was keen to fathom this putting-into-medium as a practice of everyday life, since he was constantly reformulating how much there is a "need for images, for representations, of what living now is like" (*RWT* 6). Ordinary people ceaselessly endeavor to make sense out of their experience, and to use that made-sense as the basis of higher-order connections to the other people around them. He never tired of maintaining that this anthropological and psychological observation fueled his early skepticism of Marxism, which he saw as too-often bogged down in the negative diagnosis of incessantly renewed exploitation, and too-rarely improvising the positive forecast of everyday emancipation. What do literature and art help us to think, and does the production of alternative worlds or the synthesis of alternative meanings support practical construction in this world? A commitment, then, to affirming the liberatory potential of sense making and relay, of representation and transformation, underwrites Williams's less simple elaboration of mediation as a dynamic, aleatory social exercise. To mediate is to put into medium, which is to provide an occasion and vehicle for collectivizing meaning, to provide a modality or form conducive to the content of the commons. Occasion, vehicle, modality, and form are all levers in collective social struggle.

Rooted in the radical political project of liberation from exploitation, extraction, and alienation, mediation stands at the center of Williams's conflicted engagement with Marxism, and its conceptual intensification over the course of Williams's career illustrates his increasing radicalization. Both of the late programmatic accounts of mediation Williams proffers, in *Marxism and Literature* and *Keywords*, reiterate this trajectory of the becoming-Marxist, by narrating a history of the idea that culminates in its Marxist inflection.

"Putting-into-medium" is a definition that absorbs and expands the history of the idea of mediation, which Williams reviews at multiple junctures. In colloquial usage, mediation has legalistic connotations of brokering agreements between opposing interests, like husband and wife or capital and labor. While there are, of course, more precise connotations at work in the history of philosophy, this colloquial significance is actually important for the Williamsonian/Marxist promise of the term, because it so clearly underscores relationships and their conflictuality. In classical philosophy, as exemplified in Aristotle, mediation described the action of linking the levels of a syllogism, the agent of which he referred to as a "middle" (*meson*) in distinction from the extreme (*akron*). In Latin, it similarly means halving, intercession. Tracing a line from Aristotle to medieval texts to Hegel and Marx, Lukács, and Adorno, Williams arrays three etymological and historical senses that entwine in his schematization: mediation as intercession in conflict, mediation as the middling between two otherwise separate entities (parties, facts, experiences), and mediation as the expression of the unexpressed. All three of these senses are required, Williams contends, for any coherent Marxist analysis of culture and/as representation. Interceding in class conflict, generating common grounds, and making available to thought the supervalent abstractions of ideology, totality, emancipation, and utopia, mediation encompasses *both* the mystification of capitalist antagonisms *and* their elucidation, both the adhesive of social relations and their dissolution. Enveloping such duality, mediation becomes for Williams an "active process" of relating that is "material" and "social": the creative agency of rendering ideas in material form as well as the social agency of changing relations by representing them. Here, then, is a counter to immediacy: mediation as friction, as process, as production of syntheses.

As much as this alertness to the active social practices of representation and intervention founds the essential distinction of his body of theory, Williams's concept of mediation only presents as a theoretical topic in its own right (as, indeed, a "keyword") in his later works. In what follows, I pursue the chrysalis of mediation by approaching a number of Williams's works in roughly chronological fashion—in the fashion indeed of *Keywords*. With this archaeology, I aim to sustain several concentric claims. First, even though "mediation" is mostly used today in media studies circles (and there, often confounded with "mediatization"), it should be more broadly operative in literary studies, since Williams's theory of mediation culminates his lifelong interest in literature (especially literary realism) as a resource for grappling with society and sociality. Second, Williams is passive, circumspect, and anticlimactic about his own significant theoretical contributions, tending to obfuscate their foundational and original qualities, likely out of some humble commitment to the communal nature of meaning, and a resistance to theory as "abstract." Third, his oeuvre's particular *bildung*—his becoming across his life more and more leftist—suggests that mediation should center a vibrant Marxist aesthetic and cultural theory and that any coherent theory of mediation should be explicitly Marxist; he anticipates in advance many of post- and anti-Marxist impulses of contemporary media theory and provides fodder to refute them. Happy Birthday, Raymond Williams! You gave the gifts.

Concerns and motifs in the early literary explorations prefigure and instantiate the later more explicit theory of mediation Williams develops after his intermediate explorations of media industries. In his first work of literary criticism, *Culture and Society* (1958), the novelist and homegrown, working-class intellectual set out to define several nodal terms that, he argued, could properly establish the terrain of socially minded literary criticism: industry, democracy, class, art, and culture. For each term, Williams takes a condensed, genealogical approach, describing permutations in meaning over the eighteenth, nineteenth, and twentieth centuries. In each case he arrives at a working definition that he suggests conveys relationality: industry is "our manufacturing and productive institutions and their general activities," art is "imaginative truth . . . distinguished from other human skills," and, most importantly, culture is "the relations . . . (within) a field . . . of situation and feeling . . . a whole way of life . . . a mode of interpreting all our common experience and in this new interpretation, changing it" (*CS* xiii, xvi, xviii). By focusing his study on relations, Williams, as he acknowledges, broadly connects literary and aesthetic interpretation to historical analysis and sociological survey; his solution to this multidisciplinarity is, he says, "examining not a series of abstracted problems, but a series of statements by individuals," and he thus proceeds to array political economy, nonfiction essayistic prose, poetry, novels, aesthetic criticism, and political protest as "statements" (*CS* xix). While such a melding of literary and nonliterary speech acts tends to reduce poetics to rhetoric or logic—and might obscure the paramount difference between how literary texts make themselves available to interpretation and how phenomenal cultural practices do not—what is nonetheless gained for Williams in carving out this method is that culture can be understood as the working out of life. Culture reflects and digests the structured, evolving material social world, creating meanings in, judgments of, and alternatives to, those structures and circumstances.

Theorized as this working out, "culture" distinguishes itself from inert mechanics, and comes to denominate the "moral and intellectual activities *separate* from the driven impetus of a new kind of society" (*CS* xviii; italics mine). Culture is habitual, culture is received, but at the same time culture is also interpretative. Beyond the immediate industrial drive, culture is the making of meaning, including meanings that prevision industrial reconstitution or social transformation. The critical potential of this meaning making underwrites its deceptively simple definition: "a mode of interpreting all our common experience, and in this new interpretation, changing it" (*CS* xviii). In reaching for adequate encapsulations of culture's simultaneously acclimative and transformative functions, of its bidirectional or ambivalent sum, Williams worries about confusions wrought by lurching from determinism (culture is efflux of industry) to romanticism (culture creates social reality) to relativism (culture is ungeneralizably situated):

> Either the arts are passively dependent on social reality, a proposition which I take to be that of mechanical materialism, or a vulgar misinterpretation of Marx. Or the arts, as the creators of consciousness, determine social reality, the proposition which the Romantic poets sometimes advanced. Or finally, the arts, while ultimately dependent, with everything else, on the real economic structure, operate in part to reflect the structure and its consequent reality, and in part, by parting attitudes towards reality, to help *or hinder* the constant business of changing it. I find Marxist theories of culture confused because they seem to me, on different occasions and in different writers, to make use of all these propositions as the need serves. (*CS* 274)

Left without a categorical theory of what art does in social reality, Marxists must continuously evaluate what theories are useful "as the need serves"—that is, they must judge in concrete rather than theoretical terms, in situations and contexts rather than in the abstract, whether art is transforming reality or securing the status quo. To describe beforehand the quality of representation susceptible to such judgment, Williams relies on formulations that are resolutely *copulative*, open to both trajectories of evaluation.

In "Culture Is Ordinary" (1958) we find a typical and consummate gesture of the copulative, overcoming an opposition in conventional discourse (academic and popular) by underscoring a bothness. Culture is *both* common meanings and special creative meanings, both everyday practices and exceptional artistic efforts, both a whole way of life and the engines that change the contours of that whole. Egalitarian fusion is the libido driving this copulative, since Williams viscerally rejects divisiveness: "What kind of life can it be, I wonder, to produce this extraordinary fussiness, this extraordinary decision to call certain things culture and then separate them, as with a park wall, from ordinary people and ordinary work?" (*RH* 5). Here Williams sets out to reject certain catastrophizing and disapproving tendencies he sees in Marxism that hold all culture to be bourgeois, and mass culture to be all-consuming. For Williams, culture designates authentic ways of life that intrinsically bend toward dignity and mutuality, even as it also designates the "special processes" of artistic "discovery" (*RH* 4). Both the anthropological and the aesthetic can facilitate socialist social change, but this promise can only be assessed concretely.

In the same year as "Culture Is Ordinary," Williams also wrote an essay called "Realism and the Contemporary Novel," which would become a centerpiece of *The Long Revolution* (1961). The book as a whole lends temporal dimension and phenomenal texture to the generic prospect of interventive representation; the essay in particular establishes some theses on realism that will later guide his definitional work on mediation. Revolutionary length gestures not to a specious contrast with insurgent rapidity, but rather to the lived experience of process, an essential Williamsonian term. "Process" substantializes the bidirectional potentialities of culture acting on society, the aleatory contingencies of concrete quotidianism and high art converging in the project of emancipation. Realism comes to light then as a paradigmatic "process."

Realism produces a form from its insight into "interpenetration": every feature of a realist representation is shot through with its complementary opposite, every part is inflected by the whole. As he describes it,

> Neither element, neither the society nor the individual, is there as a priority. The society is not a background against which the personal relationships are studied, nor are the individuals merely illustrations of aspects of the way of life. Every aspect of personal life is radically affected by the quality of the general life, yet the general life is seen at its most important in completely personal terms. ("RCN" 22)

The reader who encounters this dialectical fusion gains a new standard by which to evaluate other art forms. "What we have to look for is the recovery of that interpenetration, idea into feeling, person into community, change into resettlement, which George Eliot made living in *Middlemarch*" ("RCN" 25). Realism is an aesthetic of enmeshment that also sustains a notion of the whole, an inclination to dialecticity that also discretizes parts.

This initial and perpetual orientation to literature in Williams's thought assures his special contribution to the theory of mediation. Even though the concept is only robustly named by him after his work on communications technology and media, the way in which he proceeds to define the term is centrally literary. He famously studied television and film, but his career began with two novels (and others later), and his first works of criticism considered literature closely. Literature is of course an institution embedded in politics, but literature is also the use of written languages for purposes oblique to ordinary or instrumental communication, and that obliquity actualizes an agency of language, representation, and ideas to compose something more than business as usual. The literature that preoccupied Williams—from Crabbe[2] and Wordsworth, to his early unconventional reading of eighteenth-century bourgeois drama[3] and his later praise for *Ulysses*[4] and George Orwell, and even in his own novels *Border Country, Loyalties*, and others—constitutes a long arc of realism, insurgent in narrative verse and "the real language of men," and resplendent in spartan socialism or historical relay. Within this long arc, he identified three consistent characteristics of realism: social extension (keying average and working people in addition to the powerful, heroic, and rich); presentism (siting the action in the contemporary); and secularism (departure from the metaphysical and religious; preoccupation with the human). ("LR" 64). In combining these characteristics, realism wields the power of making the social thinkable, and so Williams emphatically concludes that "the realist novel alone" is the art form adequate to social transformation, because it alone is the mode that fuses individual and society in ways that contribute to the mapping necessary for tactical intervention. Realism's dialectical capacity buttresses Williams's future criteria for mediation.

Always at pains to enflesh this abstraction in particular relations, Williams turns to the study of multiple communications technology in *Communications* (1962), where he ardently articulates the mediated character of reality: "Many people seem to assume as a matter of course that there is, first, reality, and then, second, communication about it. We degrade art and learning by supposing that they are always second-hand activities: that there is life, and then afterwards there are these accounts of it" (*C* 19). Such a position on telecommunications reads, as well, like a lesson from the analysis of realism, which also exposes the constitution of reality. Zooming in on quotidian communication as the production of this mediated reality, this brief book redefines communication as a basic relation structured by genres, institutions, and technologies. University study from the most introductory writing courses to the most sophisticated theories must, Williams recommended, foreground the social determinants and social agency of relay, to substantiate acts of communication as engaged practice. The expressly programmatic tenor of the work here ("Proposals" is the last and longest chapter) brings home Williams's conviction that ordinary people in ordinary life can change their reality.

Having articulated a processual notion of culture and a continuum of daily genres and technological conglomerates, and then spending several years investigating drama, Williams's theory of mediation arrives at a decided theoretical climax in the essay "Base and Superstructure in Marxist Cultural Theory" (1973). Notably, it is the first of his works to name a political orientation in the title, leaving behind the more generic titles like "Culture and Society" or "Communications" in favor of the political and intellectual specificity of the Marxist tradition, and harkening to future works like "Socialism and Ecology," *Marxism and Literature*, and "Problems in Materialism." Taking up the central question in Marxist cultural theory of determination, and intervening, as he always did, against unidirectional, un-dialectical accounts of social forces, Williams insists on the interpenetration of the economic mode of production alongside the cultural institutions and meaning frames accruing to it. Where in previous works the verb "to medi-ate" made guest appearances, in "Base and Superstructure" the noun "media-tion" takes priority, and this conceptual substantialization should be under-stood as an effect of the expressly Marxist political purchase of the essay. In these pages, mediation is realized as the concept necessary for a nondeter-ministic theory of the "relationship" between social being and consciousness, material practices of existence and the ideas and representations thereof. Yet even in this moment of explicit naming, Williams is curiously passive, so as to conceal his own theoretical achievements.

One might of course psychologize such passivity, palpating humility of the Welsh boy made good at Oxford. Political attachments might also explain why he never trumpeted proprietary relation to his biggest, most original contribution, preferring instead to conduct many voices. But perhaps a con-ceptual explanation is also apt: in addition to his suspicions of theory's abstractions, Williams always intimated mediation as dialectically spanning ideology and critique, material relations and their ideal representation, contradiction and interceding; all this middling energy in the thick of things inhibits the vantage necessary to proclaim a full-fledged theory. Reviewing Williams's career for this anniversary, though, and tracking chronologically the situated ways that this notion of situatedness arises over time to solve specific questions, we can see how brightly Williams theorized, even if his own syntaxes pull down the shades.

Awkward syntax abounds in the base and superstructure discussion. As he describes a quasi-history of base-superstructure notions, he points to an "operational qualification" in which the determination of the superstructure by the base is nuanced by "delays in time, with complications, and with certain indirect or relatively distant relationships." He then points to another "more fundamental" evolution, when qualification passes to reconceptualiza-tion. Here is the passive construction: "The relationship itself was more substantially looked at. This was the kind of reconsideration that gave rise to the modern notion of 'mediation,' in which something more than simple reflection or reproduction—indeed something radically different from either reflection or reproduction—actively occurs" ("BSS" 5). The strangely unat-tributed agency and activity of who or what "gave rise" buries the bombshell of Williams's own advances, which are to situate mediation not only in the base-superstructure relationship (an incredibly important contribution), but also in the very notion of the base itself: "When we talk of the base, we are talking of a process and not a state," asserting that this emphasis on process in turn means that "we are then less tempted to dismiss as superstructural, and in that sense as merely secondary, certain vital productive social forces, which are in the broad sense, from the beginning, basic" ("BSS" 5, 6). This renovation of the spatial model reconfigures the structural foundations of determination, finding an active, agential construction of the economic base via representations, practices, institutions, meanings.

The essential brilliance of the essay is Williams's demand that this emphasis on process, relationship, and mutuality—requisite for any suitably refined Marxism—must never veer into a dispersive, celebratory indeterminacy that refuses causality, determination, and totality. In a formidable and prescient riposte to our own hegemonic Latourianisms in media theory, cultural studies, and literary criticism, Williams starkly warned that the dialecticity actuated by the concept of mediation risked disappearing into the encomium of complexity, and that vigilant theorizing was necessary to avoid the risk. Recommending, in the Lukácsian vein, "totality" as a more useful concept than the traditional base-superstructure model, Williams concisely cautions,

> It is very easy for the notion of totality to empty of its essential content the original Marxist proposition. . . . [T]he key question to ask about any notion of totality in cultural theory is this: whether the notion of totality includes the notion of intention. For if totality is simply concrete, if it is simply the recognition of a large variety of miscellaneous and contemporaneous practices, then it is essentially empty of any content that could be called Marxist. ("BSS" 7)

Totality may be a more suitable spatial model than that of the *uberbau* but its acumen dissipates under the fetish of the concrete. Abstraction must also animate the theory of totality, and that abstraction pertains in part to the ways that capitalist domination and determination of social existence do not always readily appear in the realm of the concrete. To analyze culture, to recognize mediation, we must not only revel in the concrete and preach complexity, but also hail what lacks immediate presence. Williams continues by unambiguously defining intention as class rule: "Intention, the notion of intention, restores that key question, or rather the key emphasis. For while it is true that any society is a complex whole of such practices, it is also true that any society has a specific organization, a specific structure, and that the principles of this organization and structure can be seen as directly related to certain social intentions, intentions by which we define the society, which in all our experience have been the rule of a particular class" ("BSS" 7). With this incisive distinction, Williams parries upfront the lukewarm Latourian diffusions that dominate media and cultural studies today. The sheer fact of power's dispersal does not gainsay the other sheer fact of its concentration. Recognizing distributive agency too often lets the ruling class off the hook; Williams never lets his considerations of localized, concrete, processual situations becloud the intensive totality of class relations.

After this transformative working through of mediation in "Base and Superstructure," Williams has a new vantage from which to return to some of the cultural products with which he began his critical career: nineteenth-century literature. *The Country and the City* (1973) tremendously actualizes the distinction between complexity and totality, ambivalence and mediation, showing how major literary realism must be judged according to its figuration of the problematic of totality. If *Culture and Society* was conceptual but digestible literary history, *The Country and the City* foregrounds contradictions, oppositions, and tensions in tangibly Marxist ways. For Williams, what is essential in George Eliot and Thomas Hardy, and superior to Jane Austen and Anthony Trollope, is the dynamic with which their novels transcend the country-city opposition. Instead of casting the pastoral against the urban or the past against the present, Eliot and Hardy consistently show, Williams argues, the constitution of the country by and through urbanization, as well as the configuration of the individual by and through social relations that we have already noted. Realist novelists mediate vast socioeconomic transformations by refusing simple binaries of past and present, country and city, focusing instead on interanimation and mutual constitution. This sense of total subsumption within a mode of production keeps the intention of capitalism in mind. That novelists are able to do so by virtue of their use of description, plot, and objective narration points to the ways in which a mode known for its worldliness uses its formal elements to mediate. Mediation, in this phase, entails semi-autonomy, since representations that emerge from the context of the capitalist mode of production make that mode thinkable, making its processes of determination delimitable and its prospects of emancipation palpable. Even though novels are the ultimate capitalist art form, they retain the possibility of recognizing their own socioeconomic enmeshment and of gesturing toward other modes of production. Mediation is the name of this interventive, copulative movement of instantiation and critique, of symptom and cure, of ideology and utopia.

Shaping up by this time as such a driving topos in his thought, mediation begins to appear much more frequently by name in and after the early 1970s. *Television: Technology and Cultural Form*, his 1974 intervention into McLuhan-mode media debates around technological determination, stands as a fitting turning point in this regard. Williams sets out to offer a theory of television, rooted in its different function from the equally visual medium of cinema. Where cinema is, he attests, "a special kind of theater, offering specific and discrete works," the revolution of television stems from "the social complex that is the intersection of the visual with the space of the household and the time of the lived day (*TV* 22). Television's distinction is its rendering visual of everything, from theater-like dramas to radio-like news broadcasts, which, Williams carefully notes, it does at a level of technological inferiority to the cinema, but with great appeal anyway.

Introducing the concept of "flow" to describe the saturation of stimulation and information issuing from the interweaving of different programs and their commercial breaks, Williams spotlights both the political economy of broadcasting and the counterpoint of consumer agency as democratic cultural meaning making. "Mediation" in this text refers consistently to the way the visual medium of television relates social reality, especially through the news and its reporters, anchormen, cameramen, and directors, who "select and present what is happening" (*TV* 70). It also carries a tacit argument that the way television makes perceptible the selection and presentation of what is happening in turn makes visible that "the orthodox political process" itself is one of selection and presentation, that what we take to be immediate reality and its conduction by democratic republicanism is indeed a construction resulting from a selective, almost editorial, fabrication of meaning. Television mediation, with all its "producers," therefore succinctly encapsulates the ways that social reality itself is produced.

The immediate and immediacy are crucial motifs in *Television*, so we can read the evolving interest in mediation as a function of these reflections of immediacy as an apparent property of the televisual medium. As he puts it,

> The unique factor of broadcasting—first in sound, then even more clearly in television—has been that its communication is accessible to normal social development; it requires no specific training which brings people within the orbit of public authority. If we can watch and listen to people in our immediate circle, we can watch and listen to television. Much of the great popular appeal of radio and television has been due to this sense of apparently unmediated access. The real mediations will have to be noted, but again and again they are easy to miss. (*TV* 135)

Unlike literature or writing, which require literacy for individual consumers, and unlike theater or art or music that evidently require that consumers put themselves into the "orbit of authority" (by countenancing the institutions that purvey the media, by heeding the guidance of the critics and channels that promote the music), the social space of the living room and the technology of the on button lend television the sensation of immediacy between the consumer and the consumed.

Immediacy effects itself as "an intrinsic element of television: its capacity to enter a situation and show what is actually happening in it"; but this effect occludes the reality that "in all such cases there is mediation: directors, cameramen and reporters select and present what is happening. There is thus an intrinsic overlap between what is classified as factual report and what is classified as dramatic presentation. This overlap if often confusing" (*TV* 70). Several things to note here: the specter of immediacy is what continually raises the concept of mediation; the more the cultural media that engross Williams excel in their production of immediacy, the more mediation has to accrue to the heft of a concept. The essential case of television newly high-lights how selection and shaping, direction and lighting, narration and editing go into the relay of reality. And this relay threatens always to fall out of perceivability qua medium. The more visual our culture, the more important the concept of mediation; the more something seems immediate, the more mediation must be thought to be at work.

McLuhan famously argued that new media forms often theorize them-selves with reference to the older forms they imagine they are superseding. Williams's substantive denomination and uptake of mediation after his turn to communications technology and television suggests a reverse dynamic: only with thinking through the new media of television did he arrive at an adequate vocabulary for what he had all along described good literature as doing. For this reason, it is necessary to track a common confusion stemming from today's rapidly expanding landscape of media theory. Although these theories often invoke a concept of mediation, ultimately they confuse media-tion with mediatization. This conflation happens no doubt because media-tion, as John Guillory recently remarks, "remains undertheorized"[5] —be-cause, in short, Williams's formulations were so deceptively lucid as to preempt further elucidation. But it also happens because "mediation" enjoys a fate no different from that of its sibling Marxist concepts as they were absorbed into the neoliberalizing academy: the heft and bite are diffused by a tepid broadcast descriptivism. Where the specifically Marxist notion of me-diation evokes forms of appearance and their transfiguration, the Latourian complexus traces diffuse polylateral comminglings that "obviate determina-cy."[6] This rhizomatic complexity of indeterminacy avowedly courts para-doxical identities; as Richard Grusin puts it, "Radical mediation also insists upon an immediacy that transforms, modulates, or disrupts experienced rela-tions . . . Mediation is not opposed to immediacy but rather is itself immedi-ate."[7] The paramount ambition of these Latourian models is to impute dual-ism to the Marxist philosophical tradition and then to promote as an alterna-tive the monism of immanence. Williams's thought has the virtue, I suggest, of refusing in advance this immanentism; Williams is able to conceptualize mediation differently from mediatization because he develops his account *after* turning to the study of media technologies like radio and television, but *through and as* a consummation of his extensive study of older print modes. At the same time, he is able to avoid philosophical dualism because his anthropological ethos and his socialist politics propel his thought away from idealism. Williams's critique of technological determinism in McLuhan, for instance, already makes clear that for him the analysis of mediation requires full attention to the agential human uses to which media are put. The empha-sis on agency, process, and human meaning making with which Williams anchors his theory of mediation anticipatorily undoes mediatization theory's habit of collapsing message into medium.

Having centered mediation in his riposte to mediatization, Williams importantly elevates it to an everyday phenomenon by including it as a dedicated term among the 228 entries in *Keywords* (1976). The synoptic effort that saw Williams offering one-page, working genealogies of "family," "organic," and "welfare" casts mediation as an ultimate processual practice. In the entry there, Williams carefully notes how the first use of the word "mediation" in English comes from Chaucer, who already incorporated its multiple connotations of intercession, transmission, and division. Williams goes so far as to share the quotations from Chaucer for all three senses, and interestingly one of the quotations is a self-reflexive moment of literary purposefulness: "By mediacion of this litel tretis, I propose to teche . . . (*Astrolabe*, c. 1391)" (*K* 204). Mediation harkens the quality of writing to intervene and educate, transform a situation, create new states of affairs. These early meanings and the literary dynamics of education, relating, and the performative have been obscured, Williams notes, by the emergence of modern media technologies and their saturation of what "mediation" might signify. Via a reference to Adorno, and an insistence that "mediation is positive and in a sense autonomous," Williams de-obscures, stipulating a "complexity" of uses of the term: the "political" use of "intermediary action designed to bring about reconciliation or agreement"; the "dualist" use of "an activity which expresses," with varying degrees of veracity and opacity, "a relationship between otherwise separated facts and actions and experiences"; and what he fascinatingly calls a "formalist" use, "an activity which directly expresses otherwise unexpressed relations" (*K* 206). It is this formalist use, we cannot fail to notice, which most engrosses Williams in works like *The Country and the City*, where realism is the putting-into-medium of the historical, psychological, and spatial operations of the capitalist mode of production.

Arriving at this summit of restoring to its original literary richness the multiple facets of mediation, Williams's *Keywords* entry on mediation ends rather deflatingly, with the predication that the plurality of meanings of "mediation" might be replaced by "a better word" for each of the specific meanings: for the political sense, "conciliation"; for the dualist sense, "ideology or rationalization"; and for the formalist sense, "form" (*K* 206–7). This fractional parsing of terms might be another explanation for why Williams's own efforts at theoretical coherence haven't been received. So it seems worth affirming that mediation can name as a unity the divergent effects of rationalization and illumination, ideology and autonomy, that both conciliate us to our conditions of existence and confirm those contradictions that cause the very need for conciliation. In its plastic multivalence, mediation might be unsatisfying theoretically—but for just this reason it vividly actualizes dialectics. *Keywords* are not just names; they are points of view from which to undertake sociocultural analysis. The importance of dialectics for Marxism is its flexibility to address the charges of reductivism and determinism that had earlier concerned Williams. Mediation achieves precisely this function.

As mediation comes to figure the promise of dialectics, it constitutes the core of the expansive and programmatic embrace of Marxism that Williams finally makes in *Marxism and Literature* (1977). In that book, "mediation" takes center stage as the sine qua non of Marxist cultural analysis. The problem of multiple connotations is again rehearsed, but Williams settles quickly on the solution that mediation poses for many traditional debates around Marxist approaches to representation and cultural production. Specifically, Williams is at pains to show that "reflection" has dominated not only Marxist but also generally culturalist, generally historicist, generally contextualist approaches to art and representation, and to argue that reflection is wholly inadequate as a concept: "what is wrong with the theory is that it is not materialist enough" (*ML* 92). The materialism Williams proposes in contrast is one that doesn"t just elevate the situation of representation or something like its causes, but that dialectically comprehends as well the action of representation and something like its effects. As he clarifies,

> The most damaging consequence of any theory of art as reflection is that, through its persuasive physical metaphor (in which a reflection simply occurs, within the physical properties of light, when an object or movement is brought into relation with a reflective surface—the mirror and then the mind), it succeeds in suppressing the actual work on material—in a final sense, the material social process—which is the making of any art work. (*ML* 97)

At the crest of this fascinating and lucid assertion that Marxist concepts can only be materialist enough if they encompass how artworks act upon the material world (including their medium and their imaginative synthesis of something beyond instrumental relay or already-existing values), Williams is again curiously passive, in the same fashion as in the "Base and Superstructure" essay. In the midst of theorizing agency and activity, he buries his own theoretical action: "By projecting and alienating this material process to reflection, the social and material character of artistic activity—of that artwork which is at once 'material' and 'imaginative'—was suppressed. It was at this point that the idea of reflection was challenged by the idea of 'mediation'" (*ML* 97). Williams modestly does not identify himself as the source of the challenge, but his careful summations of intellectual history here and in *Keywords* make it glaring that he is describing an enormous theoretical development without attributing it to a proper name or historical conjuncture. The idea of mediation enters his summation free-floatingly: "'Mediation' was intended to describe an active process" (*ML* 97). Eventually he embeds it: "The negative sense of mediation [as distortion] . . . has coexisted with a sense which offers to be positive. This is especially the contribution of the Frankfurt School. . . . [A]ll active relations between different kinds of being and consciousness are inevitably mediated, and this process is not a separable agency—a 'medium' but intrinsic to the properties of the related kinds. 'Mediation is in the object itself, not something between the object and that to which it is brought.' Thus mediation is a positive process in social reality" (*ML* 98). The leap from Adorno to Williams's crystallization of the "positive" is unintuitive, and bespeaks the elision of his own theoretical agency.

A similar deflation transpires at the end of the "From Reflection to Mediation" chapter in *Marxism and Literature*. While Williams underlines the "positive and substantial" definition of mediation as "a necessary process of the making of meanings and values, in the necessary form of the general social process of signification and communication," he worries that such a definition unwittingly reinscribes a dualism between "concrete reality" and "meanings and values" (*ML* 100). The only solution to this worry seems to point outside of theory: no single concept can be adequate to social activity. But if mediation is not a concept so much as a point of view or method, then it instantiates the analysis of representational activity in concrete situations even as it also prevents that analysis from being dead on arrival, convinced of its findings of determination before the beginning.

In their repetition, these passivities and deflations explain why mediation has remained only partially theorized. Intrinsically, however, they also bespeak how much the theory of mediation cannot ascend to a theory at all, since it pitches itself at the intercessional strata between theory and practice, between abstract and concrete, between making capitalist totality thinkable and pinioning the power of thought. Williams's ambivalence about fully proclaiming the importance of this fundamental motif or fully gauging his own prodigious gifts leaves mediation fittingly, decently, on middling ground.

From its earliest formulations in his work, mediation transudes the problematic of *writing*, through the institution of literature across the realist novel and romantic poetry. To write is in some ultimate sense to mediate, to reach out for phenomena whether existent or merely possible, and grant to those phenomena outline, syntax, names. Writing is rules and their breaking, writing is essential and luxurious, writing is mundane and marvelous. Such an exercise of contradiction is thus a great figure for mediation, and through it a certain symmetry of Williams's oeuvre comes into relief, since his last big works resume the centrality of writing in society.

In *The Sociology of Culture* (1981), where Williams unassumingly offers an integrative resume of his own career by returning to the earliest questions of *Culture and Society*, culture looks different than it did when literary criticism was his main terrain, but retains the fundamental aspect of a "signifying system" (*SC* 207). Literature anchors the innovative cultural studies method of a revisionary sociology because it "shares its specific medium, language, with the most general medium of all kinds of social communication" (*SC*

212). Disposed thereby to disclose the relations of society, literature models culture's mediating faculty, its outpacing of determined reflection. As he puts it, "The basic process of writing and printing retained at least some elements of mediation. It is, after all, an inherently notational rather than a direct system" (*SC* 110). Thus Williams has occasion to reiterate his sublation of reflection into mediation, arriving at the quintessential formula of "composition in a specific medium." Composition always involves exclusion, and pressing rather than expressing, so this mediation, he clarifies, "refers to an indirectness of relation" (*SC* 24). Phenomena are direct; writing is indirect; mediation is the name of this indirection.

The literary current of mediation accrues a certain felicity in *Writing in Society* (1983), a kind of capstone essay collection that Williams himself assembled, which announces "writing" as the name of the mediations to which his career was devoted. Writing is a social practice extraneous to "the basic process of growing up in a society" in its difference from and difficulty compared to oral communication (*WS* 3). Williams thus urges thinking of writing as "a new form of social relationship," the unique technological and historical status of which directly effects the content of "what was written and what was read" (*WS* 3). These gradings of the socially constitutive power of writing distill the generative representation connoted by mediation. Williams again here attributes the conceptual development of mediation to thinkers other than himself (this time Benjamin, Adorno, and Lucien Goldmann), but arrives at signature Williamsonian copulative that mediation must be located in literary form rather than in its content, and that this formal angle cannot sink into a kind formalism that would preclude situated interpretation. Marxism elevates this practice of writing and reading, and "instead of privileging a generalized Literature as an independent source of values insists on relating the actual variety of literature to historical processes in which fundamental conflicts had occurred and were still occurring" (*WS* 211). Writing as situated praxis parallels the meaning making that simultaneously constitutes society as signifying system and reconstitutes society in stressing its contradictions. A Marxist theory of mediation pinpoints these contradictions, and their pursuant struggles, qualifying the agency of representations with the scoreboard of the class war.

That mediation could prove for Williams a tactic in that war returns us to the fetish of immediacy with which we began. For already in 1983, when he selected "writing" as a culminative signifier of his life's work on process and transformation, he offered writing as a means of traversing instrumentalism and immediacy. The concluding words of *Writing in Society* jauntily rouse:

> There are periods in a culture when what we call real knowledge seems to have
> to take priority over what is commonly called imagination. in our own image-
> conscious politics and commerce there is a proliferation of all instrumental

professions which claim the sonorous titles of imagination and creativity for what are, when examined, simple and rationalized processes of reproduction and representation. To know what is happening, in the most factual and down-to-earth ways, is indeed an urgent priority in such a world. A militant empiricism claims all; in a world of rearmament and mass unemployment seems rightly to claim all. Yet it is now the very bafflement and frustration of this militant empiricism, and especially of the best of it, that should hold our attention. . . . [O]nly imagination, in its full processes, can touch and reach and recognize and embody. If we see this, we usually still hesitate between tenses: between knowing in new ways the structures of feeling that have directed and now hold us, and finding in new ways the shape of an alternative, a future, that can be genuinely imagined and hopefully lived. There are many other kinds of writing in society, but these now—of past and present and future—are close and urgent. (*WS* 267–68)

Amid unrelenting emergencies and the militant empiricisms they assuredly commission, imagination, projection, writing, mediation become more, rather than less, urgent. Against the crush of immediacy, Williams commends and instantiates mediation as synthetic, reflective, processing necessary to adequately fathom what confronts us and to generatively build better orders.

Over the course of his fantastic career, Williams's blossoming commitment to socialist politics supported an intensifying theory of mediation. Williams worked in a way that attested to his disdain for what he saw as the abstract premises of both academic and Marxist frameworks, but only as he became more leftist did he become more committed to systematic conceptualizations. Marxism distinguishes between the generality of abstractions, relationships, practices, and their appearance in specific forms. To launch analysis of general phenomena, specific forms of appearance are indispensable; "mediation" describes how these generalities render themselves into specificities. "Capitalism," for instance, does not readily appear before the eye or present itself for deixis, but commodities do and wages do; ideology cannot be touched but a commercial or political speech or a film can give it contour. Mediation is a precondition for the analyzability of the contingency of a given social order. But because mediation names the putting-into-medium of abstractions, it also denotes that analysis itself. Critique of the kind Marx invented is a mediation, a naming and limning of social phenomena like "mode of production" and "ideology" so as to enable reconfiguration, sublation, transformation. The concept of mediation is thus inherently bidirectional, since it connotes the putting-into-medium of abstractions like "value" and "sociability," and it simultaneously connotes the revelation that this putting-into-medium could assume other forms.

Attending to the bidirection of mediation is slow work. So, too, the blend of close reading, rhetorical analyzing, technological contextualizing, historical embedding, anthropological observing, and political interpreting that the best of Williamsian cultural studies performs requires interdisciplinary dexterity and careful coordination. These slownesses of criticism concomitant upon the theory of mediation ill fit the pace of precarious academics absorbed in self-branding wars and crushed by instrumentalist, vocational whittlings of the university, fascinated by the glitter of rapid-uptake computational humanities or stirred by the righteousness of expressivist anti-aesthetics. But only the capacious study of mediation, with all its risks of inconclusiveness and all the unfinished business of history, renders fuller gradations of that flatness galvanizing the immediacy mania in culture and in theory.

Williams's exploration of mediation as the social activity of representation furnishes a conceptual and practical link between the sense making in everyday life and the cognitive mapping requisite for transforming everyday life. It underscores that representation is neither ex nihilo nor reducible to what preexists it, that art is not a reflection of life but a production of life, that culture is not epiphenomenal to the economic base but integral to it. That the theory encompasses both phenomenal meanings (the quotidian chatty stories we tell ourselves in passing) and aesthetic representation (writing, literature, theater, television, film) can compound efforts to differentiate the activity of constative communication from the activity of performative art. This is a problem if one expects a theory of mediation to account for what is mediated and what is not, what is merely phenomenal and what is extra- or anti-phenomenal in ways that extend the bounds of the knowable. But because Williams charges theories with revealing the intentions of the capitalist mode of production and with fostering human flourishing, we can say that the theory of mediation does not solely name *that there is* social activity in progress, but rather names the possibility of judging that social activity.

The cumulative theory of mediation as social process involves, therefore, a corollary theory of critique as social process. To fully dialectically behold the force and promise of representation requires situated attentiveness to the specificities of a work and the relations it enables, and this attentiveness must change as the context in which the work is consumed changes. Critique of representation is a local, relational, punctual activity, and not one that is possible to definitively end for all time. There cannot be a last word on what *Middlemarch* or *Black Mirror* helps us to think.

Critical judgment emerges then as one of the practices of mediacy that intervenes in the cult of immediacy. The critic studies and educes the processual and relational milieus of meaning and aesthetics, the production, consumption, and agency of the image. Then criticism itself becomes another layer of mediation, open to further judgment. As countless Marxists have riotously debated for a few hundred years, interpreting the world is not equivalent to changing it. Mediation in Williams's gaze sublates this pat opposition—as arguably Marx's original thesis did too. Mediation is a dialectical concept in the most perverse way, since it attunes Marxist theory—that materialism that contextualizes ideas within their fields of social causes and constraints, that space where academics genuflect to action in their essays—to the power of ideas in their own right.

NOTES

1. Karl Marx and Friedrich Engels, *The German Ideology* (Amherst, NY: Prometheus Books, 1998), 67.

2. What Williams calls Crabbe's "own intention of realism" (*CC* 13).

3. In his "A Lecture on Realism," Williams refers to "the crucial development of realism as a whole form" ("LR" 63).

4. On *Ulysses,* Williams writes, "Ordinary language [is] heard more clearly than in anywhere in the realist novel before it" (*CC* 245).

5. John Guillory, "Genesis of the Media Concept," *Critical Inquiry* 36, no. 2 (Winter 2010): 354.

6. Alexander R. Galloway, Eugene Thacker, and McKenzie Wark, "Introduction: Execrable Media," in *Excommunication: Three Inquiries in Media and Mediation* (Chicago: University of Chicago Press, 2014), 10.

7. Richard Grusin, "Radical Mediation," *Critical Inquiry* 42, no. 1 (Autumn 2015): 128–29.

Chapter Two

Experience, Culture, Utopia

The Long Politics of Raymond Williams

Mark Allison

> Not in Utopia,—subterranean fields,—
> Or some secreted island, Heaven knows where!
> But in the very world, which is the world
> Of all of us,—the place where, in the end,
> We find our happiness, or not at all!

> —William Wordsworth, *The Prelude* (1850)
> slightly misquoted by Raymond Williams, "Utopia and Science Fiction"
> (1978)

> We are always in danger of taking too short a view—history is much slower than any of us can bear.
> —Raymond Williams, ("FM" 59)

"One of the latent *leitmotivs*" of *Culture and Society* (1958), the editors of the *New Left Review* observe, is a "direct counterposition of the social core of the thought of successive thinkers against a mere political surface that can be somehow detached or dismissed" (*PL* 100). After citing several examples, the editors complain that the text draws a consistent contrast between "a truth which is necessarily social, and politics which is a brittle and ephemeral adjunct separable from it" (*PL* 101). As its very title appears to confirm, *Culture and Society* neglects "the middle term of politics" (*PL* 108).

In a pattern that will be familiar to readers of *Politics and Letters* (1979), Raymond Williams responds to this critique by making a number of self-abasing concessions before digging in his heels. He acknowledges that his reputation-making book is "negatively marked by elements of a disgusted

withdrawal . . . from all immediate forms of collaboration," including political collaboration (*PL* 106). Its tone betrays an "element of fatigue with the
complexities of politics" (*PL* 103). But having offered these self-criticisms,
he roundly defends his work. *Culture and Society* is not merely "a contribution to a different kind of politics," but an attempt to precipitate "the redefinition of what politics should be, and the remobilization, at every level, of the
forces necessary for it" (*PL* 106, 106–7).

In this essay, I seek to illuminate this alternative understanding of politics, which we might term (with nods to Fernand Braudel's *longue durée* and
Williams's own long revolution) a "long politics." For all of his subsequent
ambivalence about *Culture and Society*, Williams affirmed in the introduction to its 1983 reissue that "it was in this book that I first found a position
which expressed my sense of what had happened and was still happening in
industrial civilisation, and in its art and thought" (*CS* ix). The ensuing developments and departures in his own scholarship and activism could occur
because he had "found a position"—a theoretically grounded, independent
democratic socialism—that constituted a bedrock commitment and basis for
action. As I will demonstrate in my first section, investigating Williams's
long politics sheds light on some of the most debated subjects within his
oeuvre, including the epistemological status of the category of experience
and the relationship of his work to the tradition of Cambridge literary studies
in which he was trained. Through a reading of *Culture and Society*'s conclusion, the second section explicates Williams's long politics, paying particular
attention to its tacit utopianism. In my last section, I take up Williams's
neglected final book, *Towards 2000* (1983), which Williams conceived as a
renewal of the investigation that *Culture and Society* and *The Long Revolution* (1961) inaugurated—and in which he considers the theoretical and political value of the utopian mode directly.

Before I begin my analysis, a few qualifications are in order—all the
more so, given Williams's famous methodological scrupulousness. First,
Culture and Society made what might justifiably be characterized as political
interventions on a number of fronts; here, I focus solely on the long-political
outlook that the book adumbrates.[1] Second, I take it as given that significant
elements of the book's historical analysis are superannuated; the same might
be said of any scholarly work, however seminal, published more than six
decades ago.[2] Here, I am less interested in approaching *Culture and Society*
as a work of historiography than as a feat of political stocktaking and an
example of method. Finally, I want to clarify that Williams did not view what
I am calling his "long politics" as a replacement for the day-to-day political
engagement and struggle he calls "immediate politics" (*PL* 106). Rather, the
former complements the latter, by equipping political actors with a theoretical self-consciousness and sense of historical perspective that are difficult to
achieve in the cut and thrust of day-to-day struggle. The present—another

moment of acute disorientation and rolling crisis in the Anglosphere, and, indeed, the world—seems a particularly appropriate time to revisit Williams's exemplary act of self-reckoning and affirmation.

"EXPERIENCE" AND THE SUBLATION OF CAMBRIDGE ENGLISH

In response to his *NLR* interlocutors' accusation that *Culture and Society* systematically neglects the category of the political, Williams draws an instructive distinction: "Politics often functions, not as I think you are using the term, as a conscious struggle or strategy formed by history and by theory, but as a routine reproduction of controversies or competitive interests without relation to the basic deep movements of society" (*PL* 103). Such unreflective maneuvering for immediate advantage, he continues, "positively prevents people from seeing what is happening in society" (*PL* 103). Against this routinized, blinkered, and superficial activity, Williams valorizes "a politics which is based on an understanding of the main lines of force in society and a choice of sides in the conflict between them" (*PL* 103). An efficacious politics, in other words, requires the historico-theoretical comprehension of the dominant contending forces within the social body, as well as a deliberate decision about which side of the struggle to take.[3] Although Williams did not undertake *Culture and Society* to attain the critical lucidity required for effectual political practice, this ambition inexorably became central to the project.

As is well-known, Williams intended to write an "oppositional work" aimed at rescuing the discourse of culture from its reactionary appropriation by T. S. Eliot, F. R. Leavis, and their acolytes (*PL* 97). With this critical task complete, he would delineate his own views in *The Long Revolution* (*PL* 98). But Williams's sense of disillusionment and anomie overrode this tidy scheme. As he later reflected, "I did not write it [*Culture and Society*] only as a history, as the Conclusion sufficiently shows. I began it in the post-1945 crisis of belief and affiliation. I used all the work for it as a way of finding a position from which I could hope to understand *and act* in contemporary society, necessarily through its history" (*CS* xii, emphasis mine). During its protracted, and often haphazard, composition between 1948 and 1956, *Culture and Society* evolved into the very historical-cum-theoretical investigation that its author considered the prerequisite to effective political activity; it became, that is, an inquiry already inclining toward praxis.[4]

In the process, the book outgrew its methodology as well; it strains against the Cantabrigian literary-critical paradigm in which it is couched. From its first reviewers onward, commentators have argued that *Culture and Society*'s essentially literary approach to its materials is inadequate, given the book's extraordinary scope and ambition. While I will not contest this judgment, I do want to underscore the ways in which Williams's formation in "Cambridge English" made possible the long-political investigation the text performs.[5] Even "experience," that most mystified of Cambridge school concepts, grew supple and complex in Williams's hands, so that opened onto the social and, ultimately, the utopian.

Primed by Terry Eagleton's infamous attack on just this subject, the *NLR* editors pounce on the deference to lived experience that *Culture and Society* evinces.[6] Particularly when engaging with conservative figures, Williams appears to make an implicit distinction "between the truth of ideas as usually understood—the sort that help us to understand history or politics—and a deeper or more durable experience that does not necessarily correspond to any kind of ordinary discursive truth" (*PL* 120). As their allusion to "politics" intimates, this line of questioning is closely connected with the editors' unease with the book's tendency to neglect the political in favor of putatively more essential categories, be they social insight or lived experience. Williams admits that this deference to textually mediated experience is a residue of his instruction in practical criticism: "The hard-learnt procedure of literary judgment was a kind of suspension before experience"—and avers that he now believes that the highly asymmetric relationship between reader and text that traditional literary criticism prescribes "is unsustainable and destructive" (*PL* 121, 122).

Williams can retroactively critique the literary critical paradigm of the "passive-active reader," however, because he has already reaped the benefits of having employed it (*PL* 122). He recalls that while writing *Culture and Society*,

> I was making a conscious effort to understand what someone like Burke or Coleridge must have been as a mind. Indeed, there was a sense in which as I was writing about each of these people I felt that I was looking at things so entirely in their terms that I was almost becoming them. . . . I found that I was sinking so much into the material that it was a positive effort to control my own writing back from the mode of writing I was reworking. I think this enabled me to get nearer to some of the ideas of these writers than I might have otherwise done. (*PL* 121–22)

This empathetic reading allowed Williams to push beyond the rote "marshalling of who were the progressive thinkers and who were the reactionary thinkers"—a method that the *NLR* editors would appear to prefer he had continued under the sign of ideology critique (*PL* 105). Far from an avoidance or trivialization of the political, his sympathetic engagement with conservative authors enabled Williams to achieve more nuanced understandings of the sensibility underlying and informing their political thought.

Crucially, the reading practice Williams describes in the above-quoted passage owes less to Richards or Leavis than to an earlier Cambridge literary giant. Williams lamented that *Culture and Society* gives short shrift to Wordsworth, a writer who figures prominently in "The Idea of Culture" (1953), the essay-length precis of the book (*PL* 100). But Wordsworth, slighted at the level of content, is ubiquitous at the level of methodology. In the preface to *Lyrical Ballads* (1802), Wordsworth memorably asserts that "it will be the wish of the Poet to bring his feelings near to those of the persons whose feelings he describes, nay, for short spaces of time perhaps, to let himself slip into an entire delusion, and even confound and identify his own feelings with theirs."[7] By imaginatively submerging his own identity into that of his subjects, the poet is able to produce language that more closely approximates what would be spoken in the situation he depicts. Williams's own acts of imaginative identification led to a similar affective and stylistic blurring ("I was sinking so much into the material that it was a positive effort to control my own writing back from the mode of writing I was reworking").[8] But the yield of this method in his case is political insight, rather than mimetic verisimilitude. In particular, it enabled Williams to recognize that, for most of the long nineteenth century, both protosocialist themes and a sense of "radical disturbance" were more prevalent among canonical romantic conservatives than their liberal and radical counterparts (*CS* xi). This realization lies behind the book's greatest polemical achievement: its bravura demonstration that British socialism can claim intellectual descent from both sides of the political spectrum.

This is not to assert that Williams achieved a clean break from the early twentieth-century exemplars of Cambridge English. *Culture and Society* holds in high esteem those authors who exhibit what Leavis famously called "a vital capacity for experience, a kind of reverent openness before life, and a marked moral intensity," and it lavishes praise on writers who allow their direct observations to modify—or, better still, simply bypass—their own political commitments.[9] Yet both his passionate disagreements with Leavisism and the very nature of his theme drive Williams beyond the master's literary vitalism. *Culture and Society* takes as its governing conceit Britain's industrial modernization, a climacteric so vast and unprecedented that all extant conceptual and linguistic resources are brought up short before it.[10] The social ramifications of this transformation are such that "at the beginning, and indeed for two or three generations, it was literally a problem of finding a language to express them" (*CS* x). In such an unexampled and dynamic milieu, the experience of even the most perceptive and cerebral witnesses will, inevitability, be of equivocal value.

As Williams warms to his theme, this recognition exerts an ever-greater influence on his analysis. Thus in the concluding flourish of the second chapter, "The Romantic Artist," he writes, "The whole action has passed into our common experience, to lie there, formulated and unformulated, to move and to be examined. 'For it is less their spirit, than the spirit of the age'" (*CS*

48). Here, several of *Culture and Society*'s central methodological supposi-
tions cinch into place. First, individual testimonies are sublated within a
shared field of "common experience"; collectively, they document a pivotal
episode in the nation's social being. (Because Britain was the first country to
industrialize, moreover, this is an epochal event in the species being of humanity as a whole.) Second, some quantum of this common experience remains "unformulated"—that is, incompletely assimilated and inarticulate.
Most of this inchoate experience, Williams would soon acknowledge, is
irretrievably lost with the passing of the "lived culture of a particular time
and place" (*LR* 70). But the recovery and interpretation of the salvageable
remnant of this inert experiential material is one of the cultural historian's
essential tasks.

Despite his oft-mooted skepticism of Freud and his heirs, the theoretical
procedure Williams delineates in this passage is strongly reminiscent of the
psychoanalytic approach to trauma: unassimilated psychical material must be
dredged up and "examined," so that it can be successfully integrated into the
analysand's identity.[11] Deepening the similarity to psychoanalysis, the surviving collective experience of industrial modernization, although only partially formulated, retains its strong capacity "to move"—a locution that
underscores the centrality of emotion to Williams's hermeneutic. Like the
analyst in talk therapy, the critic can "follow the feeling," using powerful
affect to locate the unassimilated, ideational material that must be worked
through. Here the parallel to psychoanalysis breaks down, since Williams's
ultimate concern is social and political, not individual and therapeutic. Accordingly, he uses the experiential material he excavates for a transindividual
purpose: the reconstitution of the ascendant structure of feeling in a particular
historical moment. His attention to this horizon of meaning enables him to
transcend not just the confines of individual experience, but the manifest
ideological oppositions that characterize immediate politics as well.

To be sure, the *NLR* editors are correct to protest that *Culture and Society*
systematically underweights the expressed political ideas and commitments
of the conservative writers it examines (*PL* 107–8). But the virtue of
Williams's approach is its capacity to make visible the "strange affiliations"
that obtain between contemporaries ranged on opposing sides of the political
spectrum (*CS* 20). These unexpected convergences "in thought and feeling"
occur as individuals respond to "the basic deep movements of society": para-
digmatically, the unfolding of the industrial and democratic revolutions (*CS*
vii, *PL* 102).[12] These are "the momentous social changes," as Williams says
in relation to the Romantic poets, "which were eventually to determine all
politics"—and, simultaneously, to relegate many topical political debates to
the status of historical curios (*PL* 102). By pursuing its synchronic recon-
structions of the structure of feeling in chronological succession, *Culture and
Society* reveals the uneven but inexorable course of the long revolution. It is

with reference to this extended temporality—and the ongoing struggles that propel and attend it—that a theoretically self-conscious political actor must plant his or her flag in the present. It is this task that Williams takes up in the book's conclusion.

LOCATING THE SEEDS OF LIFE:
THE LONG REVOLUTION SURVEYED

"When we confirm our deepest alignments, but now very consciously and deliberately, something strange has happened and we feel quite differently committed," Williams observes in "The Writer: Commitment and Alignment" (1980) (*RH* 87). In the conclusion of *Culture and Society* we witness just such a confirmation, as Williams embraces the very determinations that have shaped him. The result is what he characterized as a "renewal of belief"—and a rededication to political engagement on the basis of newly clarified principles (*PL* 106). Here, I will examine Williams's anatomy of the long revolution's political field, before investigating the ways in which Williams seeks to intervene within it. The conclusion extends Williams's productive defamiliarization of the concept of "experience" to include his own—and lifts the utopian dimension of his political thought into high relief.

Because the conclusion is staged as a succession of mini-essays, it will be helpful to begin by abstracting its political analysis. Admittedly, this procedure would be anathema to Williams; however, I maintain that the celebrated subtlety of his arguments has, as their very condition of possibility, their author's sure grasp of a handful of fundamental political struggles, as well as his affiliations within them. According to the Williams of *Culture and Society*, the essential politics of the long revolution is structured by two abiding, and inter-articulated, conflicts: aristocracy versus democracy, and individualism versus collectivism.[13] Consequently, we might visualize the epoch's politics as a field demarcated by two axes: a vertical axis with aristocracy and democracy at its extremes, and a horizontal axis with individualism and collectivism at its antipodes. While there are innumerable possible positions within this field, we can nonetheless identify four primary tendencies, which we might reasonably label as follows: socialism, Toryism, bourgeois liberalism, and enlightenment democracy.[14] The result is represented in table 1.

Williams's primary antagonist is, of course, bourgeois liberalism, which weds "class-democracy"—a mode of aristocracy that dare not speak its name—to an individualist conception of society (*CS* 299). In (roughly) the first half of the conclusion, Williams seeks to expose and subvert Britain's class democracy through imminent critique; in the latter half, he draws upon his historical and semantic investigation of "culture" to challenge the bourgeoisie's claim to cultural stewardship and, ultimately, its individualist ethos.

Table 2.1.   Primary Political Tendencies of the Long Revolution

↓ Political Axes →	Individualism	Collectivism
Aristocracy	Bourgeois Liberalism	Toryism
Democracy	Enlightenment Democracy	Socialism

Initially, Williams fall back—or, rather, appears to fall back—into the familiar Leavisite strain: "What we receive from the tradition is a set of meanings, but not all of these will hold their significance if, as we must, we return them to immediate experience," he writes. "I have tried to make this return, and I will set down the variations and new definitions that have followed from this, as a personal conclusion" (*CS* 297). While "immediate experience" is indeed central to the rhetoric of the conclusion, both the modesty and the emphasis on the "personal" in this statement prove highly misleading. Throughout, Williams favors the first-person plural—the "we" of the first sentence of the quotation rather than the "I" of the second—implicitly denying that there is anything markedly individualized about the observations he proffers.

Eagleton was astute to link Williams's readiness to treat his "own experience as historically representative" and "socially 'typical'" to the precedent of Wordsworth.[15] Once again, however, it is not Wordsworth the introspective lyricist that Williams takes as his lodestar, but Wordsworth the ventriloquist. In the conclusion, Williams aims to do the poet one better, by ventriloquizing *social experience* itself. Rather than imaginatively channeling the language of a particular, situated individual, in other words, he tries to vocalize the experience that members of the social collective share—or can summarily confirm by testing for themselves. Far from betraying a belief that experience and ideology are antithetical (as Eagleton claims is true of Williams's method more generally), the efficacy of this technique presupposes their substantial, albeit not total, overlap.

Consider the demystification of the spurious concept of "the masses," one of the conclusion's central interventions. It provides a particularly clear example of Williams's technique of social ventriloquism at work:

> I do not think of my relatives, friends, neighbours, colleagues, acquaintances, as masses; we none of us can or do. The masses are always the others, whom we don't know, and can't know. Yet now, in our kind of society, we see these others regularly, in their myriad variations; stand, physically, beside them. They are here, and we are here with them. And that we are with them is of course the whole point. To other people, we also are masses. Masses are other people.
>
> There are in fact no masses; there are only ways of seeing people as masses. (*CS* 299–300)

As is characteristic of the conclusion, the "I" is not particularized.[16] Rather, it momentarily precipitates out of the collective "we" to invite readerly introspection (i.e., Do *I* think of my relatives, friends, etc. as masses?) before dissolving, again, into first-person plural. Taken in isolation, this passage almost reads as a parody of syllogistic reasoning: An initial sensory input—I do not see people with whom I am familiar as masses—sets into motion a deductive cascade that culminates in the realization that that "there are in fact no masses." A central ideological prop of bourgeois-class democracy is thus shaken.

In arguing in this fashion, Williams is motivated neither by naïve empiricism nor self-regarding hubris, but strategy. Because bourgeois ideology is hegemonic—because "the ideas of the ruling class are in every epoch the ruling ideas"—even those members of the social formation who belong to other classes are fluent in (and, to varying degrees, ensnared by) it.[17] This enables Williams to sap the dominant ideology from within through internal critique, rather than challenging it from a position of exteriority.[18] But when he turns, in the latter part of the conclusion, to the question of who possesses "culture," Williams can no longer sustain his equanimity. "None of us are referees . . . ; we are all in the game, and playing in one or other direction," he admits (*CS* 319). Consequently, he changes tack to contest the bourgeoisie's assertion of cultural stewardship and its individualist conception of society.

As the sports metaphor insists, all of the participants in the debate about culture are players, not referees. But the book's historico-semantic and discursive investigations radically delimit the field of play, enabling Williams to demonstrate that many of the opposing players are, in effect, standing out of bounds. In the argumentative climax of *Culture and Society*, Williams discloses the unifying thread of the British discourse of culture:

> The development of the idea of culture has, throughout, been a criticism of what has been called the bourgeois idea of society. The contributors to its meaning have started from widely different positions, and have reached widely various attachments and loyalties. But they have been alike in this, that they have been unable to think of society as a merely neutral area, or as an abstract regulating mechanism. The stress has fallen on the positive function of society, on the fact that the values of individual men are rooted in society, and on the need to think and feel in these common terms. (*CS* 328)

Any position that wishes to claim the sanction of "culture" must reject laissez-faire atomism. Having already exposed the hypocrisy of the bourgeoisie's professed adherence to democracy, here Williams vindicates the collectivist conception of society by divulging the essence of the idea of culture. The ground is thus cleared for the presentation of his own stance: a democratic-socialist common culture founded on the recognition of "equality of being" and imbued with coherence by a collectivist spirit of solidarity. These are the essential, guiding commitments that Williams would maintain for the rest of his life, albeit with ongoing refinement and periodic shifts in emphasis.[19]

Williams articulates his own social commitments by referring to the actualization of a particular facet of the idea of "culture." In so doing, he reveals the utopian impulse that animates his conception of that term. Indeed, for Williams a kind of weak utopianism inheres in language more generally. In the peroration of *Culture and Society*, he declares that "we are coming increasingly to realize that our vocabulary, the language we use to inquire into and negotiate our actions, is no secondary factor, but a practical and radical element in itself. To take a meaning from experience, and to try to make it active, is in fact our process of growth" (*CS* 338). Because words' meanings evolve in response to changes in collective life, language is a repository of "meaning from experience"—of different social configurations and the life possibilities they engender. Collective "growth" in the present is facilitated by deliberate efforts to activate particular lived experiences abeyant in language, so that they become the basis of subsequent social development. To be sure, Williams recognizes that the "major material barriers" to democratic socialism will not be swept away by changes in linguistic "emphasis" alone (*CS* 337, 338).[20] But he expresses his exalted sense of the generative potency of language by adopting, in the book's closing sentences, an uncharacteristic Biblical register: "There are ideas, and ways of thinking, with the seeds of life in them, and there are others, perhaps deep in our minds, with the seeds of a general death. Our measure of success in recognizing these kinds, and in naming them making possible their common recognition, may be literally the measure of our future" (*CS* 338). With this quasi-apocalyptic flourish, Williams's long political investigation races past the struggles of the present to anticipate the outcome, utopian or catastrophic, of the future.

Although it has a basis in the past, the figure of "the seeds of life" confirms that Williams's utopianism is prospective, rather than nostalgic. As Patrick Parrinder cogently put it, Williams judges "present culture unsatisfactory, not by comparison with an idealised past, but from the perspective of a possible future."[21] But this possible future can nonetheless claim to be "organic" to Britain, because "it builds on the meanings and experiences of the recorded past, by a process which is 'at once the idea of a natural growth and that of its tending'"—the idea, that is, of culture.[22] In light of this orientation toward future possibility, Parrinder declares Williams "our [Britain's] only utopian critic."[23] The ideal of a common culture Williams extols in *Culture and Society*'s conclusion is a veritable "cultural utopia reflecting the instincts embodied in the vocabulary of an intellectual and literary tradition—a tradition, moreover, which had grown out of, and had influenced, everyday speech."[24] To return to Williams's own image, "the seeds of life" contained within the language and the literary tradition, if properly tended, blossom as a democratic common culture, which is rooted in an ethos solidarity and (to strain the metaphor) trellised by socialism.[25] This outcome is at once organic and utopian.

There is one final aspect of Parrinder's account that warrants our attention, due to its relevance for the argument of my final section. Parrinder hypothesizes that Williams's utopian ideal emerges as an implicit rejoinder to the dystopian nightmare of another quintessentially British author: George Orwell. Orwell is the subject of the last chapter of *Culture and Society*, and a figure "with whose legacy Williams has engaged in a lifelong struggle."[26] Yet Williams's agon with the most iconoclastic democratic socialist of the preceding generation is fueled as much by their similarities as their differences: "Where for Orwell England appeared as a 'family with the wrong members in control' [in "The Lion and the Unicorn" (1941)], for the Williams of *Culture and Society* it is a native language and literary tradition with the wrong meanings in control; in each case there is a strong sense of cohesion"—the legacy of their shared experience of wartime Britain—"and a feeling that putting things right may only be a matter of time."[27] Both the correspondences Parrinder identifies and the pressure that he speculates Orwell's legacy exerted on Williams's thought are persuasive. They become more so when he adds that it is particularly *Nineteen Eighty-Four*, and Orwell's depiction of the debased laboring-class proles and enfeebled "Ingsoc," that haunted Williams's imagination. The utopian valence of Williams's own politics becomes most pronounced when Williams feels compelled to respond to a threat he perceives as dystopian.

I have argued that Williams's long politics were his effort to orient present political activity by linking it to the abiding, deep-structural conflicts of the long revolution. With the establishment of these theoretical linkages, many pressing controversies are revealed as ephemeral, and "themes and issues" of perennial importance assume their rightful place as guides to struggle (*PL* 106). This is the "redefinition of what politics should be," and its very articulation, Williams's attempt to rouse "the forces necessary for it." As Parrinder's analysis helps us grasp, Williams's inquiry culminated in the elaboration of a utopian ideal of a democratic socialist common culture. But Williams was not yet willing to reckon with the utopian imperative in his own thought; that acknowledgment was still decades away, and far from straightforward when it came.

TOWARDS 2000: FROM "CULTURE"
TO THE "UTOPIAN IMPULSE"

As his conversation with the *NLR* interviewers reveals, Williams's desire to formulate and practice a "different kind of politics" sprang from a conjunctural sense of disillusionment and isolation. Nearly a quarter of a century after *Culture and Society*'s publication, it was a strikingly analogous disappointment with the status quo that prompted Williams to return to his long political project. The deprivations of Thatcherism, the intellectual bankruptcy of the Labour Party—these pressures were compounded by Williams's growing concern with the global impacts of deindustrialization and environmental degradation. In his under-studied *Towards 2000* [American title: *The Year 2000*] (1983), Williams announces his resumption of the project begun "in *Culture and Society* and *The Long Revolution*."[28] Recalibrating his political position in response to new circumstances—and in the face of an emergent threat—drove him to engage with utopianism directly. Williams's consideration of the "utopian impulse" stopped short of a recognition of its animating presence within his own work (*T* 14). Nevertheless, harnessing its resources enabled him to renew his long-political analysis—and project it into futurity.

Towards 2000 is explicitly a rewriting of "Britain in the 1960s," the final, prognostic section of *The Long Revolution*. Williams seeks to revise and expand the analysis of this text in order to transcend its nation-state frame and extend its prospective gaze. While *The Long Revolution* is thus the book that Williams foregrounds in *Towards 2000*, I believe that *Culture and Society* is just as constitutive.[29] "Culture," we recall, came to designate the "effort at total qualitative assessment" of the social formation; it provided a normative standard against which contemporary society, or "civilization," could be judged (*CS* 295, 63). The tradition of invoking "culture" against "civilization" comprises nothing less than "a slow reach again for control"— a protracted effort to reform the "is" of civilization in light of the "ought" of culture (*CS* 295). In *Towards 2000*, Williams again seeks an instrumentality that will provide "some effective common controls of our future" (*T* 11–12). This entails surveying the available modes of "thinking about the future, in their real sense as ways of making it" (*T* 5). As with *Culture and Society*, the vacuousness of immediate politics and its future-oriented discourses (the party program, the manifesto) compels Williams to seek elsewhere for analytical tools.

The "most widely known" of these extra-political anticipatory modes is "utopianism," here understood as a way of thinking about the future, rather than in its strict etymological sense of imagining another place (*T* 12). As Williams had already observed in "Utopia and Science Fiction" (1978), utopian discourse was enjoying a resurgence; here, he adds that "there is an obvious relation between this revival and the recurrent disappointments and despairs of orthodox politics" (*T* 12). But this recoil from "orthodox politics" should not be understood solely as a negative phenomenon:

> The utopian impulse still runs, not only against the disappointments of current politics or a more generalised despair, but also against the incorporated and marketed versions of a libertarian capitalist cornucopia . . . . Its strongest centre is still the conviction that people can live very differently, as distinct both from having different things and from becoming resigned to endless crises and wars. In a time of scarce resources, of any such kind, there can be no question of dispensing with it. (*T* 14)

Utopianism has indubitable value as a stay against nihilism and a means of sustaining belief in the possibility of alternative, noncapitalist forms of collective life. This passage reveals, moreover, that the utopian impulse shares with "culture" qualities that render it especially suited for the rejuvenation of Williams's long-political project. Like the idea of culture, the utopian impulse provides a locus of alternative values—a vantage outside "current politics" from which contemporary civilization can be judged. Again like culture, it serves as a "mitigating and rallying alternative" to existing social and political conditions (*CS* xviii). Most important, utopianism shares with culture the drive to undertake the total qualitative assessment of civilization.

Williams makes the utopian impulse's totalizing vocation explicit in his discussion of the "systematic utopia," the genre of imagined ideal societies, in which the utopian impulse finds its traditional literary expression.[30] "What is strongest about the systematic utopias," he suggests, "is that they are formed by a kind of whole analysis and whole constructive formation. They may then be weak in their particularity or their narrow uniformity, but this procedure of whole analysis and whole formation is intellectually very important" (*T* 14–15). The systematic utopia, that is to say, is a totalizing form that shares with culture the "impulse to wholeness" (*T* 15). The act of depicting a society that is qualitatively superior to contemporary civilization entails, as one of its compositional moments, the "whole analysis" of that civilization. The utopian mode is thus a near relation to the idea of culture; it performs the same compensatory, constructive, and critical tasks.

Here we might pause to ask what prompted Williams to acknowledge, in his final book, the efficacy of the utopian mode for serious analytical and political work. While a utopian strain had been implicit in his own outlook from the first, his corpus also contains unmistakable traces of a vestigial, orthodox Marxist suspicion of utopianism.[31] As late as 1980, in his laudatory review of Rudolf Bahro's *The Alternative in Eastern Europe* (1977; trans. 1978), Williams was still signaling his wariness. In *The Alternative*, Bahro acknowledges that "Marxists have a defensive attitude towards utopias," but insists that "today utopian thought has a new necessity."[32] Yet despite his fundamental sympathy with Bahro's utopian socialism, Williams closes a section of his review with the warning: "Utopia, . . . as a singular noun, is not an emancipatory concept; indeed it is often and at its best frankly compensatory."[33] Given Williams's reluctance to cast off his residual suspicion of utopianism, how we do we account for his positive assessment of it in *Towards 2000*?

I submit that this reevaluation of the utopian impulse can be understood in relation to the emergence of a new, dystopian political logic that Williams felt must be confronted. Williams calls this logic Plan X, "a new politics of strategic advantage" that constitutes "the emerging rationality of self-conscious elites" (*T* 247). If, as Parrinder argued, the spectral presence of Orwell spurred Williams to delineate his utopian ideal in *Culture and Society*, Plan X appears to have played a comparable role in *Towards 2000*. It motivated Williams to assert the value of utopianism as a conceptual and political, as well as an affective, resource.

Plan X is so named because it deliberately refuses to posit an ultimate goal or imagine "lasting liberation" (*T* 245). Instead, its practitioners accept futurity as a condition of "unending and unavoidable struggle"—a permanent state of extreme crisis (*T* 245). Once the future is conceived in these Hobbesian terms, the practice of politics contracts to the maintenance of relative advantage: "an effective even if temporary edge, which will always keep them at least one step ahead" (*T* 244). But what renders this modality truly dystopian—and a source of enormous concern for Williams—is that it takes many of the worst features of immediate politics and elevates them into a strategy for conducting the class struggle itself.

In Plan X thinking, several of the most pernicious traits of immediate politics reappear: the exclusive concern with short-term advantage, as well as the obliviousness to deep-structural social dynamics. It combines these traits with an acute class consciousness, and thereby comprises "a way—a limited but powerful way—of grasping and attempting to control the future" (*T* 248). The myopia and superficiality of immediate politics are essentially side effects—the lamentable but predictable consequence of the rhythms of day-to-day struggle and the dust of combat. What renders Plan X properly dystopian is that it takes these involuntary, debilitating features of immediate politics and *knowingly adopts them*. It thereby transforms the unintended consequences of routine political engagement into a strategy for controlling the future itself.

Contemplating the inexorable diffusion of Plan X thinking, Williams avers that "the only serious alternative to it is a way of thinking about the future, and of planning, which is at least as rational and as informed in all its specific policies, and which is not only morally much stronger, in its concern for a common wellbeing, but at this most general level is *more* rational and *better* informed" (*T* 248). Such an alternative can only emerge from the crucible of utopianism. This is so because of one final affordance the systematic utopia possesses:

> What the systematic utopia offers, at its best, is an imaginative reminder of the nature of historical change: that major social orders do rise and fall, and that new social orders do succeed them. . . . [T]he value of the systematic utopia is to lift our eyes beyond the short-term adjustments and changes which are the ordinary material of politics, and thus to insist, as a matter of general principle, that temporarily and locally incredible changes can and do happen. (*T* 13)

The utopian mode prompts its readers to look beyond the noisy but ultimately minor oscillations that comprise "the ordinary material of politics"—and that have now been transvalued, at the level of political strategy, in Plan X. By making tangible the epochal character of civilization ("major social orders do rise and fall") and by reminding its readers that temporality is characterized by rupture as well as continuity, the utopian mode cultivates a rich sense of historicity. Plan X's calculated refusal to imagine futurity as anything other than a progressively worsening extension of the present is fundamental to its efficacy. But this refusal to entertain the possibility of qualitative historical change also renders Plan X thinkers vulnerable to those who possess a more capacious historical sensibility. This is doubly so because humanity makes its own history; consequently, Williams observes, "A major element in what is going to happen is the state of mind of all of us who are in a position to intervene in [industrial civilization's] complex processes" (*T* 5). By adopting a bunker mentality, the practitioners of Plan X risk succumbing to a self-fulfilling prophecy.

At this stage of the argument, one last similarity between the idea of culture and utopianism must be addressed. While the utopian mode shares many of the affordances of the idea of culture, Williams suggests that it is marked by many of the same deficiencies. As *Culture and Society* argues, the hypostatization of "culture" lifted it into the realm of secular transcendence; its capacity to underwrite totalizing critique and provide a "higher Court of Appeal" to the injustices of civilization is wholly bound up with its detachment from everyday life (*CS* 48). Analogously, the utopian impulse manifests itself through the elaboration of an ideal society with no real world correlative. The idea of culture had to be demystified to realize its emancipatory potential; the recognition that culture is "a whole way of life," is ultimately what enables Williams to turn the tables on Leavis, Eliot, and the bourgeois class (*CS* xviii).

Williams argues that utopianism must undergo an analogous correction. "What is most deficient in the strictly utopian mode," he observes, "is that this [social] wholeness is essentially *projected*, to another place or time. What we have to learn, beyond utopian thinking, is this impulse to wholeness without the accompanying projection" (*T* 15). Just as "culture" had to be returned to earth to unleash its full store of liberatory vitality, the utopian impulse must be rendered immanent, and thereby moored in real world possibility. The result is a discourse equipped to perform "constructive analysis of the present and of possible and probable futures"—a radical futurology that has assimilated the totalizing imperative and historicist sensibility of utopianism (*T* 15).[34] It is this discourse that Williams practices in *Towards 2000*, culminating in his delineation of an environmentally sustainable, post-capitalist international order whose salience has only increased in the years since its publication. He thereby continues and updates the long political project *Culture and Society* began.

Guided by the "map" of culture, Williams had plunged into Britain's history in his groundbreaking study (*CS* xvii). He thereby attained perspective on the political struggles of the present and uncovered the potentialities of "culture" that could be realized in the near future. *Towards 2000* replicates the earlier book's procedure, but in the opposite temporal direction. Williams, that is, draws upon the capabilities of utopianism to attain critical distance from the impoverished political debates of the present from the vantage point of the immediate future. Finally, he limns an eminently realizable prospect: an ecologically responsible, global democratic socialism that lies on the other side of the long revolution. "Not in Utopia," as Wordsworth urged, "But in the very world, which is the world / Of all of us."

NOTES

1. As I have explored elsewhere, the category of the "political" is exceptionally (and, to some degree, unavoidably) amorphous in literary and cultural analysis; see Mark Allison, "Politics," *Victorian Literature and Culture* 46, no. 3/4 (2018): 806–9. Clearly, the analysis and tactics of the New Left marked a decisive—and self-conscious—step in the blurring of the boundaries of the political sphere.

2. *Culture and Society*'s catastrophist understanding of the industrial revolution as a swift and total social transformation is arguably its most shopworn feature. For a succinct intellectual-historical criticism of *Culture and Society*, see Stefan Collini, "From 'Non-Fiction Prose' to 'Cultural Criticism': Genre and Disciplinarity in Victorian Studies," in *Rethinking Victorian Culture*, ed. Juliet John and Alice Jenkins (Hounsdsmills, Basingstoke, UK: MacMillan, 2000), 22–24. Its weaknesses notwithstanding, I also take it as a given that *Culture and Society* remains an indispensable historiography.

3. The vocabulary Williams utilizes in this interview is frequently Gramscian, recalling, especially, Gramsci's attempt to theorize the interrelation of "organic" (deep-structural and permanent) and "conjunctural" (immediate and transitory) movements within a social formation. See Antonio Gramsci, *Selections from the Prison Notebooks*, ed. and trans. Quintin Hoare and Geoffrey Nowell Smith (New York: International Publishers, 1971), 175–85. While there are many affinities between the thought of Williams and Gramsci, the former's position is more distinctive and idiosyncratic than his belated adoption of a Gramscian idiom suggests.

4. On the dating of *Culture and Society*'s gestation, see Andrew Milner, *Re-Imagining Cultural Studies: The Promise of Cultural Materialism* (London: SAGE, 2002), 50–51. The *Long Revolution* (1961) further describes the way that *Culture and Society* evolved during its writing, necessitating that Williams rethink the connection between these two books. It would

be fruitful to consider the relationship between what I have termed "long politics" and what Williams later referred to as "operative theory": "a theory carrying practice" (*CM* 237–38).

5. For a helpful analysis of the chief figures of "Cambridge English" in its golden age, see Chris Baldick, *The Social Mission of English Criticism, 1848–1932* (Oxford: Oxford University Press 1983), esp. 134–86. For studies of the major print organ of Leavisism and its influence, see Francis Mulhern, *The Moment of "Scrutiny"* (London: New Left Books, 1979) and Christopher Hilliard, *English as a Vocation: The "Scrutiny" Movement* (Oxford: Oxford University Press, 2012). For Williams's own reflections, see, especially, "Cambridge English, Past and Present," and "Beyond Cambridge English," in *Writing in Society* (London: Verso, 1991), 177–91, 212–26.

6. See Terry Eagleton, "Criticism and Politics: The Work of Raymond Williams," *New Left Review* 1, no. 95 (January/February 1976), esp. 6–9.

7. William Wordsworth, preface to *Lyrical Ballads, with Pastoral and Other Poems*, in *Selected Poems*, ed. John O. Hayden (London: Penguin Books, 1994), 442.

8. Williams subsequently refers to the result of this deeply sympathetic reading as "unconscious ventriloquism" (*PL* 252). As he undoubtedly knew, Coleridge used the latter term to characterize Wordsworth's poetic identification with his imagined speakers (*Biographia Literaria : Or, Biographical Sketches of My Literary Life and Opinions*, ed. James Engell and W. Jackson Bate [Princeton, NJ: Princeton University Press, 1983], 2:135). *Culture and Society* is a Wordsworthian enterprise in more than its utilization of ventriloquism. Consider Williams's preoccupation with "common experience," "common life," and "common language," as well as his methodological privileging of affect (*CS* xiii, xx, xx). As Wordsworth declared, "It is the hour of feeling" ("To My Sister," in *Selected Poems*, 21).

9. F. R. Leavis, *The Great Tradition: George Eliot, Henry James, Joseph Conrad* (London: Chatto & Windus, 1948), 9

10. Moreover, Williams's thinking was always productively exceeding the limits of even this frame. In "The Idea of Culture," for example, he observes, "The Industrial Revolution is a myth"—a folk designation for a much more geographically and temporally uneven phenomenon ("IC" 61). And in the postscript to the 1963 edition of *Culture and Society*, Williams announces, "I feel increasingly that the creative social thinking of the Commonwealth is a major source for the later tradition," effectively locating the origins of the long revolution in the 1640s, rather than the 1780s ([Hammondsworth, Middlesex, UK: Penguin, 1963], 326).

11. Catherine Gallagher and Stephen Greenblatt's affectionate criticism of Williams's use of "experience" is incisive (*Practicing New Historicism* [Chicago: University of Chicago Press, 2000], 62). However, their claim that Williams depicts "the modern as a state of experiential lack or repression" risks conflating the traumatizing *transition* to modernity with modernity tout court (64). *Culture and Society*'s conception of the industrial revolution as a traumatic event anticipates Williams's *Modern Tragedy* (1966) and the argument that the long revolution as a whole is "the inevitable working through of a deep and tragic disorder" (*MT* 75). In true dialectical fashion, Williams understands revolution as at once liberation and catastrophe.

12. "The idea of *culture* would be simpler it had been a response to industrialism alone," Williams writes in *Culture and Society*'s original introduction, "but it was also, quite evidently, a response to the new political and social developments, to *Democracy*" (*CS* xviii).

13. *The Long Revolution*, via the category of "cultural revolution" would introduce a third structuring conflict: minority culture versus common culture (*LR* 11). The struggle for a common culture is already thematized, though not formulated as such, in *Culture and Society*'s conclusion, in its detailed discussions of education, communication, and transmission (*CS* 295–338 passim).

14. I extrapolate this last designation from Williams's discussion of "that old kind of democrat" who is "often too sure of man's natural nobility to concern himself with the means of its common assurance" (*CS* 311). Note that the designations I have chosen might easily be replaced by others; they serve merely to identify what Williams considers longstanding tendencies within British politics.

15. Eagleton, "Criticism and Politics," 9.

16. Even the moment that Williams affirms his own alignment is rendered impersonally. Discussing the trope of the "educational ladder," he writes, "The boy who has gone from a

council school to Oxford or Cambridge is of course glad that he has gone . . . , but he sees no reason why it should be interpreted as a ladder" (*CS* 331–32). With the repudiation of the ladder figure, "interest is returned to what is, for him, its proper object: to the making of a common educational provision; to the work for equity in material distribution; to the process of shaping a tradition, a community of experience, which is always a selective organization of past and present" (*CS* 332).

17. Karl Marx and Friedrich Engels, *The German Ideology* (Amherst, NY: Prometheus Books, 1998), 67.

18. Williams even ventriloquizes the bourgeois structure of feeling, "that half-world of feeling in which we are invited to have our being," as if he wholly shares it (*CS* 304). This structure is characterized by acceptance of "the principle of democracy" accompanied by fear of "its full and active practice" (*CS* 304).

19. Perhaps foremost among these modulations was Williams's increasing awareness of the constitutive importance of his Welsh identity.

20. For a pellucid discussion of language as itself a material site of struggle, see Daniel Hartley, "On Raymond Williams: Complexity, Immanence, and the Long Revolution," *Mediations* 30, no. 1 (Fall 2016): 46–51.

21. Patrick Parrinder, "Utopia and Negativity in Raymond Williams," in *The Failure of Theory: Essays on Criticism and Contemporary Fiction* (Brighton, Sussex, UK: Harvester Press, 1987), 74.

22. Patrick Parrinder, "*Culture and Society* in the 1980s," in *The Failure of Theory*, 68.

23. Parrinder, "Utopia and Negativity in Raymond Williams," 75.

24. Parrinder, "*Culture and Society* in the 1980s," 71. While his analysis is remarkably insightful, Parrinder does err in characterizing the utopia Williams envisions as "monolithic" (68). While the common culture Williams calls for will be integrated through the spirit of solidarity, he is forthright that it will be complex and reticulate: "A culture in common, in our own day, will not be the simple all-in-all society of old dream" (*CS* 333). This difference is clarified by the subsequent distinction between (the democratic and participatory) "common culture" and the (top down) "culture in common" in his "The Idea of Common Culture" (1968) (*RH* 32–38).

25. Parrinder notes in passing that Williams's ideal of a democratic common culture has marked similarities with Jurgen Habermas's normative project ("On Disagreement and the Public Domain," in *The Failure of Theory*, 50). Both Williams and Habermas eschew specifying the content of the common culture; instead, they concentrate on identifying the conditions that will enable a democracy to chart its own course through a process of shared decision-making. The similarities between Williams's and Habermas's utopian ideals are further explored by Paul Jones, *Raymond Williams's Sociology of Culture: A Critical Reconstruction* (Houndsmills, Basingstoke, UK: Palgrave Macmillan, 2004), 181–94; and Patrick Brantlinger, *Crusoe's Footprints: Cultural Studies in Britain and America* (New York: Routledge, 1990), esp. 180–98.

26. Parrinder, "*Culture and Society* in the 1980s," 71.

27. Ibid.

28. Raymond Williams, *The Year 2000* (New York: Pantheon Books, 1983), xii. The preface only appears in the American edition. Citations hereafter will be to the English version. The most important discussion of this book remains Francis Mulhern, "Towards 2000, or News from You-Know-Where," in *Raymond Williams: Critical Perspectives*, ed. Terry Eagleton (Boston: Northeastern University Press, 1989), 67–94.

29. Perhaps the continuity between *Culture and Society* and *Towards 2000* is best illustrated by Williams's claim that replacing the social emphasis on "production" with an orientation toward "livelihood" will facilitate a richer conception of society as "a way of *life*" (*T* 266). This, in effect, expands the concept of culture—"a whole of life"—so that it is coextensive with "society."

30. For ease of exposition, I am bracketing the distinction that Williams, following Miguel Abensour, draws between "systematic" and "heuristic" utopias. On this distinction see Williams, "Utopia and Science Fiction" (*CM* 202–4).

31. On Williams's skittishness about utopianism, see Andrew Milner, *Tenses of the Imagination: Raymond Williams on Science Fiction, Utopia and Dystopia* (Oxford: Peter Lang), 125–26; 149.

32. Rudolf Bahro, *The Alternative in Eastern Europe*, trans. by David Fernbach (London: Verso, 1981), 253.

33. Raymond Williams, "Beyond Actually Existing Socialism" (*CM* 261).

34. We might question whether a spatiotemporally immanent futurology necessarily lies "beyond utopian thinking," or whether this assumption is simply another manifestation of Williams's inherited distrust of utopianism. That fellow son of a railway signalman, Ernst Bloch, would identify the mode Williams desires as an anticipatory hermeneutic keyed to "concrete utopia": the genuinely utopian that is nonetheless latent within the historical process itself (*The Principle of Hope*, vol. 1, trans. Neville Plaice, Stephen Plaice, and Paul Knight (Cambridge, MA: MIT Press, 1986), 146.

Chapter Three

Unlearning and Relearning the Future

Raymond Williams's Timely Utopia

Mathias Nilges

In 2021, we are celebrating Raymond Williams's one-hundredth birthday, and, as is often the case when we celebrate such milestones, especially those of great critics and theorists, this moment is an opportunity not only for praise, but also for detailed retrospection and reevaluation. Attempts to re-examine a critic's work and thought benefit from widening the scope of our engagement with the source material by reminding ourselves not only of what was said but also of how things were formulated. That is, we should not only examine the content of the oeuvre, determining which aspects of the work remain relevant or may in fact be endowed with a new salience in our own time, but we should also look at how Williams thought about the world, how he approached a problem, and how he formulated his analyses—focusing, that is, on questions of method. Doing so, allows us to determine which aspects of Williams's methodology may help us make sense both of our own historical moment and of the social and cultural constellations in which we find ourselves. In short, as part of my own celebration of Williams's one-hundredth birthday, I wish to return to some aspects of his work that strike me as particularly important for our own time; in order to highlight these aspects, I shall focus less on what Williams said than on how Williams thought about and approached a specific set of topics and problems. This re-examination of Williams's methodology and some of his most characteristic forms of thought strikes me as fitting for the important occasion marked by this book.

Since the attempt at historicizing Williams is in line with his own metho-dology, focusing on method and forms of thought is also an exercise in fidelity aimed at honoring Williams's emphasis on matters of methodology.

After all, Williams himself stressed throughout his career the importance of studying the historical flow of specific forms of culture and imagination and the material and social structures with which this historical development was for him, at every point, bound up. And yet, what follows is more than a dry assessment of the structures and methods of Williams's thought and work, however helpful such a discussion might be. I also wish to suggest that we remember Williams as one of the great theorists of hope of the second half of the twentieth century. For although those who know Williams's work will readily associate him with the study of utopia, critical discourse ordinarily does not count Williams among the big theorists of hope (such as Ernst Bloch or Richard Rorty). But one important reason why we should revisit Williams in our time, I shall suggest, is that hope is not just a topic of Williams's work but might be more significantly understood as a consequence of Williams's method. And it is this striking ability to find hope in dark times through a particular commitment to materialist social and cultural analysis that is endowed with new significance and urgency today, when so many of us struggle to find a glimmer of hope in the murkiness of our increasingly troubled times.

For the better part of the new millennium, academic and popular commentary has been proliferating the notion that we live in an era defined by a crisis of the utopian imagination. In fact, the suggestion that we cannot imagine alternatives to the present has become so ubiquitous that it is situated somewhere between an axiomatic account of our present and a cliché that, through repetition *ad infinitum*, transforms itself into lived reality. Our historical moment, we keep hearing, is defined by our struggle to conceive of substantive social change, and, indeed, by our increasing inability to imagine futures that would constitute positive improvements of our lives compared to the conditions of our present existence. In a recent article published with the political news website and polling data aggregator *RealClear Politics*, Robert J. Samuelson observes that the phenomenon that literary and cultural critics, economists, political philosophers, and a wide range of writers and artists have long stressed has, in fact, become a widely measurable global phenomenon. "It has long been an accepted axiom . . . that the future would be better than the past. People took it for granted that living standards would rise and that life would become more comfortable and stable," Samuelson writes.[1] In our moment, however, we have reached the limits of this narrative; we must, Samuelson concludes, "kiss that optimism goodbye." Samuelson reports that a new survey of twenty-seven countries finds that "confidence in the future is weak" and that "among the 18 advanced countries surveyed, only Poland (59 percent) and Russia (51 percent) had majorities who felt the future would be better than the present."

What is striking here, aside from the not entirely surprising notion that a strong belief in the future only exists among a small majority of people living in countries that are rapidly drifting toward far-right authoritarianism, is that even the recent, gradually rising confidence in *the present*, following a big dip in confidence in the immediate aftermath of the 2008 crash, does not translate into a rise in confidence in *the future*. On the contrary, optimism and the belief that the future may end up better than the present continue to erode, leaving politicians, economic analysts, and pollsters to wonder how we can account for this significant, widening gap between present and future. But while he notes that "losing faith in the future is a big deal," Samuelson concludes his inquiry without advancing any significant insights into the matter, merely expressing his hope that what we are seeing "reflects a passing moment and not a permanent new reality."[2]

This hope has no doubt been thoroughly dashed by the events of recent months; the year 2021 is sure to see not only Williams's one-hundredth birthday, but also an all-time low in our level of confidence in the future. For most of us who have lived through months of the COVID-19 pandemic, optimism and hope for a better future (or even the return to the now mythical pre-pandemic "normal") are becoming increasingly rare, especially as capital once again tightens its grip on the mechanisms of crisis management, leading many to conclude, with a significant degree of dismay, that the pandemic and its long-term effects may cause nations to roll back the few, fledgling efforts at working toward advanced societies (such as facilitating an energy transition and other large-scale projects that may grapple with the climate crisis) that have emerged in recent years. Already as I write, such initiatives, new tax codes, governmental incentives, and emergent support for progressive social initiatives moving toward a greener economy are being widely canceled in the general effort to ramp up capitalist production to make up for lost productivity. In this situation, we seem caught in a moment that, as William Gibson stressed in a recent conversation with Joshua Rothman on *The New Yorker Radio Hour*, leaves us without the kind of future imagination that was still available to him as a child. One simple yet clear sign of this, Gibson suggests, is that while generations looked ahead and excitedly anticipated the future of "the twentieth century" or "the twenty-first century," barely anyone today hears or utters the phrase "the twenty-second century."[3]

The causes of this crisis of futurity are highly complex but, as I show elsewhere in great detail,[4] they can be traced back to specific sociopolitical, cultural, and indeed epistemological crises that result from the gradual transition into the current stage of neoliberal capitalism. In other words, while mainstream commentary has been reiterating the same diagnosis for more than two decades now—namely, that we seem unable to imagine progressive futures or alternatives to contemporary capitalism, resigning ourselves to the proliferation of cultural and political fantasies of the end times and of large-scale catastrophes—it is important, I argue, to understand the current crisis of futurity as a symptom of a specific set of changes in material history. Doing so, allows us not only to historicize the purported end of the future in our time but also to find ways to think and ultimately move beyond what we can then understand as self-imposed limits. In this context, the work of Williams is of central importance, in part because his late work offers the beginnings of a historicization of the crises of our time. Additionally, while the general context of this crisis surpasses the frame of what can be examined here, it is important to ask, as I will do in what follows, how we may read Williams's work in our historical moment. In short, why should we read Williams in our temporally troubled time? In the pages that follow, I argue that we have much to gain from revisiting Williams's writings on utopia as a form of thought because his analyses of the limits of our (utopian) imagination offer us remarkably timely tools for making sense of our present. After all, it is precisely in moments of foreclosure and crisis, Williams shows, that the question of the renewal of the utopian impulse raises itself with particular urgency. And it is through an examination of the emergence of utopia under dire constraints, Williams's work illustrates, that we are able to get at the heart of the utopian imagination. Utopia, Williams demonstrates, lies not in images of harmonious futures or picturesque alternatives to the present. Rather, utopia should be understood as a form of thought itself, as the first step toward what he describes as a "transformed this-world" (a term that we will interrogate in more detail below), a step that must be taken within a situation of confinement by confronting the limits of utopia in a given historical moment.[5] Examining our moment from the standpoint of Williams's account of the dialectic of foreclosure and utopian impulse, this chapter argues that Williams's conception of the politics and method of utopia offers us a method for historicizing the present that lays bare the self-imposed limits of our cultural and political imagination by tearing at the fissures of the now. Today, Williams's work provides us with powerful ways to wrest a sense of renewal from the grip of a present that obscures the relation between the utopian imagination and the possibility of a "transformed this-world." What we find in Williams's account of the self-renewal of the true utopian impulse, which can only emerge out of a confrontation with its own limits and foreclosures, is a form of thought aimed at transporting our imagination and ultimately our world beyond the limits imposed upon it by the capitalist imagination.

When asked, in an interview with Terry Eagleton conducted in 1987, after retiring from his position at Cambridge (Williams retired in 1983) and years of teaching, writing, and fighting against fascism for a more just society, if the rise of Thatcherism left him disillusioned, Williams responded by making a simple yet instructive distinction: The turn to the right left him feeling disappointed yet not disillusioned. More importantly, precisely as a consequence of what he describes as the "open reaction of the Thatcher governments," Williams stresses that "it is clearer to me than ever that the socialist analysis is the correct one" (*RH* 315). The problem of the Left was, in a sense, that the "perspectives which had sustained the main left organizations were simply not adequate to the society they were seeking to change" (*RH* 315). The problem, in other words, was not a new one and could not be reduced to the rise of Thatcherism alone. Instead, it must also be understood as part of a self-reflexive analysis of Left strategy and logic, in particular in relation to what he describes as the well-known "attempt on the left to reconstitute old models" that were not appropriate to their context, the continued deployment of received models of analysis and political strategy "as if what's happened in international capitalism over the past forty years simply hadn't happened" (*RH* 315). Instead of feeling disillusioned, Williams emphasizes, it is important for the Left to ask not only in what ways the rise of the Right or the continued power of capital may be said to have resisted the efforts of Left critique and activism. We must also examine the terms of Left critique itself. Capitalism is not necessarily proving unassailable; rather it is Left critique that has failed to adapt itself to new historical conditions as effectively as capitalism and the new Right have been able to do. In our own moment, we would surely benefit from the same line of inquiry, focusing not only on the no doubt profoundly disappointing and worrying rise of a new (far) Right or the remarkable resilience of a neoliberal capitalism that is proving more resistant to systemic crises than Left critique would have liked or hoped, but also on those strategies and methods of Left critique that may no longer be appropriate for our changed times and that may have lost the force they had under different historical conditions. Doing so will ensure that we do not mistake the regressive movement of recent years as an indication of the limits of Left critique itself. Just as important as analyzing which forces of capitalism and which modes of domination characterize our moment, then, is the need to determine which "old models" of analysis and politics "history has ruled out"—for these old models constitute blocks on strategy (*RH* 315). Thus, it is important to recognize that it is not only reactionary politics with which we have to contend, but that the disillusionment and loss of hope that we encounter so frequently may, to an important degree, result from the internal blockages of Left thought, culture, and politics. Possibility and, indeed, hope and optimism for us may therefore in part lie in our ability to identify and erase these blockages in order to rejuvenate Left critique for our time.

The murkiness of our times is to an extent self-imposed. It results from our continued reliance on what Williams describes throughout his work as "received ideas," those ideas that in a new historical context obscure rather than illuminate, that may serve altogether different interests under changed conditions, and that become untimely due to our inability to update them, those methods and conceptions that have that belong to different historical moments and no longer allow us to illuminate the situation with which we are confronted in the present. One may think here of the Left's continued inability to reconcile the value of class critique and one's membership in the category of class, with the new significance that class-based social problems assume within the latest wave of (white) nationalism, racism, and xenophobia, exemplified by the identitarian, far-right populism across North America and Europe. In recent years, the populist Right has effectively preyed on the working class and the working poor's experience of the exploitative structures of contemporary capitalism, displacing their concerns with economic struggles and massive increases in poverty and economic inequality onto the terrain of identity. In other words, the category of identity—once a weapon in the arsenal of a Left organized around the inclusion of previously excluded groups—has now been taken over quite successfully by the Right. The Right has been able to build its rapid and deeply troubling rise in part on its successful ability to turn fledgling structural critiques of capitalism (say, working-class objections to the effects of globalization, austerity politics, economic inequality, and the politics of corporate bailouts and subsidies that stand opposed to the rapid decline of the social-welfare state) into concerns with identity (the purported loss of national heritage, the purity of culture, and white masculinity overwrite the actual threat to the existence of many—capitalism). What disappears is a politics of transformation and futurity (undoing and moving beyond the exploitative and violent structures of capitalism), and what emerges in its place is a politics of static protectionism (leaving the actual sources of alienation and exploitation untouched and focusing instead on the reactionary defense of identity categories and cultural traditions).

But while the Right has managed to manufacture and capitalize on a new concern with identity—the global rise of the identitarian movement is one of the most notorious examples of this—Left critique has by and large proven strikingly unable to offer convincing analyses of and mainstream responses to the new ways in which identity politics, anti-globalization (or, in the context of the new Right, anti-globalism), and the politics of class operate in the contemporary moment. And while the Right continues to expand its vast network of mainstream agitation and public "intellectuals," Left commentary all too often continues to fight old battles that appear particularly unhelpful and untimely in the context of the current conditions.[6] Ongoing debates about "race reductionism," for example, not only remain stuck in familiar binary thinking that simplistically pits identity politics and a politics of class against each other, but they also strikingly miss the urgency of the new meaning that the relation between class and identity have assumed in the context of the new populism.[7] Out of time and out of context, it is no wonder that such ongoing debates on part of the academic Left, paired with the paucity of mainstream Left commentary and analysis that is able to counteract the meteoric rise of right-wing agitation and demagoguery, would leave many of those who occupy political positions to the left of neoliberal centrism without a strong sense of futurity and without a strong sense of trust in the possibility of change. But, once examined from the standpoint of Williams's work, it becomes clear that this crisis of futurity and hope is to an important extent self-imposed and methodological in nature—and it is from this insight, one might add, that hope can emerge.

The lack of change and the collapse of utopian thought that commentators associate with our moment is therefore not an actual historical problem as much as it is the consequence of a lack of historicization. And this, it is important to foreground, is one of the crucial arguments to which Williams returns time and again throughout his work, whether in his emphasis on the need to examine the relation between the city and the country anew each time the historical context undergoes significant changes that in turn change the meaning and function of each of the two terms, or in relation to the conceptual lexicon upon which cultural studies and Left analysis is based, a vocabulary of culture and society that, Williams stresses, is constantly in flux precisely because culture and society cannot be understood as static, transhistorical entities but can only be grasped in their historical development.[8] Disappointment must thus take the place of disillusionment, for disillusionment merely reaffirms the current status quo. Disappointment, on the other hand, must lead, as Williams stresses, to the renewal of Left critique, asking what new version of Left critique, which methods and strategies, might be appropriate to our times. The crisis of our own era, therefore, once examined in the way that Williams recommends, should be understood not as an endpoint that would call into question the effectiveness of the Left, as some have suggested,[9] (as well as the very possibility of advanced, progressive societies or, in fact, categories like change, hope, and the future themselves) but rather as an important occasion to return to and rejuvenate the basic principles of Left social, cultural, and political analysis. Such a project is not only important for our historical conjuncture, since it allows us to understand the purported foreclosures, of our time, as a methodological problem, but it also foregrounds the important connection between the grounding methodology of cultural studies and the politics of academia that Williams traced in his later work.[10]

Williams reminds us that when old modes of analysis and established models for creating social change fail, it does not mark the end of social change or of the future. It merely indicates the historical exhaustion of the old models and the need to create new futures and ideas appropriate for the political struggles and the material conditions of our time. And while we must understand moments of crisis and transformation in this manner, Williams is also well aware that such times of transition tend to create precisely those crises of futurity that we are once again witnessing today. In fact, critics like Steven Connor foreground just this important area of emphasis of

Williams's late work: "The future that Williams warns against is . . . a future in which futurity itself is indefinitely deferred."[11] Connor's essay on Williams's examination of utopia and our understanding of the future appears in a 1997 collection titled *Raymond Williams Now: Knowledge, Limits and the Future*, which traces the importance of Williams's conception of utopia as the "*fin de siècle* approaches."[12] The essays in this collection illuminate not only Williams's work on utopia and on the conception of "the limit," but, taken together, also provide us with an engagement with Williams in a moment that we may understand as a prehistory of our present. Additionally, Connor stresses that in *Towards 2000*, Williams emphasizes those "distractions from the business of considering and preparing for a future in which it will have been recognized that there are unsurpassable limits to economic . . . growth" and, Connor continues, "Williams writes of the dangerous and artificial limiting of the processes whereby one might generate knowledge and acknowledgement of this limitation."[13] It is thus helpful, I would suggest, to return Williams's conception of "the limit," which, the editors propose, "can be seen as subtly crucial to the active contestation of available versions of the future," while emphasizing the importance, for Williams, of "maintaining a notion of an open, indeterminate and unforeseeable future, directed by the limitless potential of human creativity."[14]

And yet, as enjoyable as it may be these days to return to such a conception of the future, it is admittedly difficult to maintain this notion of utopia in the midst of a global pandemic, the ongoing climate emergency, the global rise of authoritarian and repressive governments, and the continued, forceful repression of those who seek to make visible the myriad unsolved social problems that continue to exist in our midst. As I write, it is clear that the forces in power aim to defend at all cost a system whose limits are clearly legible, curtailing the possibility of happiness, health, peaceful existence, and the ability to construct caring, sustainable societies for all too many. That is, the limits of the capitalist system are reified in everyday life as the limits of our collective imagination, as boundaries beyond which we may not stray and that our imagination is increasingly unable to traverse. Under such conditions, when the limits of capitalism reinforce themselves as the limits of our imagination, devaluing and rendering implausible all those demands for a better life that dare to venture beyond that which exists, how is it possible not to fall prey to anti-utopian thinking? How do we defend ourselves against the dominant assumption, reinforced not just by overt rhetoric but all too often by lived experience, that capitalism is definitive of the limit of the possible and of our imagination? How is it possible not to lose trust in the power of desire itself, which time and again is vanquished by the pragmatism that binds our reality and its possible alternatives to the limits of capital? For Williams, the ability to resolve this problem is bound up with his definition of utopia as a method that requires a process of unlearning and relearning, a constant process of historicizing and updating our own modes of thought and analysis. Williams's conception of utopia models for us a form of thought that wrests change and historical mobility from the forces of stasis and from the grip of a dominant ideology that wishes to convince us that there is no alternative or better way forward. Utopia for Williams becomes particularly important when it responds to situations of constraints in the context of which it emerges as thought and desire in practice.

Critique for Williams, in part, designates the process by which we "unlearn . . . the inherent dominative mode," as Wallace, Jones, and Nield remind us (*CS* 336). In *Towards 2000*, Williams insists that "it is not some unavoidable real world . . . that is blocking us;" rather that the impression of a social, political, and indeed imaginative dead end instead results from "a set of identifiable processes of *realpolitik* and *force majeure*, of nameable agencies of power and capital, distraction and disinformation, all these interlocking with the embedded short-term pressures and the interwoven subordinations of an adaptive commonsense" (*T* 268). What is required in such a situation is a conception of utopian thought understood as the unlearning of reified thought, a mode of critical imagination driven by the desire to lay bare the sociopolitical and material context out of which different modalities of our imagination emerge that can then help us transcend the blockages maintained by capitalist adaptive commonsense.

To reconstruct the logic of this line of argumentation—one that runs across Williams's work—we may look toward his engagement with the different modalities of utopian literature that he formulates through his famous examination of the relations between science fiction and utopian thought. "It is tempting to extend both categories until they are loosely identical and it is true that the presentation of *otherness* appears to link them, as modes of desire or of warning in which a crucial emphasis is obtained by the element of discontinuity from ordinary 'realism,'" Williams writes (*TI* 97; emphasis original). "But this element of discontinuity is itself fundamentally variable," he insists. "What most has to be looked at, in properly utopian or dystopian fiction, is the continuity, the implied connection, which the form is intended to embody" (*TI* 97).

Surveying works of utopian literature across different historical moments, Williams finds one constant—namely, that the "alternative images" the works depicted were "rooted, in each case, in a precise social and class situation" (*TI* 99). Thomas More's humanism, for example, must be understood as being "deeply qualified," Williams insists, since "his indignation is directed as much against importunate and prodigal craftsmen and labourers as against the exploiting and engrossing landlords—his social identification is with the small owners, his laws regulate and protect but also compel labour" (*TI* 99). More importantly, it "is qualified also because it is static: a wise and entrenched regulation by the elders" (*TI* 99). Therefore, Williams emphasizes, we must interpret it as "socially the projection of a declining class, generalized to a relatively humane but permanent balance" (*TI* 99). Similarly, Francis Bacon's *Atlantis* advances notions of experiment and discovery in pursuit of a scientific revolution that in effect are "research and development in an instrumental social perspective" (*TI* 99). That is, Williams argues, by "enlarging the bounds of human empire," Bacon is not only expressing a desire for "the mastery of nature," but he also importantly advances "a social projection" connected to "an aggressive, autocratic, imperialist enterprise," namely "the projection of a rising class" (*TI* 99).

What is of crucial importance here is Williams's insistence on the category of "continuity," which becomes a problem central not only to the development and function of utopian literature and SF (that is, as an aesthetic problem expressing the relations of work to material context) but also to questions of method, naming the possibilities and limitations associated with the relation between thought and the historical and material conditions out of which it emerges and to which it responds. In fact, throughout his work, Williams is interested in continuity as an aesthetic, and simultaneously, a critical and political problem. In *The Country and the City*, for instance, Williams interrogates the effect of inherited ideas and cultural modes on our ability to conceive of historical change. As indicated above, *The Country and the City* is a work that examines the changing constellation of what we often construct as a stable binary: the opposition between the urban and the rural. The meaning of the terms and of their relation to each other, Williams shows, is determined by specific historical and material conditions that give rise to, and, in turn, are influenced by particular intellectual and cultural forms. As material history develops, in other words, the meaning of the concepts "country" and "city," as well as the relation between the concepts, changes and expresses new social logics, desires, and aspirations. In our own time, we might think of how the *City Slickers*–syndrome endows the relation between city and country with new meaning. That is, as the city, the locus of progress and change throughout much of modernity, becomes the expression of stasis and of the dead-ends of capitalist life, we see the emergence of new cultural narratives that project images of a different kind of change—of a better, simpler life—onto a notion of the country newly determined under these conditions. One only need to tune into the wealth of popular "back to the land" reality TV series to see a wide range of examples of this recent trend, which transforms the country—in modernity often understood as a site of "backwardness" and uneven development—into the locus of strangely distorted ersatz-futurity. A sense of change emerges here not from moving into a better future but in returning to a better version of life, a life constructed as purportedly simpler and thus less alienated than a city life that is, by contrast, understood as no longer offering the prospect of a better tomorrow. The meaning of the relation between country and city is thus redefined in our moment in this escapist return to the country, where a sense of simplified futurity is recovered, arising from a life that is imagined as offering clear and attainable goals and rewards otherwise unavailable.

We return, here, to Williams's dialectical reading of inherited ideas: While we must understand the meaning of concepts and indeed their relation to each other as always in flux and as at every point determined by their social and material history (as in the case of the terms "country" and "city"), the meaning of these terms is nevertheless crucially determined by inherited ideas. While the relation between country and city assumes a very specific meaning in our own moment, the logical operation of the nostalgic return to country life that replaces true utopian longing for change in our time is mounted on conceptions of nature that we inherit from a long history of cultural constructions of country space throughout modernity. Simply put, trading in a notion of change defined as the recovery of futurity in the present for a nostalgic notion of change realized through the return to the romanticized backwardness of the rural ("Let's all move to Alaska to solve the problems of alienated life without perspective under contemporary capitalism!") is only able to rise to popularity in our moment because the association of the rural with backwardness and uneven development is so firmly anchored in modern cultural constructions of the relation between country and city—the fact that uneven development forms a central aspect of the modern sociocultural imaginary; that is, makes possible the rise of nostalgia for uneven development, a cynically distorted version of a longing for change that is altogether bound up with the crisis of futurity of our moment. Throughout modernity, Williams reminds us, the changing relation between city and country casts into relief the imagination of those who are "accustomed to perceiving their immediate environment through received intellectual and literary forms" (*CC* 142). And, although they must be understood as deeply involved in the ongoing reinterpretation and function of concepts and ideas, inherited ideas and received forms are also crucially bound up with self-imposed stasis and, therefore, as Williams stresses, received forms can significantly limit our ability to conceive of historical process, constraining our ability to imagine the future. After all, Williams argues, "out of an experience of cities came an experience of the future" (*CC* 272). And we only grasp the complex relation between historical change and the limits and possibilities of our imagination fully if our method of inquiry is centrally aimed at tracing the relation between material context, imagination, and cultural form.

From such a critical standpoint, Williams insists, we are able to see that as a result of a "crisis of metropolitan experience, stories of the future went through a qualitative change" (*CC* 272). What is striking here is the utterly persuasive, straightforward insistence on the fundamental historical connection between modes of thought, cultural formation, and historical/material form/context, a historicism that stands opposed to the histrionics of contemporary commentary that conflate the exhaustion of a historically specific imagination of the future with the exhaustion of our ability to imagine change, with the end of utopia *tout court*.

We can find examples that illustrate how important it is to historicize futures—which is to say, to understand the rise and fall of specific conceptions of the future in direct relation to the rise and fall of those material and social structures with which a given future imaginary is bound up—in the work of science fiction authors like Gibson. After all, "the problem isn't whether or not . . . we have a future," Gibson reminds us in a 2020 tweet, "but that we do, absolutely, have a future."[15] What Gibson wishes to stress here is that the phenomenon of the waning of a specific conception of the future itself is not actually very interesting. It is simply an indication of the flow of history. What is more problematic and what deserves our attention, however, is that we do have a future and that it is this future that we must help imagine and shape through our critical engagement with the present. Gibson's oeuvre strikingly illustrates this point, since it is centrally characterized by his commitment to tracing the waxing and waning of futures, charting the rise of, for instance, techno-optimism or the emergence of 1930s-style imaginations of rocket-shaped futures that celebrate modernism's futurism. Futures change, and the fall of such conceptions of the future is inevitable, as they are either exhausted by the flow of history or rendered untenable by new historical conditions, as in the collapse of modernist futurism into fascism and the horrors of World War II. Much like Gibson, therefore, Williams proposes that futures and the thought forms and imaginaries with which they are bound up perpetually change, and they do so quite naturally—because the material world also changes and must be grasped in its process. Central to Williams's examination of the utopian imagination, therefore, is the insistence on the importance of the work of our imagination for material transformation and social change, and the significance of examining the limits placed upon our imagination by a given historical context. Such an analysis allows us to understand both the possibilities and limitations of the utopian mode. After all, Williams argues, "to imagine a whole alternative society is not mere model-building, any more than the projection of new feelings and relationships is necessarily a transforming response" (*TI* 102).

Williams therefore distinguishes between four types of fictions ordinarily grouped under the category "utopian," but only one of which ought to be recognized as truly utopian—as a fiction aimed at transforming both our imagination *and* material reality. This is not the place to rehearse Williams's full taxonomy of utopian fiction, although it remains of great importance for scholars of SF today, especially since we are finding ourselves in a moment in cultural history in which some of the most exciting artistic developments are emerging out of the field of speculative fiction. What matters for our purposes, however, is Williams's distinction between "the willed transformation" and "the externally altered world" (*TI* 95). While the willed transformation is a narrative characterized by "a new but less happy kind of life" that "has been brought about by social degeneration, by the emergence or re-emergence of harmful kinds of social order, or by the unforeseen yet disastrous consequences of an effort at social improvement," it is, in fact, "the characteristic utopian or dystopian mode" (*TI* 98). In its focus on possibility as practice and on human, collective agency, the willed transformation stands opposed to the externally altered world insofar as the latter imagines large-scale change for humanity by reifying notions of "human limitation or indeed human powerlessness" (*TI* 98). "The event saves or destroys us," Williams writes, "and we are its objects" (*TI* 98). It is not surprising, thus, that cultural production in our moment, which is so thoroughly preoccupied with a focus on limitations and impossibilities, turns more readily toward narratives of externally altered worlds (as are common in contemporary cinema and long-form TV) than to depictions of willed transformation.

The replacement of cultural depictions of willed transformation by representations of externally altered worlds is readily exemplified by disaster narratives and apocalyptic fictions in which the solution to any given social problem emerges not from the transformative actions of those who seek to improve our world by addressing the structural problems that underlie crises, but rather from the conveniently "auto-revolutionary" effects of heavy weather, asteroids, and pandemics. Here, one may think of striking examples like Roland Emmerich's 2004 blockbuster movie *The Day After Tomorrow*, which opens with a range of scenes that seeks to establish the movie's commitment to an examination of social problems—including US-Mexico border relations and the grave environmental consequences of the capitalist plunder of our planet's resources. A central part of the movie's attempt to pass off a purely gestural engagement with social issues as robust politics is a scene in which a homeless man and his dog, seeking shelter from torrential rains, are not allowed entry into the New York Public Library. But, *The Day After Tomorrow* tells us, this problem can be solved. And, indeed, as we see later in the movie, it is possible to transcend a society in which the homeless are barred from the fundamental spaces of public life. All it takes is a second Ice Age, which destroys New York City and, with it, all of the global North. The grand scale of the imagined solution to the social problem is thus bound up with its tragic inverse—namely, the impoverishment of analytical rigor, political insight, and transformative imagination. Instead of solving problems resulting from the violent structures of capitalism by attempting to imagine alternative social and economic systems and instead of imagining truly revolutionary means of transformation based on the insights and the will of the

people, the contemporary culture industry confines narratives of transformation to the realm of large-scale disasters that alter a world that people seem
no longer able to change.

Opposed to such narratives of passivity, which further amplify the perceived stasis of our moment, stands the kind of writing and imagination that
Williams associated with authors like William Morris and that we find in the
work of contemporary authors like Gibson and Kim Stanley Robinson. Morris's utopian imagination, Williams argues, is characterized by an "active,
engaged, deeply vigorous mind" that is bound up with and enables "the
commitment to urgent, complex, vigorous activity" (*TI* 105). The work of the
active imagination and its direct connection to "vigorous activity" stands
opposed to the reliance on narratives of external transformation that allow us
to shirk responsibility for transformation by understanding change as something that happens *to* us (environmental catastrophes, asteroid impacts, or
global pandemics), rather than something that is the result of human agency
and committed action. William's insistence on the link between the utopian
imagination and the practical transformation of lived reality remains of crucial importance for us today—not only due to its insistence on agency and
the connection between imagination and transformative practice, but also
because it helps us to unlearn our relation to the present in order to free
ourselves from the limits imposed upon both thought and practice by the
repressive continuity of the material structures of our moment and our inherited ideas.

Here, Williams's distinction between heuristic utopia and systematic utopia is also helpful. In contradistinction to systematic utopia, heuristic utopia—which, following E. P. Thompson, Williams associates with the "education of desire"—projects "the substance of new values and relations . . . with
comparatively little attention to institutions" (*TI* 102).[16] "The whole alternative society rests, paradoxically, on two quite different social situations,"
Williams explains: "either that of social confidence, the mood of a rising
class, which knows, down to detail, that it can replace the existing order; or
that of social despair, the mood of a declining class or fraction of a class,
which has to create a new heaven because its Earth is a hell" (*TI* 102). The
basis of the systematic mode, on the other hand, "is a society in which
change is happening, but primarily under the direction and in the terms of the
dominant social order itself" (*TI* 102). This, Williams argues, "is always a
fertile moment for what is, in effect, an anarchism: positive in its fierce
rejection of domination, repression, and manipulation; negative in its willed
neglect of structures, of continuity and of material constraints" (*TI* 102).
"The systematic mode is a response to tyranny or disintegration; the heuristic
mode, by contrast, seems to be primarily a response to a constrained reform-
ism," Williams explains, adding that while "the heuristic utopia offers a
strength of vision against the grain; the systematic utopia a strength of con-

viction that the world really can be different" (*TI* 103). And yet, each mode also has distinct weaknesses that we must keep in mind if we are to adequately assess their ontology and function in a given historical moment. The heuristic utopia, Williams explains, "has the weakness that it can settle into isolated and in the end sentimental 'desire,'" which Williams associates with "a mode of living with alienation" (*TI* 103). The systematic utopia, on the other hand, "has the weakness that, in its insistent organisation, it seems to offer little room for any recognisable life" (*TI* 103).

For our moment, the tension between both weaknesses is highly instructive, since it restores our attention to those limits of our imagination that erode the foundations of utopian thought. One might add here that the emphasis on the shortcomings of systematic utopia tellingly highlights the limitations of the pseudo-utopian thought of the contemporary oligarchy and the super-rich, of systematic futurists like Elon Musk, whose conception of the future not only fails to address any of the substantive social and political problems of the present, but, by reserving the future for the few who can afford it, evacuates their plans for the future of humanity of any notion of life that would be recognized as such. After all, the mere survival of the ultra-wealthy on a few space outposts of humankind, while the vast majority of humanity is left to die on a planet that is better abandoned than defended and sustained, cannot truly be counted among the valid, complex conceptions of what may qualify as life. We may find out, in other words, just what *Star Trek* tried to teach us by suggesting that "survival is insufficient." On the other hand—or, in the case of oligarchic futurism, "the other side of the same coin"—we are becoming increasingly aware of the frequency with which the utopian imagination collapses into populist versions of itself in a situation of great constraint. Right-wing pseudo-utopias, including the idealized version of pure and unified notions of nation and identity to which populists promise to return those on whom they prey for support, hold out immediate gratification in place of true, long-term change and improvement, turning the heuristic utopia's investment of working "against the grain" into precisely a sentimental, reactionary, dangerously distorted version of itself.

Ruth Leys makes a similar argument in *Utopia as Method* when she writes:

> Williams argues that this willed transformation of the social world was an essential characteristic of the utopian mode, and that without it, there was the danger of utopia settling into "isolated and in the end sentimental 'desire.'" Such willed transformation is the target of political and ideological anti-utopianism. But it demands a holistic, sociological approach, normative judgment and political commitment, all called into question by the social and cultural conditions of late modernity. [17]

Williams's analysis is thus endowed with renewed urgency in our present, in a time when the challenges of contemporary capitalism and of new forms of far-right demagogy can be helpfully understood as anti-utopian projects that join forces in their assault on our imagination, strategically erecting limits that foreclose avenues of imagination and thus of political possibility and social change. Williams's work importantly outlines an analytical method that cultivates modes of our imagination that refuse the limits of the present. At the same time, Williams insists on the significance of a self-reflexive engagement with our own analytical and critical methods and with the limits of possibilities of the utopian mode itself, which requires constant histori-cization. "The utopian mode," Williams insists, always has to be read before the backdrop of a constantly changing context that "itself determines whether its defining subjunctive mood is part of a grammar which includes a true indicative and a true future, or whether it has seized every paradigm and become exclusive, in assent and dissent alike" (*TI* 108). Only in this way can the true utopian mode emerge: "when utopia is no longer an island or a newly discovered place, but our familiar country transformed by specific historical change, the mode of imagined transformation has fundamentally changed" (*TI* 105).

This account of utopia as method or, we may also say, as a form of historical, transformative imagination that binds thought to practice, is con-nected to Williams's general account of the methodology of cultural studies as a form of critique that is always linked to historical change. The methodo-logical heart of cultural studies as formulated by Williams—and indeed one of the foundations of Williams's own method—is the dialectic of project and formation. "You cannot understand an intellectual or artistic project without also understanding its formation," Williams writes, stressing that "the rela-tion between a project and formation is always decisive" (*PM* 151). The core value of cultural studies that must be defended, Williams argues, "is precise-ly that it engages with *both*, rather than specializing itself to one or the other" (*PM* 151). "Indeed," he continues, "it is not concerned with a formation of which some project is an illustrative example, nor with a project which could be related to a formation understood as its context or its background" (*PM* 151). Put differently, this can be seen as "the refusal to give priority to either the project or the formation—or, in older terms, the art or the society" (*PM* 152). This suggestion matters greatly for the quality of cultural analysis, since it emphasizes the ability of cultural critique to generate complex inter-rogations of dialectical mediation instead of simply tracing homologies. It also refuses the popular (and indeed in some instances populist) strategy to limit agency and imagination alike by construing our present as a homoge-nous totality ("the future has died!") while pointing to individual cultural objects that are said to confirm this generalizing suspicion ("here's a novel that illustrates our inability to imagine the future"), reducing culture to the status of mere confirmation of truths held to be self-evident until the artwork itself can finally be pronounced exhausted in our time ("the novel is dead, too! Again!"). The return to the foundational methods of cultural studies and the basic operations of cultural critique matters greatly, therefore, not just because of the particular problems of our time, but also because problematic versions of the relation between culture and formation are far from new and arise with regularity. Relating culture to society, Williams stresses, has been done frequently and for a long time, "just as there [is] a whole body of work—for example in history—which describe[s] societies and then illustrate[s] them from their characteristic forms of thought and art" (*PM* 152). But "what we were then trying to say, and it remains a difficult but, I do believe, central thing to say, is that these concepts—what we would now define as 'project' and 'formation'—are addressing not the relations between two separate entities, 'art' and 'society,'" Williams emphasizes, but "processes which take these two different material forms in social formations of a creative or a critical kind, or on the other hand the actual forms of artistic and intellectual work" (*PM* 152). This methodology thus commits cultural studies to a process of self-examination that, as we saw at the beginning of this essay, is of great significance for our moment. "We have to look at the kind of formation out of which the project of Cultural Studies developed, and then at the changes of formation that produced different definitions of that project," Williams writes. "We may then be in a position to understand existing and possible formations," he concludes, "which would in themselves be a way of defining certain projects toward the future" (*PM* 152).

Williams advances a similar argument in "The Uses of Cultural Theory," in which he discusses cultural theory's ontology. "Many suppose," he writes, "that the making of useful cultural theory is in some intermediate area between, on the one hand, the arts and, on the other hand, society. On the contrary, these now a priori but historically traceable categories, and the conventional forms of their separation and derived interrelation, are just what useful cultural theory most essentially and specifically challenges" (*PM* 164). Cultural theory and the practice of critique, in other words, is a method for imagining the future out of the critical, dialectical interrogation of the present. Williams reminds us,

> Cultural theory is at its most significant when it is concerned precisely with the *relations* between the many and diverse human activities which have been historically and theoretically grouped in these ways, and especially when it explores these relations as at once dynamic and specific within describably whole historical situations which are also, as practice, changing and, in the present, changeable. . . . It is then in this emphasis on a theory of such specific and changing relationships that cultural theory becomes appropriate and useful. (*PM* 164).

Here, we may return to the conversation between Williams and Eagleton with which we began. Toward the end of the conversation, Williams recalls that he was "sometimes told by good Marxist friends that [cultural analysis] was a diversion from the central economic struggle" (*RH* 319–20). And yet, for Williams, cultural analysis and critique must accompany or, indeed, centrally inform other forms of leftist struggle and politics, for it allows us to historicize our own moment, to study the ideas and imagination that are part and parcel of it, and to create an area for political struggle when education itself is no longer adequate. After all, already in his own moment—and thus significantly more so in our time—"manipulative methods are too powerful, too far below the belt" for education alone to be held out as a viable way to work toward an advanced society (*RH* 319). The simple belief in the power of education is not sufficient in a moment when the forces of reaction know no shame or limits, and when they seize hold of the media and of culture to wage their battles far more effectively than the Left has been able to do.

In this moment, Left cultural analysis is crucial not just as an academic tool but must be transported into the public realm, as part of Left political practice, in our moment possibly even more so than in Williams's own. Williams's model of cultural analysis binds the educational mission of critique and cultural analysis to social and political activism, in particular in the realm of culture and media. In the age of the new culture wars—and in a moment when capital seeks to limit possibility by constraining our imagination—cultural critique must also be aimed at practice by seizing the means of communication. We may do well, therefore, to recall William's emphasis on and faith in "the infinite resilience, even deviousness, with which people have managed to persist in profoundly unfavourable conditions, and the striking diversity of the beliefs in which they've expressed their autonomy" (*RH* 322). If we manage to maintain our belief in "the possibilities of common life," as Williams did, then we may be able to keep hope and the future itself alive. And, indeed, Left cultural critics are called upon today to do just this, for, in Williams's words, "we must speak for hope, as long as it doesn't mean suppressing the nature of the danger" (*RH* 322).

NOTES

1. Robert J. Samuelson, "Losing Faith in the Future?" *RealClear Politics*, September 18, 2018, https://www.realclearpolitics.com/articles/2018/09/18/losing_faith_in_the_future_138105.html.

2. Ibid.

3. Alex Barron, "William Gibson on the End of the Future" *The New Yorker Radio Hour*, March 6, 2020, https://www.wnycstudios.org/podcasts/tnyradiohour/segments/william-gibson-end-future.

4. See Mathias Nilges, *How to Read a Moment: The American Novel and the Crisis of the Present* (Evanston, IL: Northwestern University Press, 2021), and *Right-Wing Culture in Con-*

temporary Capitalism: Regression and Hope in a Time without Future (London: Bloomsbury, 2019).

5. "Transformed this-world": Raymond Williams, "Utopia and Science Fiction" *Science Fiction Studies*, 16.5 (1978). N. pag. https://www.depauw.edu/sfs/backissues/16/williams16art.htm.

6. What is particularly notable here is the dangerous naivete of the continued commitment to identity politics of the 1980s and 1990s and their classic texts that we continue to find on the syllabi and in the works-cited lists of a notable set of academics whose centrist (or, in their minds, leftist) investment in the fight for identity categories, unhistoricized and without concern for the new meaning of such arguments, loses its analytical purchase and creates unintended consequences in the context of the contemporary Right's cynically distorted version of identity politics.

7. The work of Touré Reed is of central importance here, not only because of his ability to lay bare the illogic in the history of Left accounts of "race reductionism," but also because he illustrates the danger of continuing to frame arguments and analyses in this manner in the contemporary moment. See, for example, his recent book *Toward Freedom: The Case against Race Reductionism* (London: Verso, 2020).

8. See *The Country and the City*, as well as the introduction to, and a range of definitions in, *Keywords*, in which Williams explains that the very project that yielded *Keywords* began as an attempt to trace the historical emergence and changes of key concepts in order to interrogate their ability to explain and also obscure or falsify thought and analysis.

9. See T. J. Clark, "For a Left with No Future," *New Left Review* 74 (March/April 2012): 53–75.

10. See, for example, "The Future of Cultural Studies" (1985), in (*PM* 163–76).

11. Steven Connor, "Raymond Williams's Time," in *Raymond Williams Now: Knowledge, Limits and the Future*, ed. Jeff Wallace, Rod Jones, and Sophie Nield (Houndsmills, Basingstoke, UK: Palgrave Macmillan, 1997): 164.

12. Jeff Wallace, Rod Jones, and Sophie Nield, "Introduction: 'Somebody Is Trying to Think . . . ,'" in Wallace, Jones, and Nield, *Raymond Williams Now: Knowledge, Limits and the Future*, 1.

13. Connor, "Raymond Williams' Time," 163.

14. Wallace, Jones, and Nield, "Introduction," 1.

15. William Gibson, @greatdismal, January 14, 2020, 7:06 p.m., https://twitter.com/GreatDismal/status/1217221448038637568.

16. The phrase "education of desire" is in E. P. Thompson, "Romanticism, Moralism, and Utopianism: The Case of William Morris," *New Left Review* 1/99 (1976): 83–111.

17. Ruth Leys, *Utopia as Method: The Imaginary Reconstitution of Society* (Houndsmills, Basingstoke, UK: Palgrave Macmillan, 2013): 108.

Chapter Four

Structures of Feeling

Raymond Williams's Progressive Problemshift

Thomas A. Laughlin

The element of thought itself—the element of thought's living expression—
language—is of a sensuous nature.
>—Karl Marx, *The Economic and Philosophic Notebooks of 1844*

We are talking about characteristic elements of impulse, restraint, and tone;
specifically affective elements of consciousness and relationship: not feeling
against thought, but thought as felt and feeling as thought: practical consciousness of a present kind, in a living and interrelating continuity.
>—Raymond Williams, *Marxism and Literature* (1977)

Tom Pinkney has called "structures of feeling" Raymond Williams's "most
distinctive concept."[1] That this was in the context of Tom Bottomore's *A
Dictionary of Marxist Thought* (1983) implies two things: (1) that in formu-
lating his theory of structures of feeling, Williams was in some way addressing himself to the theoretical tasks and preoccupations of a shared intellectual project, Marxism; and (2) that this project, in turn, should respond or even
adapt itself to Williams's intervention and conceptual innovation. But herein
arises the problem of what Pinkney identifies as the concept's *distinctiveness*: "structures of feeling" is not a concept "native" to classical Marxism
itself, but rather a "foreign" introduction by the Welsh critic.[2] Such introduc-
tions produce a certain amount of intellectual anxiety. Will the new concept
weaken the preexisting system of thought? Or will it be so powerful as to
displace the old system, producing what used to be called a paradigm shift?
In which case, is it actually a contribution to Marxism at all, or, in fact, the
coming into existence of something else altogether, some new Williams-*ism*
(or as Williams himself sometimes called it, for reasons that will be explored

later, *cultural materialism*)? Or, on the other hand, if the concept is, in fact, perfectly synthesizable with the old system—and can be assimilated and subordinated to its protocols and procedures—was it even necessary in the first place, if everything has changed only to remain the same? These are questions that have often plagued what gets called Western Marxism.[3] Such lines of questioning, however, turn too much on notions of theoretical purity, which preserve "Marxism" at the cost of erecting borders around what inevitably starts to look like an arrested thought system or ossified doctrine no longer capable of conceptual development or refinement. But if an insistence on purity risks stalling Marxism's theoretical development, this same problem is just as little solved by a turn toward a liberal—or postmodern—pragmatic pluralism, which would mean the abandonment of Marxism as a privileged explanatory system worthy of *collective* research and refinement. In a little-known article first published in 1961, Williams, for his part, declares, "I think it is wrong to assume that Marxism as a set of *active* doctrines is finished" ("FM" 63; emphasis mine).[4]

One's attitude to this question of Marxism's *active* legacy will very much depend, as Williams's comment makes clear, on whether one views it as a closed or open mode of scientific inquiry. It would be naive to argue that Marxism has not known periods in which its development has seemed—largely as a consequence of twentieth-century politics—ossified and summarily closed. The question of a system's openness, however, is not determined by its periods of stagnancy, but by whether the system of thought can brook and absorb new data, which, in turn, can then be assimilated to evolve and refine a theory's initial hypotheses rather than explode them. As John Bellamy Foster has persuasively argued, Marxism is best characterized as an open system or, as he calls it, an "open-ended critique": "the 'greatness' and 'vitality' of Marxian social science," he writes, "derives primarily from its inner logic as a form of *open-ended* scientific inquiry. . . . This openness can be seen in . . . Marxism's ability constantly to reinvent itself by expanding its empirical as well as theoretical content, so as to embrace ever larger aspects of historical reality in an increasingly interconnected world."[5] Foster, in addition to pointing to the open-ended nature of Marx's own researches (one need look no further than the ever-evolving and never-completed project of *Capital*), draws on conceptual terminology developed by the Hungarian philosopher of science Imre Lakatos, who differentiates between "degenerative" and "progressive" research programs.[6] The former, Foster and his colleague Paul Burkett explain, have "a shrinking rather than a widening empirical content, and [are] no longer able to generate novel facts."[7] Such a "degenerative" research program is "unable to carry out what Lakatos calls a progressive problemshift, by introducing 'auxiliary hypotheses' emanating from the logic of its scientific model, so as to increase its overall content (and create a 'protective belt' around its hard core)." Such ossifying research programs instead become caught in a "degenerative problemshift" and "resort to 'ad hoc hypotheses,' borrowing from outside" their own scientific model and "hard core."[8] In what follows, I propose to treat Williams's conceptualization of the structure of feeling as a progressive problemshift *within* Marxism that maintains its "hard core" while simultaneously evolving the Marxist thought system as a whole, introducing new "auxiliary hypotheses" that can radiate out from the center of its initial hypotheses as so many "belts" of expanded meaning, absorbing ever-more material content in a dialectic of mutual elaboration.

Broadly speaking, Williams's progressive problemshift brings the whole area of cultural activity and production—the so-called ideological super-structures erected on top of the socioeconomic base—back into the ambit of a rigorously materialist (and dialectical) criticism. Here, culture becomes the location not only of legitimating ideologies mechanically thrown up by the corresponding mode of production, but also the site of an active and emer-gent—rather than inert and received—*practical consciousness* vis-à-vis the cultural laborer's social environment. Such *practical consciousness*, howev-er, is not the same as scientific or empirical knowledge, but is rather worked out through artistic practice and experimentation, which, in turn, can give shape to new structures of feeling arising from the conflicts and contradic-tions that pattern "a whole way of life." Crucially, these new structures of feeling are not identical or reducible to that way of life (i.e., the social totality) and for that reason can also play a role in contesting older attitudes and cultural orientations within a society, the latter of which may be ideolog-ical in the sense of serving to ratify the existing social order and the biases of the dominant class. The structure of feeling's potential for contestation, how-ever, exists only in its period of emergence, as what was once emergent can become dominant or residual as the whole adapts and evolves again. Such cultural shifts are not inherently revolutionary, then; but a new revolutionary politics will necessarily attach itself to an emergent structure of feeling if it is to become a successful counter-hegemonic force. Williams's cultural materi-alism thus leaves behind much of what was both mechanical and, as will be seen, idealist in how the base/superstructure relationship had been interpreted in the 1930s, while still preserving and developing the basic Marxist prem-ises that (1) the meaning of culture is discoverable only in its relationship to a wider society (the social-economic totality), and (2) that culture can be the site of both legitimating ideologies as well as contesting practices through which individuals and collectives become conscious of their lived conditions and, in Marx's memorable phrase, "fight it out."[9]

THE MATERIALIST OUTLOOK

In order to understand how Williams sought to effect this progressive problemshift, it is important to look further into the Marxism that Williams
inherited when he became a committed socialist at an early age. Here, we
would do well to consider Williams's own narrative about his introduction to
Marxism via the Socialist Club (run by the Communist Party Great Britain)
at Cambridge in the 1930s, which overlapped his brief period of party membership. In his interviews with the *New Left Review* (*NLR*) collected under
the title *Politics and Letters* (1979), he explains, "The central points of reference [for the Club] were Engels's *Socialism—Scientific and Utopian* and
Anti-Dühring. These were taken more or less as the defining texts, especially
the former. Marx was much less discussed, although one was told to read
Capital, and I bought a copy. I studied it during that year, but with the usual
difficulties over the first chapter. It was not till much later that I knew Marx
as much more than the author of *Capital*" (*PL* 40–41). In the Club, he
continues, "there was an emphasis on the scientific and revolutionary character of Marxism, in terms largely taken from Engels" (*PL* 42). There is nothing unusual about this filtration of Marxism through Engels in the 1930s or
the framing of Marxism as a *scientific socialism* rather than a *radical humanism*. What is interesting to note, however, is that, by and large, Western
Marxism has been characterized by its rejection of this classical Marxism,
and more specifically of Engels and his extension of the dialectic to nature,
whereas Williams—although he broke with the party and party-affiliated
cultural theory—remained committed to the problematic of scientific socialism or "Engelsian" Marxism, which sought a rigorous materialist and dialectical interpretation of a "comprehensive range of subjects."[10]

   This last quotation comes from the 1885 preface to *Herr Dühring's Revolution in Science* (1878), often referred to simply as *Anti-Dühring*, where
Engels writes that, although the popularity of Dühring's so-called scientific
revolution had greatly receded (in no small part, he does not say, due to his
own criticism), his book could still be read as an "exposition of the dialectical method and of the communist world outlook championed by Marx and
myself—an exposition covering a fairly comprehensive range of subjects."[11]
This famously involved following Dühring (Marx and Engels's intellectual
rival for influence on the German Social Democratic Party) into the natural
sciences to combat his idealist distortions of emergent scientific knowledge.
This extension of "the dialectical method" and "the communist world outlook" was later codified in Soviet Marxism as "dialectical materialism."[12]
This Soviet legacy has been contested in Western Marxism and continues to
be controversial. However, before turning to this reception history, we
should reconstruct the significance of dialectical materialism to Engels's
wider project in *Anti-Dühring*.

The Spanish, Marxist philosopher Manuel Sacristán, in a penetrating discussion of *Anti-Dühring* and the 1885 preface, argues that dialectical materialism, or what Engels in the preface simply called the "communist outlook,"
involves a dynamic interrelationship of different modes of thought: the first,
which is dialectical, is philosophical and synthesizing, whereas the second,
which is materialist, is empirical and *positivist*, producing, "a reductive analysis that by means of abstraction dispenses with the qualitative peculiarity
of . . . complex phenomena."[13] The dialectical component of the Marxist
outlook, however, presupposes at the same time that "the materialist data of
reductive analysis" are necessarily also interconnected into larger systems—
"complex and concrete 'wholes,'" in Sacristán's terminology—and that
those systems, in turn, must be interpenetrating and should therefore be theorized up to their totality, which "positive science cannot grasp," or, at least,
has yet to grasp systematically.[14] The dialectical line of inquiry is thus "both
ahead of and behind positive research. Behind because it will attempt to build
itself in accordance with the course and results of positive research; ahead
because as a general view of reality, the worldview inspires or motivates
positive research itself."[15] The materialist line of inquiry, in Marx and Engels's outlook, thus presupposes that the materials with which the dialectical
theorist works will be empirically reducible and ratified by scientific methods, and that the dialectical method of synthetic reconstruction must therefore remain open to revision and reverification as the sciences continue to
produce new knowledge. For Sacristán, this means that the "second [dialecti-
cal] feature of the Marxist worldview cannot regard its explicit elements as a
system of knowledge *superior to positive knowledge*" (emphasis mine).[16]
Historically this required Marx and Engels to put their sociological theory
into dialogue with the natural sciences (the latter of which first developed the
protocols of positive science). In embracing this "objective" side of the materialist dialectic associated with Engels (but actually overlapping with Marx
as well), Sacristán—and Williams too, I will argue—fell outside the parameters of what usually gets classified as Western Marxism.

    From the perspective of the Western Marxists, writes Russell Jacoby,
"physical and chemical matter was not dialectical; moreover the dialectic of
nature shifted attention away from the proper terrain of Marxism, which is
the cultural and historical structure of society."[17] Indeed, Engels's attempts
in the unfinished manuscripts for *Dialectics of Nature* (published posthumously in 1925) to extend the dialectic to physical and chemical processes
has struck even generous appraisers like Sacristán as a sometimes forced
translation of the dry empirical language of the natural sciences to the more
flexible, labile language of German idealism (i.e., dialectics).[18] However,
such criticisms, if not properly qualified, risk misunderstanding the historical
context and, with it, the intellectual substance and novelty of Engels's project. Against an outdated empiricism in nineteenth-century attempts to popu-

larize the natural sciences—an empiricism that, as Paul Blackledge observes "tended to squeeze real motion and qualitative change out of [its] image of reality"—Engels's dialectics of nature dramatized the incredible *motion* of the transformations occurring in the natural world through his heightened awareness of the *interconnection* of the different branches of science, which had previously dealt with these transformations mainly in isolation.[19] Engels's sought, in other words, nothing less than the rewriting of the sciences as one mobile totality and open-ended system of inquiry. Engels's open-ended dialectics of nature not only pointed the way to a new holistic approach to the natural sciences, but, by emphasizing the *mediating* role of labor in "the transition of man from ape," also undermined the attempts of Social Darwinists to subsume society to natural laws in a way that reduced "man's cultural, moral, and political behavior to biological activities *without any mediation*"—a reduction, moreover, which foreclosed class struggle as a means of addressing "social inequalities and injustices."[20] As Foster explains, in *Anti-Dühring* and *Dialectics of Nature*, "Engels was concerned . . . with combatting mechanical materialism and providing an analysis that focused on evolutionary change, coevolution, emergence, and the unity of opposites. As a result, he pushed the analysis at every point in the direction of an interconnected, ecological analysis, employing in the process the full array of dialectical categories."[21]

Western Marxism, however, renounced this legacy and sought to isolate Marx's "good" historical materialism from Engels's "bad" dialectical materialism, focusing instead on the ways in which humanity was forged in the furnace of its own history and culture *apart from natural laws*. In this perspective, humanity becomes, through the ascendant class, its own subject and object. But what is lost in the rejection of this other half of classical Marxism is precisely Engels's *holism*. Crucial components of material reality—nonhuman nature, physical geography, language, sexuality, the body, and so on—are either bracketed from historical materialism because they are seen as outside the purview of history (which is to say they are not *seen* at all), or else they are, perhaps too quickly and optimistically, assimilated into history as products of the class struggle, immediate objects of social-historical transformation in what becomes not *materialism*, but rather a kind of *humanist idealism*.

This last is what the Italian Marxist Sebastiano Timpanaro has criticized as Western Marxism's excessive "historicism": an "anti-Engelsism" in which too much is included on the side of history that should more properly be placed on the side of nature—a nature that, he argues, is "passive" and untranscendable, and therefore outside the sphere of immediate human agency or *praxis*.[22] Even those who have agreed with Timpanaro's critique of anti-Englesism have sometimes felt that his emphasis on "the element of passivity in experience"—"the external situation which we do not create but which imposes itself on us"—was an unfortunate way of retrieving Engels's legacy and the project behind his *Dialectics of Nature*.[23] In "Problems of Materialism" (1978), his review of Timpanaro's then recently translated work, Williams notes that he would have preferred "constitutive" over "passive" as the qualifying adjective to describe both social and natural inheritances beyond human control (*PMC* 108). But, setting aside this disagreement, Williams largely embraced Timpanaro's intervention and accepted as a matter of principle that materialism—historical or otherwise—must accept the *priority* of nature with which any dialectical sociology must then reckon and factor into its analysis of human social evolution.

This priority of nature plays a major role in Williams's theory of language, which is crucial, as I will argue later, to his reconceptualization of the structure of feeling in an explicitly materialist and dialectical framework in *Marxism and Literature* (1977). Here, mirroring the language he will use in the Timpanaro review just one year later, he writes,

> Thus we can add to the necessary definition of the biological faculty of language as *constitutive* an equally necessary definition of language development—at once individual and social—as historically and socially *constituting*. What we can then define is a dialectical process: the *changing practical consciousness of human beings*, in which both the evolutionary and the historical processes can be given full weight, but also within which they can be distinguished, in the complex variations of actual language use. (*ML* 43–44)

How to place Williams, if at all, in the story of Western Marxism is thus harder to determine than it might at first appear. Williams's overriding focus on cultural and aesthetic concerns aligns with those traditionally assigned to Western Marxism, but an underlying and persistent materialist "Engelsism" at the same time puts him at odds with this tradition.[24] In his interviews with *NLR*, he notes with some pride, "I am extremely sympathetic—probably more than most people on the left—to a lot of work being done in the natural sciences, which I try to follow," and even goes so far as to proclaim, "When I read Timpanaro, I had the sense of an extraordinary recovery of a sane centre of the Marxist tradition, which it seemed to me had been largely forgotten or had persisted only among the dwindling number of natural scientists who were still Marxists" (*PL* 327, 340). It is this same rigorous, materialist dialectic—the "sane centre of the Marxist tradition"—that Williams sought to animate, by fits and starts, in his cultural criticism after the war.

MEETING THE QUESTIONS

Williams's party membership lapsed during his service as a tank commander in the Second World War, but by the time he returned from the war, he had already decided not to rejoin the party. "The whole crisis," he explains to his *NLR* interviewers, "had an important bearing on my attitude when I returned to academic work in 1945. People often ask me now why I didn't carry on then from the Marxist arguments of the thirties. The reason is that I felt they had led me into an impasse. I had become convinced that their answers did not meet the questions" (*PL* 52). What had shaken his confidence? The crisis to which Williams refers was not only the crisis of the war, but also an academic conflict that preceded his entry into the army. He recounts how in the second year of his degree he was criticized by his tutor, the renowned classicist and literary critic E. M. W. Tillyard, after submitting a paper in which he "produced the Party orientation—that it was necessary to see any bourgeois novel of the past from the perspective of the kind of novel that must now be written, in the present" (*PL* 50–51). Tillyard, who was famous for his carefully contextualizing literary criticism, "told me this was not a tenable procedure; it was a fantasy." He then recalls the embarrassment and humiliation of being unable to defend this and other party orientations he had been taking in his academic work, positions that nonetheless he felt were deeply in line with his theoretical outlook and political commitments:

> I was involved in constant political activity, and other kinds of writing—practical priorities that were in keeping with my theoretical principles. In that sense I was living in totally good faith. But in my academic studies I was not able to produce the properly prepared and referenced and coherent work that I knew I needed to defend my positions. . . . I was continually found out in ignorance, found out in confusion. (*PL* 51)

From this experience, Williams resolved always to be able "meet the questions" in the future: "I had got to be prepared to meet the professional objections," he narrates; "I was damned well going to do it properly this time" (*PL* 52).[25]

Williams's phrasing in this section of the interview is interesting: he does not reject outright the premise of the "questions" put to him by Tillyard, but neither does he reject reactively his generally Marxist theoretical orientations and political commitments. What is re-interrogated instead—in a deeply personal way—is the rational basis and justification for a materialist and socialist literary criticism and cultural theory. This leads Williams, over his career, to reengage with the problematic that had first oriented Marx and Engels's own nascent theory of culture: namely the relationship of the "superstructure" to the socioeconomic "base." In his famous preface to *A Contribution to a Critique of Political Economy* (1859), Marx writes,

> In the social production of their existence, men inevitably enter into definite relations, which are independent of their will, namely relations of production appropriate to a given stage in the development of their material forces of

production. The totality of these relations of production constitutes the economic structure of society, the real foundation, on which arises a legal and political superstructure and to which correspond definite forms of social consciousness. The mode of production of material life conditions the general process of social, political and intellectual life. It is not the consciousness of men that determines their existence, but their social existence that determines their consciousness. . . . The changes in the economic foundation [like those produced by "social revolution"] lead sooner or later to the transformation of the whole immense superstructure. [26]

"Sooner or later" in the final sentence has created analytical problems for Marxism, as it seems to imply a certain level of asynchrony in the "general process" conditioning "social, political and intellectual life." Indeed, in the very next sentence, Marx writes,

In studying such [revolutionary] transformations it is always necessary to distinguish between the material transformation of the economic conditions of production, which can be determined with the precision of natural science, and the legal, political, religious, artistic or philosophic—in short, ideological forms in which men become conscious of this conflict [between the "productive forces of society" and "the existing relations of production"] and fight it out. [27]

The latter assertion implies that even though men and women are undergoing a process of conditioning, they are not passive in this process, but active—always at the same time becoming conscious of its shaping influence and the kind of society to which it is adapting them, and then disputing or reinforcing it in their superstructural activity. For the "proleptic criticism" of the party-sanctioned critics—in which, as John Higgins explains, "the literature of the present and of the past is read and evaluated in terms of future needs"—this meant that culture could articulate desires and project attitudes that actually *ran ahead* of the base and spoke to the needs of a future (socialist) society. [28] Tillyard's comments and question asking had cast this procedure in doubt for Williams and reopened the whole problem of the base/superstructure relationship for him as an area for more, not less, research.

In a hostile chapter on English Marxism in *Culture and Society* (1958), Williams takes aim at critics touting this "Party orientation" that Tillyard exposed as a "fantasy." Given the intensity of Williams's criticism in this section, one could be forgiven for reading the chapter as a rejection of Marxism *tout court*. But it is important to note that his hostility is reserved not for Marx and Engels or even Plekhanov, who are all treated fairly, but for the English Marxists attempting to make a literary criticism in Marx's name. For Williams, it is disputable how much this "proleptic criticism" actually resembles Marx's own nascent cultural theory with its emphasis on the determining influence of the material forces and relations of production. "Much of the

'Marxist' writing of the 'thirties," Williams coolly observes, "was in fact the old Romantic protest that there was no place in contemporary society for the artist and the intellectual, with the new subsidiary clause that the workers were about to end the old system and establish Socialism, which would then provide such a place" (*CS* 271). Williams, however, wonders if "this is not Romanticism absorbing Marx, rather than Marx transforming Romanticism," since it would seem, in fact, to reverse the weight of determination by making "the arts, as the creators of consciousness, determine social reality" (*CS* 274). So, far from rejecting Marxism *tout court*, Williams actually criticizes the English "Marxist" critics for deviating from the inherent materialism of the approach to culture that Marx was trying to develop, in which a certain determinate weight was given to the productive forces and social relations, not as an inert backdrop, but as an active force within the process of cultural formation. However, as Williams observes, this was "still an emphasis rather than a substantiated theory" (*CS* 269).

At the same time that Williams is at pains to criticize this Romantic idealism, cropping up in "Marxist" writing (always using quotation marks around *Marxist* when speaking of these critics), he also pushes back against the inverse notion, that "the arts are passively dependent on social reality, a proposition which," he continues, "I take to be that of mechanical materialism, or a vulgar misinterpretation of Marx" (*CS* 274). As the final words make clear, for Williams this mechanical materialism misses the complexity inherent in Marx's comments on the base/superstructure relationship. In *Culture and Society*, he associates this latter position with Christopher Caudwell (although he will later revise his opinion of Caudwell). Here, he writes, "The interpretative method which is governed . . . by the arbitrary correlation of the economic situation and the subject of study, leads very quickly to abstraction and unreality, as for example in Caudwell's description of modern poetry . . . as 'capitalist poetry'"—a label so reductive for Williams that it loses all explanatory power (*CS* 281).

Against both Romantic idealism and mechanical materialism, Williams begins to argue instead for a *holistic* approach: "For, even if the economic element is determining, it determines a whole way of life, and it is to this, rather than to the economic system alone, that the literature has to be related" (*CS* 281). Here, Williams's judgment on Marx's hypothesization of the base/ superstructure relation could apply to his own inchoate formulation: this is "still an emphasis rather than a substantiated theory" (*CS* 269). What is clear, though, is that while Williams does not yet identify his own project as a continuation or extension of Marxism, there is a clear sense of the gravitational pull he feels toward a theory that includes, as Marx's original sketch did, cultural activity within its conception of a concrete evolving totality, in which "the arts, while ultimately dependent, with everything else, on the real economic structure, operate in part to reflect this structure and its consequent reality, and in part, by affecting attitudes towards reality, to help *or hinder* the constant business of changing it" (*CS* 274). Williams thus begins to effect his progressive problemshift in Marxist cultural theory by treating the base/ superstructure relationship not as a solution, but as problem, or problematic, requiring the generation of new "auxiliary hypotheses," which will be able to expand, rather than contain and limit, the material content or empirical data that a Marxist theory can absorb and explain. Here, Williams's reorientation of cultural theory toward "a whole way of life," although not without its own problems and limitations, plays a decisive role in facilitating his progressive problemshift.

ELEMENTS IN A WHOLE WAY OF LIFE

In *The Long Revolution* (1961), Williams puts forward his "theory of culture as the study of relationships between elements in a whole way of life" (*LR* 67). In striving to ground his interpretation of culture in a materialist frame-work that avoids the pitfalls of mechanical materialism, on the one hand, and Romantic idealism, on the other, Williams emphasizes over and over again the *wholeness* of both his approach and the object of his analysis. The expression "a whole way of life," however, has proven a tricky one. In a fiery review published in *NLR*, E. P. Thompson argues that Williams's theory erases any sense of the social conflicts that might be *internal* to a culture, making it into something very far from *whole*. Thompson thus commands that the phrase, if it is to have any value, be rewritten as "a whole way of *conflict*"—or better, *struggle*.[29] There is some justice to this criticism. As Terry Eagleton has observed as well, but perhaps overstated, there is an "organicism" imported from T. S. Eliot, F. R. Leavis, and the longer nine-teenth-century tradition traced in *Culture and Society* that trickles into Williams's thinking about the "whole way of life"—another part of his Cambridge inheritance that mixes unevenly in *The Long Revolution* with his more Marxist influences.[30] This "organicism" does at times displace notions of class.[31] But Thompson's criticism misperceives the problem Williams is try-ing to address. Williams's effort is to bring what Marxism often calls "ideol-ogy" back to the ground and recontextualize it *in* "a way of life," making it, in fact, inseparable from that way of life, even if not *identical* with it (some-thing Williams also insists on). But when ideology is reduced to a blunt instrument (a whole way of *struggle*), all we hear is the sound of clashing ideologies.

Perhaps one extreme version of this, which Thompson would also abhor, is Louis Althusser's proclamation that ideology "has no history," not even a *class* history, but is reducible to a clash between materialist and idealist positions on an abstract "philosophical" plane, which, it turns out, is a peculiarly *non-materialist* way for a Marxist to discuss ideology.[32] Althusser, however, elsewhere comes very close to defining ideology also as "a whole way of life," when he argues that ideology is an *enacted ritual* embedded in daily life, orienting our thoughts and actions.[33] But here again a crucial difference arises: for Althusser, *ideology acts through us*, organizes our thoughts and actions for us, as we go through the motions that the social "apparatus" requires of us, whereas for Williams (and, for that matter, Thompson), *we act through ideology*. We are not only *passive* within ideology, but also *active*. Against ideology Althusser opposes "Theory"—namely, his own—which has for him the truth value of a science, whereas Williams, as a sociologist of culture wanting to understand how both modifying and large-scale cultural transformations work, opposes his concept of the structure of feeling to ideology, not as a "science," nor even necessarily as a moral value (although Williams sometimes seems to give it the latter), but as the location of an *internal differentiation within ideology itself*—the site of an active and emergent cultural consciousness in a moment of contestation with dominant or residual ideological forms. This is a process of emergence that will, as in Marx's nascent cultural theory, be indexed, in different ways, to transformations in the social totality—*the whole way of life*. "We are talking about," writes Williams, "affective elements of consciousness and relationship: not feeling against thought, but thought as felt and feeling as thought: practical consciousness of a present kind, in a living and interrelating continuity" (*ML* 132). This coming-to-consciousness—or what we may now term *emergence*—is a crucial component of what Williams means by a structure of feeling and it is precisely this that is bracketed when ideology is crudely reduced to the mere clash of class mentalities interpellating their subjects or competing paradigms on an abstract philosophical plane (i.e., materialism versus idealism).

DRAMA AND THE STRUCTURE OF FEELING

In *Marxism and Literature*, Williams explicitly links his concept of the structure of feeling—which he had first developed in the 1950s in his writings on drama—to *emergence*: "The effective formations of most actual art," he writes, "relate to already manifest social formations, dominant or residual"; these are *inherited* formations and, in that sense, *ideological* formations in which thought is dead or arrested, whereas "it is primarily to emergent formations (though often in the form of modification or disturbance in older forms) that the structure of feeling ... relates" (*ML* 134). In the context of his writing on drama, the structure of feeling is formulated specifically to capture the feeling that dramatic conventions and, behind those, more deep-seated social conventions are no longer adequate to life as lived and experienced—that those conventions, in other words, are no longer *representative*: "Fundamental changes of this kind, changes in the whole conception of a human being and of his relations with what is non-human bring, necessarily, changes of convention in their wake. . . . All changes in the methods of an art like the drama are related, essentially, to changes in man's radical structure of feeling" (*PF* 22–23). One of the unique advantages of Williams's auxiliary hypothesization of the structure of feeling is that it involves both gnoseological (epistemological) and mimetic (representational) questions vis-à-vis art's ability to capture knowledge of a concrete, social reality and represent or communicate that knowledge without actually reducing artistic capacity to either function. In fact, much of Williams's early work on drama can be framed as a challenge to the narrow mimeticism of naturalism with its fixation on plausible character and speech, which limits representation to mere imitation and impersonation while bracketing the dramatic and representational possibilities afforded by dramatic *spectacle*, which is not, strictly speaking, mimetic but pertains to drama as a "total performance." For Williams, "the intention of performance as *representation* becomes dangerous if it allows anyone to think that any particular set of conventions may stand for the dramatic method as a whole. I think there is real danger of this, because of the naturalist predominance in our own day; . . . it is easy to see how *imitation* or *impersonation* could acquire the same associations as *representation*" (*PF* 7–8). Williams argues instead, "*Performance*, itself, ought, in the context of drama, to carry all the necessary weight," meaning that drama's epistemological and representational capacities should be discovered in the components and composition of the performance itself—that is, in the form, and not merely in the content, of what the drama represents—for it is the *total performance* that has the possibility of giving shape to a larger and more recondite structure of feeling opposed to staid artistic and social conventions (in their own convoluted relationship of mutual reinforcement) (*PF* 8).

As Higgins observes, in his earliest writing on drama—prior to the crucial formulation of the structure of feeling—Williams was still indebted to T. S. Eliot and his notion of the "objective correlative," which he first presented in his famous essay on *Hamlet*.[34] In Eliot's conception, the objective correlative is a kind of symbolic substitute for a feeling not otherwise directly representable.[35] However, as Higgins notes, as early as the first edition of *Drama from Ibsen to Eliot* (1952), Williams was already revising this Eliotic inheritance.[36] For Eliot, the chronology is unambiguous: the poet knows the feeling he or she wants to convey; the challenge is merely to find the objective correlative, whereas for Williams, the structure of feeling is itself discovered in the author's experimentation. Hence his insistence—once he has abandoned the Eliotic paradigm —that the critical procedure being espoused is not merely a matter of putting the work of art, dramatic or otherwise, into relationship with its social context in a way that would render that context an inert, but meaningful, backdrop to the work of art. "To relate a work of art to any part of that observed totality," he writes in *Preface to Film*, "may, in varying degrees, be useful, but it is a common experience, in analysis, to realize that when one has measured the work against the separable parts, there yet remains some element for which there is no external counterpart. This element, I believe, is what I have named the *structure of feeling* of a period and it is only realizable through experience of the work of art itself, as a whole" (*PF* 21–22). This, then, is a whole new research program differentiated from the one charted by Eliot or, for that matter, Leavis, the latter of whom merely called on critics "to judge and discriminate the quality and sincerity of an author's thought with the ultimate aim of promoting discrimination, maturity and sincerity among the reading public as a whole."[37] In *Preface to Film*, Williams lays the groundwork for his progressive problem-shift in Marxist cultural criticism: although not initially identified with Marxism, the structure of feeling loses its full force and becomes conceptually unintelligible if one separates it from the base/superstructure problematic it was clearly developed to address.

I cannot agree, then, with Higgins's concluding judgment in his otherwise lucid study that "The central notion of a 'structure of feeling' amounts to little more than an ingenious instance of theoretical impressionism, in which a rhetorical figure tries to assume the explanatory force of a distinctly articulated theoretical concept."[38] For it is precisely with the concept in hand that Williams returns to the old question of how to develop a rational basis and justification for a materialist and Marxist literary criticism that reads literature neither "proleptically"—that is, by the standard of what a future society needs and wants (as had become the credo of so much of the 1930s "Marxist" criticism), nor deterministically, as he sometimes accused Caudwell of doing, as a mere reflection, however inverted, of society's economic base. Instead, Williams approaches the work of art—*art as both practice and creation*—from the standpoint of the artist situated *within* a whole way of life, producing, if not an exact knowledge or science of that totality, then at least a sense of its operation, artistically mediated and, if successfully communicated, potentially shared. To develop this further, we should look to what Williams says in his chapter on language in *Marxism and Literature*, where he examines language explicitly as a form of "practical consciousness," which is how Marx and Engels had also characterized it in their posthumously published manuscripts for *The German Ideology* (*ML* 30).

LANGUAGE AS PRACTICAL CONSCIOUSNESS

It is curious that Williams's intervention in linguistics is rarely acknowledged in popular applications of his method even though it makes up the longest chapter in Williams's most sustained engagement with Marxist theory.[39] In *Politics and Letters*, Williams says that the whole book rests, in his opinion, on the validity of the claims made in this chapter.[40] Here, Williams is at pains to challenge the hegemony of Saussurean linguistics in the humanities and social sciences, particularly its contradictory grafting onto Marxism. As he observes, "In Saussure the social nature of language is expressed as a system (*langue*), which is at once stable and autonomous and founded in normatively identical forms; its 'utterances' (*paroles*) are then seen as 'individual' (in abstract distinction from 'social') uses of 'a particular language code.'" Language, in this theory, has been abstracted to create a "formal system," which is then examined for its "underlying 'laws.'" Williams notes that Saussurean linguistics *does* mark a serious advance in scientific "descriptions of actual language operation," but emphasizes that this is achieved at the cost of bracketing language as an evolving and active part of men and women's lives. He observes with some weariness, "This achievement [of Saussurean linguistics] has an ironic relation with Marxism," which has also sought "certain fundamental laws of change" within a system. "This apparent affinity," he says, "explains the attempted synthesis of Marxism and structural linguistics which has been so influential" (*ML* 28). But crucially, he adds,

> Marxists have then to notice, first, that history, in its most specific, active, and connecting senses, has disappeared (in one tendency has been theoretically excluded) from this account of so central a social activity as language; and second, that the categories in which this version of system has been developed are the familiar bourgeois categories in which an abstract separation and distinction between the "individual" and the "social" have become so habitual that they are taken as "natural" starting-points. (*ML* 28)

The legibility of the formal system of language, in other words, is maintained in Saussurean linguistics by separating language out from lived reality and its messy "individual" applications in the form of "utterances." The Saussurean system refers only to its own separated self-consistency, as a seemingly "autonomous" objective structure. The purpose of Williams's chapter on language, then, is to reconnect these broken halves of Saussurean linguistics—the subjective use of language (*paroles*) and the objectivity of the language used (*langue*)—into one dynamic, evolving totality. To this end, Williams begins with a broad overview of developments in linguistics from antiquity to the present, which he sorts into two opposing schools of linguistics representing subjectivist and objectivist tendencies.

The subjectivist tendency comes into its own in the Romantic era with Vico and Herder and is given the honor of discovering language-capacity as a defining and evolutionary characteristic of human development. Here, what is emphasized is the *subjective* and *active* side of language as an always developing and even central component of human existence and creativity: what Williams positively describes, as "a distinctively human opening of and opening to the world: not a distinguishable or instrumental *but a constitutive faculty*" (*ML* 24; emphasis mine). The objectivist tendency, which dominates in the nineteenth century and leads to figures like Saussure, turns its attention to language itself. Here, language is viewed, not as a creative faculty of the human being, but as an inert structure. In this tradition, Williams writes, "Actual speech, even when it was available, was seen as *derived*, either historically into vernaculars or practically into speech acts which were instances of the fundamental (textual) forms of the language. Language-use could then hardly ever be seen as itself active and constitutive" (*ML* 27). Variability and internal difference, in other words, are treated, not as signs of an active linguistic malleability and, therefore, signals of a latent potential for transformation and development coming from within language, but rather as deviations from a norm, which is achieved only by abstracting language from practical use. According to Williams, both these positions face their own limitations.

The subjectivist tendency, in bracketing the objective world to which any language refers if it is to be meaningful, is capable of overemphasizing humanity as the maker of its own meanings, outside of any concrete or limiting field of determinations. As Williams observes, "It is precisely the sense of language as an *indissoluble* element of human self-creation that gives any acceptable meaning to its description as 'constitutive.'" However, he then adds, "To make it *precede* all other connected activities is to claim something quite different" (*ML* 29). If one adopts the latter position, then history becomes the elaboration of one long arc of spontaneous self-creation as in many versions of Romantic idealism. The objectivist tendency, on the other hand, insofar as it looks outside the system of language at all, is often limited to a mimetic or "reflection theory" of language, in which words refer unproblematically to things outside of themselves. With this objectivist development, Williams notes, "Language here decisively lost its definition as *constitutive* activity. It became a tool or an instrument or a medium taken up by the individuals when they had something to communicate, as distinct from the faculty which made them, from the beginning, not only able to relate and communicate, but in real terms to be practically conscious and so to possess the active practice of language" (*ML* 32).[41] In this interpretation, language is separated out from social reality, as one distinct, inert totality confronting another.

Most Marxism, "in its predominately positivist development, from the late nineteenth to the mid-twentieth century," inherited and maintained this objectivist separation of "'the world' and 'the language in which we speak about it,'" assigning language to the "superstructure" erected on the socioeconomic base, which language was then thought passively to reflect, even if in an inverted and ideological from. From the perspective of this "objectivist materialism," writes Williams, "the materiality of language could be grasped only as physical—a set of physical properties—and not as material activity" (*ML* 30). The early and influential Soviet linguist N. S. Marr, however, took this mechanical application of the base/superstructure relationship to language one step further, arguing that the kind of language that was dominant in capitalism was "bourgeois" language and that socialism was in the midst of producing a whole new "proletarian" language appropriate to the revolutionary transformation of the base.[42] None other than Stalin, Williams observes, sought to rectify this theoretical muddle with his assertion that language was not "part of the superstructure"—that is *not ideological* or class-specific, but was rather part of a *material* substratum determining human existence (which he associated with ethnicity and nationality) (*ML* 34). For Stalin, language, if anything, was more analogous to the base, but it was also clearly older than both the base and superstructure and therefore belonged properly to neither, acting instead with a machine-like neutrality as a basic communicative capacity, and, in that sense, productive force, mediating human relations: "Language," Stalin writes, "does not differ from instruments of production, from machines, let us say, which are as indifferent to classes as is language and may, like it, equally serve a capitalist system and a socialist system."[43] For Williams, Stalin's "clarification"—essentially a reassertion of the earlier objectivist position—reminds us that the base/superstructure problematic in classical Marxism was never satisfactorily resolved when it came to language and cultural creation.

Since the base/superstructure problem is the organizing problematic of Williams's theoretical work, it is largely to this question that the bulk of what follows in *Marxism and Literature* addresses itself, both as a continuation of Williams's early theory of culture as a "whole way of life," and as a new and more rigorous intervention or progressive problemshift within Marxism itself. At the linguistic level, Williams's intervention takes the following form. Between language and reality, there is a missing "middle term," which we can call *culture*—not language as structure, but as actually spoken and written. He writes,

> What we have, rather, is a grasping of . . . reality through language, which as practical consciousness is saturated by and saturates all social activity, including productive activity. And, since this grasping is social and continuous (as distinct from the abstract encounters of "man" and "his world," or "conscious-

ness" and "reality," or "language" and "material existence"), it occurs within an active and changing society. It is of and to this experience—the lost middle term between abstract entities, "subject" and "object," on which propositions of idealism and orthodox materialism are erected—that language speaks. (*ML* 37)

Language, then, is an objective and received structure, yes; but it is not inert, inflexible, or eternal. In other words, the truth of language is not the abstract *linguistic norm*, but *dialect* and the variability of the *invented form*:

> Indeed signs can exist only when this active social relationship is posited. The usable sign—the fusion of formal element and meaning—is a product of this continuing speech-activity between real individuals who are in some continuing social relationship. The "sign" is in this sense their product, but not simply their past product, as in the reified accounts of an "always-given" language system. The real communicative "products" which are usable signs are, on the contrary, living evidence of a continuing social process, in which individuals are born and within which they are shaped, but to which they then also actively contribute, in a continuing process. (*ML* 37)[44]

Human culture does not just operate *on* language, then, molding it as if it were some kind of raw material into so many shapes and forms, which it then opposes to reality, but operates *through* language and thus, also, "literature."[45] But here it is very important to be precise. There is one interpretation of Williams's so-called "culturalism" (advocated by the New Historicism) that turns Williams's strident and uncompromising materialism back into an idealism in which reality itself is interpreted as a linguistic construction, something he rejects over and over.[46] Language, he says, is *practical consciousness*. What is produced through language (especially the language *arts*—always connoting for Williams the older meaning of *arts* as *skills*) is not reality, but a kind of knowledge *about* reality. But note, also, that this is not *scientific* knowledge, but *practical* knowledge, which encodes an orientation to reality that informs and guides practical activity—which, for Williams, literally *grounds* that activity. It is in this sense that there is some legitimacy (*pace* Thompson) to the notion of culture as "a whole way of life." However, it might be better to say that culture is always part of and integral to the "whole way of life" which *could not, in fact, be whole if culture was subtracted from it*.

It is important to note the sources of Williams's argument before proceeding to outline how this shapes Williams's progressive shift within the base/superstructure problematic. As he explains in his introduction to *Marxism and Literature*, his arguments are derived from a renewed and sustain engagement with Marxist theory, which proposes not just to reevaluate Marxism through its new developments (the Western Marxism of Gramsci, the Frankfurt School, and Althusser), but also through a reappraisal of its classical tradition. Williams's argument in the language chapter is, in fact, largely indebted to the work of two previous interventions in the field of Soviet linguistic theory. The first is the 1930s work of the Soviet psychologist Lev Vygotsky, who Williams cites as one of two authorities behind his dialectical interpretation of culture as the missing "middle term" mediating the relationship between language (as inherited linguistic structure) and reality (as inherited environment and object of representation).[47] The other is, for Western readers, the more familiar figure of V. N. Vološinov (or perhaps Mikhail Bakhtin writing under that name), who sought to reintroduce social history into the petrified structuralism of Saussurean linguistics (the latter of which Williams nonetheless remained enduringly skeptical).[48] The point to emphasize, here, is that Williams's foray into linguistic debates evolves neither toward a theoretical abandonment of Marxism nor a synthesis of Marxism with some other alien thought system, such as Saussurean linguistics, as would be the case in a weakening, degenerative problemshift. To the contrary, the argument proceeds by a return, if not to first principles (the old answers), then to first problems, which posits Marxism implicitly as an open-ended system still capable of theoretical refinement and the generation of new facts and fields of inquiry, the latter of which Williams begins to theorize under the name *cultural materialism*.

THE CREATIVE MIND

Williams's adumbration of a theoretically Marxist linguistics in *Marxism and Literature* now makes possible a rereading of "The Creative Mind" chapter in *The Long Revolution*, which places it more explicitly within the Marxist framework, which, at that time, Williams was less comfortable reclaiming. Here, Williams maps transformations and evolutions of the idea of artistic creation (especially *imaginative* creations—i.e., mental rather than plastic) across the body of Western aesthetic theory. He begins by pointing out that the idea of artistic creation is relatively new: "We speak now of the artist's activity as 'creation,' but the word used by Plato and Aristotle is the very different 'imitation.' The general meaning of the Greek word *mimesis* is either 'doing what another has done,' or 'making something like something else'" (*LR* 20). In Plato, this had originally been a negative theory of artistic production, and, in fact, an admonishment against it, since for Plato what the artist created were actually degraded copies of God-given ideal forms. Aristotle, on the other hand, argued that what the artist "copied" was not any *particular* reality, "not the thing that has happened, but a kind of thing that might happen, i.e. what is possible as being probable or necessary." Imitation, then, was not *just copying*, but also *producing*, not just art, but also a kind of knowledge: poetry's "statements are of the nature rather of universals, whereas those of history are singulars" (Aristotle, qtd. in *LR* 21). Thus, Williams observes, "While Plato emphasises the dangers of fiction, as the imitation not even of ultimate reality but of mere appearances, Aristotle develops his concept of imitation as a form of learning" (*LR* 21). Here, we already have premonitions of Williams's future intervention in linguistic debates. Artistic realism, like language, isn't a mechanical "copy" of some external reality, but rather an *active* and *creative* process that requires, or even demands, artistic ingenuity and semi-autonomy *from* that reality: the *artwork* (with an emphasis on the practical connotations of *work*) functions, in other words, as the "middle term" between the impossible objectivism of mechanical materialism and the isolated subjectivism of idealism. Art becomes an extension, or even a productive refinement, of that "practical consciousness" that Marx, Engels, and Williams all locate in language.

According to Williams, this radical kernel of Aristotle's materialist poetics, which treats the artwork as a kind of learning or practical consciousness, was missed by early modern aesthetic theory. Renaissance "Platonism," which absorbed some elements of the Aristotelian argument, "came to include a theory of art directly opposed to that of the *Republic* [which had admonished *mimetic* art], arguing that the divinely inspired poet was able to teach the highest reality because he penetrated mere appearance, and embodied in his work the divine Idea" (*LR* 22). This led ineluctably to what became the Romantic idea—but which was first formulated in Sidney's "The Defense of Poesy" (1595)—that the artist, as a kind of God, was able in his or her imaginative works "to create beyond natural limits" (*LR* 25). This was a crucial turning point for Williams: "The belief in artistic creation as the medium of a superior reality seems most likely to be held in a period of transition from a primarily religious to a primarily humanist culture, for it embodies elements of both ways of thinking: that there is a reality beyond ordinary human vision, and yet that man has supreme creative powers" (*LR* 29). Since the eighteenth century, Williams says, "we have seen an alternation, but only of emphasis, between a naive realism—'describing things as they really are,' and the varying kinds of romanticism, from 'describing things as they ought to be, as they ideally are' to the simple 'superior reality' claim" (*LR* 30). These, of course, are false alternatives for Williams; and it is here that we encounter the crucial and surprising turn of argument, which had so annoyed Thompson in his review of *The Long Revolution*: "It is at this point," writes Williams, "that we can turn to recent work on perception, as a process of the brain and the nervous system. It seems to me, certainly, that it enables us to take a decisive step forward, in the necessary clarification" (*LR* 33).[49]

If the chapter on language was the pivotal entry in *Marxism and Literature*, providing it with a materialist basis for discussing literary production as a form of "practical consciousness," then one imagines Williams must have felt similarly about this section of "The Creative Mind," which draws heavily on the English neurophysiologist J. Z. Young's *Doubt and Certainty in Science: A Biologist's Reflections on the Brain* (1950) to formulate a scientifically materialist theory of artistic creation as a form of consciousness-making not reducible to a mere "copying" of reality. Here, again Williams does not follow Western Marxism in rejecting the extension of the materialist dialectic to areas of life not strictly circumscribed by social history. He writes with great approval,

> The growth of every human being is a slow process of learning what Young calls "the rules of seeing," without which we could not in any ordinary sense see the world around us. There is no reality of familiar shapes, colours and sounds, to which we merely open our eyes. The information that we receive through our senses from the material world around us has to be interpreted, according to certain human rules, before what we ordinarily call "reality" forms. The human brain has to perform this "creative" activity before we can, as normal human beings, see at all. (*LR* 35)

The brain, in other words, is always actively involved in interpreting reality: sense data does not immediately impress a picture of that reality on our mind. "Contrary to what we might suppose," writes Young, "the eyes and brain do not simply record in a sort of photographic manner the pictures that pass in front of us"; we are constantly involved in the interpretation and organization of that data into knowledge about our surrounding environments. As Young says, "We ourselves come into the process" (qtd. in *LR* 35). This does not mean, however, that we are free to create our reality as we see fit, or that reality is a matter of perspective. There are external and internal limiting factors, which are as much sociocultural as they are biological. In coming to see our social reality differently, we may desire to become actively involved in modifying or changing that reality, but it is not the change in perception itself that intercedes in reality, although a shift in perception may follow just such an intercession. For Williams, what this means is that we can only "learn to see a thing by learning to describe it," and it is only in the describing and in the "seeing" that we will also then be able to communicate that reality and be prepared to intercede in it (*LR* 42).

There is no guarantee, however, that first descriptions will be *correct* descriptions; in fact, the scientific premise of such an argument requires perpetual experimentation and reverification. For Williams, artistic production (the *work* of the creative mind) is actively involved in this "enlargement" of our perceptions and their communicability; "description is a function of communication," he writes, "and we can best understand the arts if we look at this vital relationship, in which experience has to be described to be realised (this description being, in fact, putting the experience into a communicable form) and has then . . . to be shared with another organism" (*LR* 43).

This may feel a long way from the Marxist understanding of art as "ideological" or "superstructural"—that is, until we remember that Marx also defines art as one of the key locations in which men and women become conscious of the disparity between received wisdom (their inherited ideological superstructures) and their lived reality, and then "fight it out," giving the base/superstructure relation its crucial complexity as a problem for more research, rather than as a prepared formula or solution.[50]

CULTURAL MATERIALISM

As should now be clear, Williams's ongoing intervention in the base/superstructure debates were not meant as refutations, but as refinements, a shifting of the problems that too often compromised the original hypotheses. The complaint, he explains in "Base and Superstructure in Marxist Cultural Theory" (1973), was not against the idea of a base "setting limits and exerting pressures, whether by some external force or by the internal laws of a particular development," but rather the idea that this then unilaterally "prefigured, predicted and controlled" the content of the superstructural forms (as in Caudwell's notion of "capitalist poetry") (*PMC* 32). Equally, though, he was just as little interested in solving the problem by "freeing" the superstructural activity from the base altogether: "For if we come to say that society is composed of a large number of social practices which form a concrete social whole, and if we give to each practice a certain specific recognition, adding only that they interact, . . . we are at another level withdrawing from the claim that there is any process of determination. And this I, for one, would be very unwilling to do" (*PMC* 36).[51]

As already noted, in *Culture and Society*, he criticized English "Marxist" cultural theory not for being crudely deterministic, but for being overly Romantic in its assertion that the artistic imagination could run *ahead* of the actual material conditions of production and, in so doing, imaginatively prefigure a situation at which material conditions had not yet arrived. "One of the unexpected consequences of the crudeness of the base/superstructure model," he observes in the 1973 essay, "has been the too easy acceptance of models which appear less crude—models of totality or of a complex whole—but which exclude the facts of social intention, the class character of a particular society and so on. And this reminds us of how much we lose if we abandon the superstructural emphasis altogether" (*PMC* 36). Here at last, then, is the response and correction to Thompson's criticism that the earlier conceptualization of the "whole way of life" had erased class conflict. The "whole way of life," he now says (although he doesn't use that expression anymore), is organized around a dominant "intention" or "class interest," which has become hegemonic. It is against this dominant idea that emergent forms of knowledge and practice struggle for existence as counter-hegemonic forces, all within a context in which residual elements of an older society or way of life may remain active or interfused with other elements.

This new focus on the organizational pull of a dominant "class interest" shines light on the meaning of the second part of the passage about "how much we lose if we abandon the superstructural emphasis altogether." We cannot understand resistances, or indeed the revolutionary potential within a "whole way of life" for substantive transformation, if we do not have a concept of what that process of emergence is up against—namely, the legitimatizing ideologies of the superstructure. "Our hardest task theoretically," he says, "is to find a non-metaphysical and a non-subjectivist explanation of emergent cultural practice"—in other words, a materialist interpretation of how new forms of *practical consciousness* come into being (*PMC* 42).

In *The Long Revolution*, the concept of the "structure of feeling," originally introduced in *Preface to Film*, is reprised as one way to explain just this process of emergence, when, for example, "we notice the contrasts between generations, who never talk quite 'the same language,' or when we read an account of our lives by someone from outside the community, or watch the small differences in style, of speech or behaviour, in someone who has learned our ways yet was not bred in them" (*LR* 68). These differences, says Williams, are to be found in the affective attitudes that mediate our relationships to each other and our wider contexts and surroundings:

> The term I would suggest to describe it is *structure of feeling*: it is as firm and definite as "structure" suggests, yet it operates in the most delicate and least tangible parts of our activity. . . . One generation may train its successor, with reasonable success, in the social character or the general cultural pattern, but the new generation will have its own structure of feeling, which will not appear to have come "from" anywhere. For here, most distinctly, the changing organisation is enacted in the organism. (*LR* 69)

Amid the indeed lamentable organicism of this passage there is still sense to be made of the final assertion: the structure of feeling differentiating the generations *appears* to come from nowhere because it blossoms in the very subjectivity of the new generation and their *way of seeing*, but its coordinates are objective, rooted in a concrete, external reality, for what is shaping the structure is how "the new generation responds in its own ways to the unique world it is inheriting, taking up many continuities, that can be traced, and reproducing many aspects of the organisation, which can be separately described, yet feeling its whole life in certain ways differently, and shaping its creative response into a new structure of feeling" (*LR* 69–70). Thus, although the structure of feeling may in one sense be ideological—in that, those doing the *feeling* are not fully aware of it—it is not a mere passive or instinctual response, but very specifically an actively *shaping* and *creative* response.

When Williams returns to the concept of the structure of feeling in *Marxism and Literature*, presenting it now explicitly in a Marxian framework, he describes it as "a structured formation which, because it is at the very edge of semantic availability, has many of the characteristics of a pre-formation, until specific articulations—new semantic figures—are discovered in material practice" (*ML* 134). The structure of feeling, in other words, articulates something on the "verge of semantic availability," not yet available in precise scientific discourse, "a mode of social formation, explicit and recognizable in specific kinds of art, which is distinguishable from other social and semantic formations by its articulation of *presence*" (*ML* 134). What we are starting to grasp in these formulations of the structure of feeling is a very precise shifting of the problems that had plagued the base/superstructure relationship in much received Marxism, which, as Williams had already started to realize in 1973, "suggest[s] at once the point of break and the point of departure, in practical and theoretical work, within an active and self-renewing Marxist cultural tradition" (*PMC* 49).

So what are the changes? We still have, as every Marxism must, a limiting and determining field of social and historical factors, for it is within and against these that the structure of feeling starts to take shape. However, these limiting factors, although determinate, do not in any way "preprogram" the form or content of the structure of feeling, which is a *creative* and *agential* response to a concrete situation and *shared* experience. In this context, the structure of feeling takes the form of a kind of grasping after something still on the verge of "semantic availability": "not feeling against thought, but thought as felt and feeling as thought" (*ML* 132, 134).

Clearly, then, we are not talking about what, too often, a certain kind of Marxism might dismiss as "false consciousness," for it is precisely against received and masking ideologies (associated with the residual and dominant) that the new structure of feeling responds, gropingly, as an "articulation of *presence*" (*ML* 134).[52] But, at the same time, neither is the structure of feeling an exact "reflection" of that external reality. Already, as early as *Preface to Film*, Williams had referred to the structure of feeling as that "element" in the work of art "for which there is no external counterpart" (*PF* 21–22); which is another way saying that, since the structure of feeling is not reducible to some external reality that it mirrors, it too must be an active "part" of that reality in the "whole way of life"—an actual and material form of "practical consciousness."

Nothing in the basic tenets of Marxism (its theoretical "hard core," in Foster and Lakatos's sense) is exploded by these emendations to the base/superstructure relationship. To the contrary, the whole of the Marxist theory of culture is moved forward by a very careful shifting of the problems that had made the base/superstructure relationship appear mechanical and incapable of absorbing new information and generating new insights about cultural production. And he does this not as had been attempted in the 1930s—by moving in the direction of a more Romantic or subjectivist idealism—but by re-grounding the whole Marxist theory of culture in a more rigorously materialist dialectic, evolving his theory, as Sacristán had suggested an "Engelsian" Marxism would, in open dialogue with new research in the sciences (for example, in linguistics and neurophysiology), which allows him to root his theory of language and culture between the twin coordinates of an inherited biological capacity and a historically mediating socioeconomic reality, as a missing "middle term."

In his 1976 essay, "Notes on British Marxism since 1945," with the publication of *Marxism and Literature* now imminent, Williams looked back at this long endeavor with notes of triumph, but also some battle weariness:

> It took me thirty years to move from that received Marxist theory (which I began by accepting) through various transitional forms of theory and inquiry, to the position I now hold, which I define as "cultural materialism." The emphases of the transition—on the production (rather than reproduction) of meanings and values by specific social formations, on the primacy of language and communication as formative social forces, and on the complex interaction both of institutions and forms and of social relationships and formal conventions—may be defined, if any one wishes, as "culturalism," and even the crude old (positivist) idealism/materialism dichotomy may be applied if it helps anyone. What I would now claim to have reached, but necessarily by this route, is a theory of culture as a (social and material) productive process and of specific practices, of "arts," as social uses of material means of production (from language as material "practical consciousness" to the specific technologies of writing and forms of writing, through to mechanical and electronic communications systems). (*PMC* 243)

The thing to emphasize about this characteristically lucid self-retrospection is Williams's persistent *materialism*: the painstaking search for the material substratum in the biology of the human brain and the organs of perception and communication, in language as the material basis of "practical consciousness," and in the technological means of production, from writing to electronic communication, all of which not only sets certain determinate and limiting parameters on cultural production, but also makes cultural production possible in the first place, as an important, if not crucial, component of the human story—something that cannot be ignored in any rigorous investigation of capitalism or socialism, or the struggle against the first for the latter.

NOTES

1. Tom Pinkney, "Raymond Williams," in *A Dictionary of Marxist Thought*, 2nd ed., ed. Tom Bottomore (Oxford: Blackwell, 1991), 585.

2. In 1992, David Simpson felt the concept was so distinct as not to be "exportable." "To the best of my knowledge," he continues, "no one has much picked it up, used it, or refined it." David Simpson, "Raymond Williams: Feeling for Structures, Voicing 'History,'" *Social Text*, no. 30 (1992): 15. The affective turn in the humanities and social sciences which became apparent in the 2000s has since proven the opposite; references to Williams's concept now abound. For two influential studies that invoke the concept, see Sianne Ngai, *Ugly Feelings* (Cambridge, MA: Harvard University Press, 2005), 25–26 and 359–60n28; and Lauren Berlant, *Cruel Optimism* (Durham, NC: Duke University Press, 2011), 15 and 65.

3. "The Western Marxists . . . included Gramsci in Italy, Lukács and Korsch in central Europe, while from the 1930s the Frankfurt School played an essential role in maintaining this style of thought. After world war II, Goldmann and the circles around *Les Temps Modernes* (Sartre, Merleau-Ponty) and *Arguments* (Lefebvre) constituted a French Western Marxism. Under the influence of Lukács, Gramsci and the Frankfurt School, new generations of Western Marxism emerged, especially in Germany, Italy and the United States." Russell Jacoby, "Western Marxism," in Bottomore, *A Dictionary of Marxist Thought*, 581. See also Perry Anderson, *Considerations on Western Marxism* (London: Verso, 1976).

4. See also Perry Anderson, "The Missing Text: Introduction to 'The Future of Marxism,'" *New Left Review* 1, no. 114 (2018): 33–51.

5. John Bellamy Foster, "Marx's Open-Ended Critique," *Monthly Review* 70, no.1 (2018): 1.

6. See Ibid., 1 and 14n6. See also Imre Lakatos, *The Methodology of Scientific Research Programmes*, vol. 1, eds. John Worrall and Gregory Currie (Cambridge: Cambridge University Press, 1978), 31–47.

7. John Bellamy Foster and Paul Burkett, *Marx and the Earth: An Anti-Critique* (Chicago: Haymarket, 2017), 17–18.

8. Ibid., 18. Interestingly, it is this same ad hoc borrowing from other thought systems that Anderson argues characterizes Western Marxism's attempts at innovation through "formal shifts"; see Anderson, *Considerations on Western Marxism*, 55–67.

9. Karl Marx, *A Contribution to the Critique of Political Economy*, trans. S. W. Ryazanskaya, Marxists.org.

10. John Bellamy Foster traces this rejection of Engels's dialectics of nature to an overvaluation of a footnote in Georg Lukács's *History and Class Consciousness* (1923), which Lukács, himself, would later re-qualify in a way that restored nature to Marxist dialectics. See John Bellamy Foster, "The Dialectics of Nature and Marxist Ecology," in *The Ecological Rift: Capitalism's War on the Earth*, by John Bellamy Foster, Brett Clark, and Richard York (New York: Monthly Review Press, 2010), 216–25.

11. Frederick Engels, *Anti-Dühring: Herr Eugen Dühring's Revolution in Science*, trans. Emile Burns, in *Karl Marx and Fredrick Engels Collected Works*, vol. 25 (New York: International Publishers, 1987), 8

12. Roy Edgley traces the expression "dialectical materialism" back to G. V. Plekhanov, "who probably first used [it] . . . in 1891." Roy Edgley, "Dialectical Materialism," in Bottomore, *A Dictionary of Marxist Thought*, 142.

13. Manuel Sacristán, "Engels's Task in *Anti-Dühring*," in *The Marxism of Manuel Sacristán: From Communism to the New Social Movements*, trans. and ed. Renzo Llorente (Chicago: Haymarket Books, 2015), 126.

14. Ibid. 129–30.

15. Ibid. 126.

16. Ibid. 127.

17. Jacoby, "Western Marxism," 583.

18. "This obligatory connection with Hegel often results, on account of this great thinker's profound ambiguity, in an unjustified invasion of the terrain of positive science, in a sterile, purely verbal application of the dialectic to the level of abstract and reductive analysis." Sacristán, "Engels's Task," 132.

19. Paul Blackledge, "Practical Materialism: Engels's *Anti-Dühring* as Marxist Philosophy," *Critique* 45, no. 4 (2017): 489. In *Dialectics of Nature*, Engels writes, "HARD AND FAST LINES are incompatible with the theory of evolution. . . . For a stage in the outlook on

nature where all differences become merged in intermediate steps, and all opposites pass into one another through intermediate links, the old metaphysical method of thought no longer suffices. Dialectics, which likewise knows no HARD AND FAST LINES, no unconditional, universally valid 'either-or' and which bridges the fixed metaphysical differences, and besides 'either-or' recognizes also in the right place 'both this—and that' and reconciles the opposites, is the sole method of thought appropriate to the highest degree to this stage [of evolutionary science]." Fredrick Engels, *Dialectics of Nature*, trans. Clemens Dutt, in *Karl Marx and Frederick Engels Collected Works*, vol. 25 (New York: International Publishers, 1987), 493–94.

20. Sebastiano Timpanaro, *On Materialism*, trans. Lawrence Garner (London: Verso, 1980), 82. See also Engels, "The Part Played by Labour in the Transition from Ape to Man," in *Dialectics of Nature*, in *Karl Marx and Frederick Engels Collected Works*, vol. 25, 452–64. For a discussion of Engels's antipathy toward Social Darwinism, see John Bellamy Foster, *The Return of Nature: Socialism and Ecology* (New York: Monthly Review, 2020), 258–64; for a critical overview of its genealogy, see Raymond Williams, "Social Darwinism" (*PMC* 86–102).

21. Foster, *Return of Nature*, 15.

22. See Timpanaro, *On Materialism*, 29–54.

23. Ibid., 34. See, for example, John Bellamy Foster, *Marx's Ecology: Materialism and Nature* (New York: Monthly Review, 2000), 258n16.

24. Anderson and Jacoby either ignore or exclude Williams (and British Marxism more generally) from their discussions of Western Marxism. Jacoby does not mention him, whereas Anderson and, under his editorial leadership, the *NLR* tend to champion him as a preeminent "socialist thinker," but reject him as a "Marxist." See Perry Anderson, "Socialism and Pseudo-Empiricism," *New Left Review* 1 no. 35 (1966): 32. For his own thoughts on the topic, see Raymond Williams, "You're a Marxist Aren't You?" (*RH* 65–76).

25. On Williams's conflict with Tillyard, see also John Higgins, *Raymond Williams: Literature, Marxism and Cultural Materialism* (London: Routledge, 1999), 8–9.

26. Marx, *A Contribution to the Critique of Political Economy*.

27. Ibid.

28. Higgins, *Raymond Williams*, 8.

29. E. P. Thompson, "The Long Revolution I," *New Left Review* 1, no. 9 (1961): 33. For the second part of his review, see E. P. Thompson, "The Long Revolution II," *New Left Review* 1, no. 10 (1961): 34–39.

30. Terry Eagleton, "Criticism and Politics: The Work of Raymond Williams," *New Left Review* 1, no. 95 (1976): 10. Thompson also notes that the expression a "whole way of life" is derived from T. S. Eliot's writings on culture ("The Long Revolution I," 32).

31. This occasional displacement of class in Williams's earlier work is substantially corrected in his work from the 1970s onward.

32. Louis Althusser, "Lenin and Philosophy," in *Lenin and Philosophy and Other Essays*, trans. Ben Brewster (New York: Monthly Review, 2001), 21.

33. See Althusser, "Ideology and Ideological State Apparatuses: Notes Towards an Investigation," in *Lenin and Philosophy*, 85–126.

34. Higgins, *Raymond Williams*, 30–31.

35. See T. S. Eliot, "Hamlet," in *Selected Essays* (London: Faber, 1932), 141–46.

36. Higgins, *Raymond Williams*, 30.

37. Ibid., 173.

38. Ibid., 169.

39. Although Ngai and Berlant, for instance, are clearly influenced by Williams's conceptualization of the structure of feeling, neither shows an interest in Williams's language theory or the concept's context within the wider debates staged in *Marxism and Literature*.

40. "The book," Williams explains, "was originally based on lectures which started in Cambridge about 1970. But it's very significant that in those lectures there was nothing on the theory of language, whereas now it is the longest section of the book, and I would say the most pivotal. I don't think any of the rest can be sustained unless that position is seen as its basis" (*PL* 324).

41. Stalin, however, insisted in his 1950s intervention that this was precisely the correct way to view language: "Language is a medium, an instrument with the help of which people

communicate with one another, exchange thoughts and understand each other." J. V. Stalin, *Marxism and the Problem of Linguistics*, https://www.marxists.org/reference/archive/stalin/works/1950/jun/20.htm.

42. See Roy A. Medvedev, "Stalin and Linguistics: An Episode from the History of Soviet Science," in *The Unknown Stalin*, by Zhores A. Medvedev and Roy A. Medvedev, trans. Ellen Dahrendorf, 200–209 (London: I. B. Tauris, 2003).

43. Stalin, *Marxism and the Problem of Linguistics*.

44. This is nearly the precise opposite of what Stalin had argued: "Dialects and jargons are therefore offshoots of the common national language, devoid of all linguistic independence and doomed to stagnation." Stalin, *Marxism and the Problem of Linguistics*.

45. The word "literature" is in quotation marks because Williams rejects the idea that literature is a special area of linguistic endeavor, separated out from other "lower" linguistic forms of expression or entertainment. To the contrary, he insisted from the very beginning to the end that, to use the title from an early essay, *culture is ordinary*. Raymond Williams, "Culture Is Ordinary" (*RH* 3–18). See also Williams's chapter on literature in *Marxism and Literature* (*ML* 45–54).

46. Consider, for example, Catherine Gallagher and Stephen Greenblatt's embarrassing assertion on behalf of the New Historicism that Williams fails to live up to his own purported "culturalism" (which is never something he espoused; the *–ism* was always to be found in *materialism*). For Gallagher and Greenblatt, and much of the New Historicism, Williams is of interest only insofar as he can be distanced from the materialism of the Marxist tradition, whereas Williams himself seemed to want to make the Marxist tradition *more* materialist. See Catherine Gallagher and Stephen Greenblatt, *Practicing New Historicism* (Chicago: University of Chicago Press, 2000), 60–66 and 112.

47. For his evaluation of Vygotstky's project, see *ML* 34 and 43.

48. Vološinov's work is central to Williams's own language theory and disagreement with Saussurean linguistics (see *ML* 35).

49. See Thompson, "The Long Revolution I," 31.

50. For a powerful reading of the centrality of this struggle with inheritance in Williams's life and writing and how it contributes to Williams's critique of modernism (a topic too large to be dealt with here), see Daniel Hartley, *The Politics of Style: Towards a Marxist Poetics* (Chicago: Haymarket Books, 2017), 121–29

51. Williams argues that this is one of the risks of replacing base/superstructure with the Marxist-Hegelian notion of "totality" (*PMC* 35–37).

52. For Williams's discussion of the limitations and contradictions in treating ideology as a form of "false consciousness," see his chapter on ideology in *Marxism and Literature* (*ML* 55–71).

Part II

Knowable Communities

Chapter Five

Anti-Imperial Literacy, the Humanities, and Universality in Raymond Williams's Late Work

Daniel Hartley

Towards the end of his career, and ultimately of his life, Raymond Williams returned repeatedly to a set of concerns whose interconnection is not immediately apparent upon simple enumeration: the relation of writing to power, the ideology of modernism, anti-imperial resistance, a critique of the nation-state, the history and culture of Wales, a call for a new, collaborative conception of the humanities, and the seemingly obscure term "distance."[1] Together they form a dense web of mutual presupposition which, taken in its totality, amounts to a highly original body of socialist thought that remains of paramount importance. In what follows I attempt to delineate what is at stake in each element and the ways in which they inform one another. I begin by considering the trajectory of the puzzlingly insistent term "distance" throughout Williams's oeuvre, for its various semantic permutations become central to his influential account of modernism. Likewise, his account of modernism connects directly to his reflections on nationalism, the imperial British state, and Welsh history. Having elaborated upon these interconnections, and defended Williams against Paul Gilroy's now-canonical accusation that his approach to nationalism reproduces the presuppositions of the "new racism," I shall turn to a detailed reading of a remarkable, but little-studied, presidential address to the Classical Association given by Williams in 1984, and posthumously published as "Writing, Speech and the 'Classical'" (*W* 44–56).[2] The address combines, in concentrated form, many of the recurring concerns of his late work and develops a highly suggestive theory of universality. I conclude with some brief remarks that attempt to draw together these separate strands in a more condensed manner so as to articulate the direct

relevance of Williams's late work to contemporary movements to "decolon-
ise" the university, and to spell out the Utopian potential of Williams's
unique democratic vision.

DISTANCE

On the last page of Williams's fictional autobiography *Border Country*
(1960), Matthew reflects on his life's journey: from the literal train ride he
took as a young man leaving the working-class village he had grown up in to
travel to university, to his recent return, after the death of his father, to his
wife and children: "Only now," he says to his wife Susan, "it seems like the
end of exile. Not going back, but the feeling of exile ending. For the distance
is measured, and that is what matters. By measuring the distance, we come
home" (*BC* 436). As ever in Williams, "distance" is not simply geographical:
it concerns the felt distances, induced by partial or total incorporation into a
more powerful class (for which the term "social mobility" is, at best, inaccu-
rate), to what one has previously known and lived. "Distance" also denotes
the (apparent) separation of country from city, Wales from England, and one
generation from the next. As an economics lecturer working on population
movements into the Welsh mining valleys in the middle decades of the
nineteenth century, it is Matthew's job to "measure" these movements (*BC*
4). "But I have moved myself," says Matthew, "and what is it really that I
must measure? The techniques I have learned have the solidity and precision
of ice-cubes, while a given temperature is maintained" (*BC* 4). Matthew
knows from his own experience that academic modes of measurement, statis-
tical surveys for example, are themselves symptoms of social distantiation:
as cold as ice. His own ways of measuring are "somewhere else altogether,
that I can feel but not handle, touch but not grasp," and that is why his
research has stalled (*BC* 4). By the end of the novel, however, Matthew has
found a way to measure the interrelated distances of geography, class, and
country; the event and aftermath of his father's death have led him through a
personal reckoning which, in turn, allows him to find a way back, to reach a
way of living that is no longer internally riven but true to the contradictory
reality of his own experience. Ending "exile" in this way is entirely different
from a simple rejection of one's working-class past and active self-incorpora-
tion into the dominant class. Matthew's solution is fully dialectical, tarrying
with the negative, immanently working through the maze of determinate
material contradictions, whereas simple rejection or repression would be the
experiential equivalent of an abstract negation or false transcendence.

While the term "distance—reappears periodically through all of
Williams's work, in the 1980s it recurs with increasing insistence across a
range of contexts. In *The Sociology of Culture*—entitled *Culture* in its British

edition—it names a measure of autonomy: "The degree of cultural autonomy of a cultural process is, at a first level, deducible from its practical distance from otherwise organized social relations" (*SC* 188). In capitalist societies, the "closer" a given practice and its conditions are to those of wage-labor, the more likely it is to reproduce the dominant social relations; inversely, "relative distance is in practice only a definition of marginality" (*SC* 190). In "Distance," a 1982 article in the *London Review of Books*, Williams critically analyzes the "culture of distance" inculcated by television coverage of the Falklands War (*W* 36). The article begins by noting the etymology of "television" from the Greek for "afar." As in *Border Country*, however, this literal spatial distance becomes inseparable from other modalities: the "war of technical distance" (via long-range missiles), the *critical* distance afforded Williams by a short stay in Ireland, and various complex forms of *social* distance. The result is a conception of distance as that which reduces the lived realities of battle to "fantasies of models and of convictions without experience," within which "men and women are reduced to models, figures and the quick [patriotic] cry in the throat" (*W* 42, 43). Taken together, it adds up to a new political form that Williams names "constitutional authoritarianism" (*W* 42).[3] Its opposite is precisely that fully dialectical mode of immanent reckoning at which Matthew had arrived.[4]

A year later, Williams gave two retirement lectures at Cambridge: "Cambridge English, Past and Present," and "Beyond Cambridge English." The first was his attempt to make clear his own "social and intellectual distance" from so-called "Cambridge English" (*WS* 190). The second took aim at two formations that Williams saw as interconnected: modernism and "theory" (particularly structuralism). His account of modernism lays the groundwork for the more detailed elaborations to be found in the later essays collected in the posthumously published *The Politics of Modernism*. He views modernism and theory as "major intellectual formations through which the unevenness of literacy and learning has been lived with and either mediated or rationalized" (*WS* 220). As in the later accounts, Williams stresses modernism's origins in the new social form of the metropolis. He notes that a number of modernist innovators were "immigrants":

> Distanced from, though often still preoccupied by, more local cultures, they found the very materials of their work—their language, which writers had once fully shared with others; their visual signs and representations, which shared ways of life had carried—insufficient yet productive in one crucial way: that writers, artists and intellectuals could share this sense of strangeness with others doing their kind of work but who had begun from quite different familiarities. From the initial strangeness what was forged was a specific form of a possible aesthetic universality. (WS 222)

Whereas in previous historical eras such estranged and estranging aesthetic forms could not have achieved cultural dominance, their hegemony was made possible by the "increasingly mobile and dislocated society" embodied in the imperial metropolis (*WS* 222).

Williams argues that "theory"—those approaches to culture and society that emerged in one way or another from structuralism—shares with modernism this "deep form": it views society with the "eyes of a stranger" (*WS* 223). Here, he echoes the earlier remarks in *Border Country*: "I can feel the bracing cold of their inherent distances and impersonalities" (*WS* 223). Williams does not dispute the explanatory power of structuralist approaches, but argues that the "form and the language" of its explanations "are at a quite exceptional distance from the lives and relationships they address, so that what is reaching furthest into our common life has the mode of a stranger, even the profession of a stranger" (*WS* 224). There will be more to say below about a puzzling strain of what appears like nativism in Williams's thought, but suffice it to say that the problem as he sees it is that unless the distance between writing, theory and "general life" can be overcome, the hegemony of capital will go unchallenged precisely because even the "most shallow and adaptive forms of commercial popular art" remain closer to people's everyday concerns than the alienated "theory" that imagines itself to be a locus of critique (*WS* 224). The same holds true for the most "inertly reproduced traditional art" (*WS* 224). Maintaining this distance reproduces the unevenness of learning and literacy, condemning the majority to a basic form of alienation from the dominant culture.

Modernism thus begins for Williams in a distance from "general life." As he sees it, as a first break with the dominant culture, this was inevitable. Yet its practitioners then had a choice pertaining directly to the unevenness of learning and literacy: a rejection of the dominant culture through an option for the past, for tradition and "clearer authorities and privileges," as a way of stabilizing the unevenness (whether Eliot's "Tradition"—"the many unconscious, the few conscious"—or that, say, of *Scrutiny* with its clerisy of enlightened critics who safeguard the popular vitality of the English tradition on behalf of—or in the place of—the people) (*D* 204). Or, alternatively, there existed the minority option of absolute revolution as a way of overcoming the unevenness and structural alienation of literacy, of sublating the distance between culture and everyday life.[5] Williams locates himself firmly in the latter camp, and seems to recognize both a continuation in the present of the necessity to choose between these two options and, more importantly, a possibility for a contemporary way out of the dilemma. For "theory" is not the only collective agent in the present to have inherited this problematic; in the period of the emergence of "interdisciplinarity" as a watchword of higher education, Williams senses new possibilities for "a much wider collaboration of the humanities" (*W* 46). Such new work had already begun "on the periphery of the old systems; in some of the new universities, in several polytechnics, in the Open University, and in many practical initiatives beyond the settled institutions" (*WS* 226). One senses here a moment in British history in which the expansion of various kinds of higher education among a widening range of popular strata acted as a potential institutional mediation between "literacy" and the "people" which, in the process, expanded the very nature of literacy as such beyond "literature" to include critical facility with other media.[6] Needless to say, the operations of neoliberalism came to exert a serious power of incorporation upon this brief moment of emergence: the zombie-like managerial incantation of "interdisciplinarity" across all university contexts today stands as a testament to its downfall.

Ultimately, then, "distance" for Williams consists primarily of two interrelated elements: social alienation and a tendency to abstract from, simplify, or repress the true complexity of social and personal mediations. As in the theory of alienation from Hegel to Marx, such abstractions become socially functional aspects of ruling class power. Literacy is caught in the cross hairs. As will become clearer in Williams's presidential address to the Classical Association, high literacy harbors true anti-authoritarian potential, but its calculatedly uneven distribution across the social body is a cultural constituent of ruling class power.

WALES, ABSTRACT UNIVERSALITY,
AND THE CULTURE OF NATIONS

Many of these concerns reappear in slightly altered guise in Williams's writings on nationalism, nation-states, and Wales. It is well-known that Williams turned increasingly to questions of Welsh history and national identity from the 1970s onward.[7] Less remarked upon is the continuity between these concerns and his late work on modernism and literacy.[8] A useful distillation of Williams's thinking on nationalism in this period is the chapter "The Culture of Nations" in *Towards 2000* (1983). To return to it in the era of Brexit is to encounter a crystalline account of a set of sociocultural contradictions that remain uncannily contemporary. There are two main targets of Williams's critique: those who uphold abstract forms of universality as a way of distancing themselves from the immediate particularities of place and nation, and the capitalist state's strategic use of patriotism as a means of hegemonic incorporation.

Abstract universality, for Williams, is a symptom of social alienation in the sense that it mistakes intellectual insight into the supposed universality of humanity as a sufficient means of concretely realizing universality in practice:

> It is ineffective and even trivial to come back from a demonstration of the universality of the human species and expect people, from that fact alone, to reorganise their lives by treating all their immediate and actual groupings and relationships as secondary. For the species meaning . . . is in practice only realised, indeed perhaps in theory only realisable, through significant relationships in which other human beings are present. No abstraction on its own will carry this most specific of all senses. To extend it and to generalise it, in sufficiently practical ways, involves the making of new relationships which are in significant continuity—and not in contradiction—with the more limited relationships through which people do and must live. (*T* 180)

Who are the purveyors of such abstract "demonstrations of the universality of the human species"? Williams seems to have three groups in mind: the elite, "relatively detached or mobile people" who mock modern nationalism and patriotism as backward or primitive; the "minority liberals and socialists, and especially those who by the nature of their work or formation are themselves nationally and internationally mobile, [who] have little experience of those rooted settlements"; and, by implication, university intellectuals who, by inheritance or learned class disposition, often overlap with both camps (*T* 180, 195–96). The argument is thus similar in key respects to Williams's critique of the ideology of modernism. Just as the dislocated and mobile modernists constructed from their shared social alienation an abstract *aesthetic* universality, so internationally mobile liberals and intelligentsia tend toward the attempted, though usually only *intellectual*, construction of an abstract *social* universality. Yet precisely because, like the conservative wing of the modernists before them, they are incapable of reconnecting this universality to ordinary people's everyday lives, they remain trapped in a sphere of alienation: unable to ground their own lives in anything other than a disposition that is often, in reality, a practically induced class habitus.[9] On Williams's reading, then, abstract universality pertains to the lived and representational modalities of capitalist abstraction; it is an extension of, rather than a challenge to, the rule of capital.

It has been alleged, however, that this logic aligns Williams with postwar proponents of the so-called "new racism," as famously argued by Paul Gilroy in *There Ain't No Black in the Union Jack*. The primary focus of Gilroy's critique is a section in which Williams states,

> It is a serious misunderstanding . . . to suppose that the problems of social identity are resolved by formal (merely legal) definitions. For unevenly and at times precariously, but always through long experience substantially, an effective awareness of social identity depends on actual and sustained social relationships. To reduce social identity to formal legal definitions, at the level of the state, is to collude in the alienated superficialities of "the nation" which are the limited functional terms of the modern ruling class. (*T* 195)

Gilroy draws a direct connection between the logic of this passage and that of Enoch Powell's far-right conceptions of race, national identity, and citizenship. If social identity is a product of "long experience," asks Gilroy, "how long is long enough to become a genuine Brit?"[10] Williams has minimized "the specificities of nationalism and ideologies of national identity" and diverted attention from "analysis of the political processes by which national and social identities have become aligned."[11] Ultimately, Williams's critique of the merely legal definition of national identity is said to underestimate the extent to which the contradictions surrounding citizenship remain important constituents of the political field: "Where racial oppression is practised with the connivance of legal institutions—the police and the courts—national and legal subjectivity will also become the focus of political antagonism."[12] Williams's argument amounts to "an apparent endorsement of the presuppositions of the new racism."[13]

I shall not rehearse here Daniel Williams's powerful rebuttal of these accusations, but I would like briefly to reconstruct what I take to be the actual "presuppositions" of Raymond Williams's work in general, and then move on to exemplifications of these presuppositions in his writings on Wales and the nation-state.[14] I should stress initially, however, that Williams does indeed consistently underestimate the extent to which racism is structurally constitutive of British social identity. Just as his theory of "cultural materialism" was an attempt to apply historical materialist principles to those areas of analysis—culture and the arts—of which historical materialism's own conception remained residually idealist, so one might challenge Williams's own views of "race" and "racism" as themselves insufficiently materialist and institutional. Yet there is a major difference between this kind of (immanent) critique and the quite serious misreading that aligns Williams with Powell from whom, as Williams himself might have said, his distance was absolute. First and foremost, Gilroy simply elides the fact that Williams was a Welsh socialist from the "border country" whose earliest lived experiences were of a society characterized by a fundamental geopolitical, class, linguistic, and social complexity that his later work would raise to a methodological principle.[15] Indeed, Williams's basic conception of social ontology always presupposes two interconnecting levels: a present in which a totality of potentially infinite social relationships, values, and activities intersect, and an attempted integration of this present into a selective tradition, which is active within it and attempts to suture it to a selected past as a way of ratifying the prevailing sociopolitical order.[16] Williams's is also a processual social ontology that is deeply averse to reified "images" of society that work, in his view, both to deny and control true social complexity.[17] Williams's signature method, time and again, is to tackle ideologically dominant "images" of society—country and city, nation-state, mode of production, economy—and to identify the ways in which they simplify an actually existing complexity. He then shows that this operation of imagistic simplification is intrinsic to the hegemony of the dominant order. Crucially, he shows that resisting the dominant order on the ground of its own simplified images of the social totality is a fatal mistake for the Left because it risks incorporation into that very order and because the social breadth and energy of its counter-hegemonic strategy will be limited. As he writes in *The Long Revolution*, "the alternative society that is proposed must be in wider terms [than those of its opponents], if it is to generate the full energies necessary for its creation" (*LR* 139). Complexity is thus an intrinsic element of both Williams's critical method and his political vision.[18]

In his writings on Wales and the nation-state, Williams combines his critique of "distance" with his habitual methodological emphasis upon complexity. In both "The Culture of Nations" and "Wales and England" he opposes reductive, state-backed, selective traditions of patriotism by emphasizing the millennia-long history of the British Isles in all its true complexity—what he calls "a long process of successive conquests and repressions but also of successive supersessions and relative integrations" (*T* 193–94). In doing so, he seeks to reinstate the real, historical complexities of mobility, ethnicity, and the long sequence of historical rulers and victims (the one often dialectically reversing into the other).[19] His real opponent is the contemporary British *state*, and by extension, those who "mistake the state for the real identity, or the projections for the people" (*W* 66).[20] This is no coincidence: ever attentive to symbols or buildings of power and authority, in this late period Williams became increasingly attentive to the material and institutional embodiments of colonial rule, perhaps inspired in part (but only in part) by Michael Hechter's influential *Internal Colonialism: The Celtic Fringe in British National Development, 1536–1960.*[21] When Williams speaks of the state in "Wales and England," published in 1983, it is "alien" not simply in the Hegelian or Marxist sense, but as the literal embodiment of foreign rule:

> English law and political administration were ruthlessly imposed, within an increasingly centralised "British" state. The Welsh language was made the object of systematic discrimination and, where necessary, repression. Succeeding phases of a dominant Welsh landowning class were successfully Anglicised and either physically or politically drawn away to the English centre. Anglicising institutions, from the boroughs to the grammar schools, were successfully implanted. All these processes can properly be seen as forms of political and cultural colonisation. (*W* 70)

Finally, English capital penetrated Wales's relatively underdeveloped economy in a manner that closely resembles what Samir Amin has called the "internal disarticulation" of colonial economies: "Lines of communication . . . were driven through Wales on bearings evidently determined by the shape of the larger economy and trading system . . . Few of these were ever related to the internal needs of Wales, as a developing country or . . . to the customs and needs of the traditional rural economy" (*W* 70).[22] In the same period in which Williams penned the chapter "The Culture of Nations," then, he increasingly saw himself as a Welshman writing from within the history of Wales's cultural, political, and economic colonization. While most historians would now firmly reject this account of Welsh history—preferring to see it as a "dependent periphery" rather than a colony in the strict sense—it is surely significant when evaluating Williams's reflections on the British state and national identity.[23]

In his view it was the integration of Wales into Britain's imperial economy that generated both resistance (from the Merthyr Rising to the Rebecca Riots) and three successive and overlapping modes of incorporation: the ideology of Empire (with the Welsh becoming "avid contributors to the British imperial project"),[24] the ideology and organization of Liberalism, and the ideology and organization of Labourism. Within and against these modes of incorporation into British hegemony, Welsh social identity tended to go one of two ways: to a residual nationalism that asserted "a received, traditional and unproblematic identity" or to "pseudo-modernist rejections of the specificities of Welshness" (an extension of his critique of both liberal and modernist universalities) (*W* 72). Williams's own preference was for the "painful recognition of real dislocations, discontinuities, [and] problematic identities" embodied in an emergent "anti-nationalist nationalism" opposed to a "centralised state" (*W* 72). Just as Roberto Schwarz would later connect the internal dislocations of Brazilian culture to its status as a dependent periphery of the capitalist world system, so Williams extends an emphasis on discontinuity that had characterized all of his major work to date by insisting on locating the core of Welsh culture in "the complex of forced and acquired discontinuities," of "certain autonomies hard won within a subordination" (*W* 68).[25] In a crucial argument, he directly counterposes the actuality of Welsh cultural dislocation to the "version of cultural nationalism, in which the continuity and inner essence of a people is discovered in a (selective) version of its 'national' literature," and which he sees as itself "one of the strongest and least noticed English influences on Welsh thought" (*W* 67–68). In other words, "continuity" and "essence" are not only rejected by Williams but are seen to be the *very ideological modality of English hegemony*.

Returning to Gilroy's accusations, we can now offer a more specific defense of Williams's argument. Contrary to Gilroy's account, Williams states very clearly the necessity of "asserting the need for equality and protection within the laws" and the "most active legal (and communal) defence of dislocated and exposed groups and minorities" (*T* 195). Yet to reduce social identity to formal legal definitions is to remain trapped within the functional abstractions of the imperial state, which are themselves the geopolitical modalities of capital.[26] The state performs a short-circuit between the most immediate bonds of neighbors and family with the artificial totality of the nation-state form. It is "abstract" precisely because it leaps over all inter-mediate-level social bonds or geopolitical mediations such as town, place, region, and country; in doing so, it constitutes a ruling, "distanced" institution. Williams shows that it is capitalism that is the principal force of social dislocation, but that by reproducing selective traditions of cultural national-ism (itself, as we have seen, the hegemonic form of the British nation-state), state institutions—not least schools—are able to suture the individual-family unit to the abstraction of the nation-state within a falsely continuous whole. To fight battles of social belonging solely at the level of legal rights and citizenship is to remain incorporated into the state's hegemony. A *socialist* strategy must instead learn from the painful experiences of discontinuity embodied in Welsh history, connecting the "complex actualities of settled but then dislocated and relocated communities" to the "practical formation of social identity" as a lived reality in the present.[27] It must work, in other words, toward new, more complex forms of self-governing societies beyond the alienating form of the nation-state.

HUMANITAS, ANTI-IMPERIALISM, AND SUBSTANTIVE UNIVERSALITY

In this light, it is significant that Williams's 1984 presidential address to the Classical Association pivots on Tacitus's literary rendering of a speech by Calgacus, a Celtic chieftain of the Caledonian Confederacy who fought the imperial Roman army in northern Scotland in 83/84 CE. Williams notes in "The Culture of Nations" that "it is a common ruling-class cultural habit, carefully extended by most schools, to identify with the Roman imperial invaders of Britain against what are called the mere 'native tribes'" (*T* 194). His address is thus, at one level, a continuation of his sustained critique of the British state, now under the guise of the classics. Somewhat more surprising, however, given his trenchant critique of abstract universality in his other writings of the period, is Williams's subtle attempt to develop an alternative version of universality grounded in anti-imperial humanism. The result is a highly original fusion of anti-imperialism with a democratic conception of literacy that extends his calls of the same period for a "new humanities." *Humanitas* thus becomes the site of a struggle on three fronts: against the British state, against empire, and against the privatization of literacy.

Williams begins the talk by noting that the "classical" has been associat-ed, historically, both with the practice of writing and with the facts of educa-tional and civil authority. It has gone hand in hand with what he calls a "distancing education"—that is (as we have seen), historically specific education systems that effect an artificial separation between "high literacy" and the world of "everyday labour" (*W* 46). Yet Williams then goes on to observe that there is a danger that (justified) resentment of such systems might eventually lead to rejecting or diminishing the skills and materials traditionally identified with them (i.e., high literacy). He rejects the position of those who defy such attitudes only by setting themselves up as what he calls—tellingly, given what follows—the "last bastion of civilisation" against "the barbarian onslaught" (*W* 45). The barbarians in this analogy are precisely those wider popular forces now beginning to infiltrate the British university system. Channeling the cautious optimism of this popular turn in higher education, Williams calls for "a much wider collaboration of the humanities than has yet been realised" so as to rethink what the traditions of learning and literacy really are, and from this to find new directions for an extending practice (*W* 46).

Williams then moves on to a brief reflection on the reductive representation of Britons—"the troop of frenzied women and the Druids lifting up their hands to heaven and pouring forth dreadful imprecations"—in Tacitus's *Annals* (*W* 47). This argument echoes his earlier condemnation of the British press's distanced representations of the screaming Argentinian crowds during the Falklands War. His point here, though, is to draw attention to the ways in which Roman soldiers, who committed systematic violence, are usually seen as representatives of true civilization whilst the Britons are seen as barbarians: the truth is precisely the inverse. The Britons enjoyed "a distinctive native culture, with its own highly organised order of scholars, philosophers, poets and priests" (*W* 47). What they lacked was *writing*, and those social orders that have developed literacy tend to enjoy disproportionate historical advantages. Echoing Walter Benjamin's dictum that there is no document of civilization that is not at the same time a document of barbarism, Williams states, "It is a terrible irony that writing, until our own century incomparably the greatest skill of accurate record, should so often, within the realities of historical conquest and repression, have become a medium of obscurantism and falsification" (*W* 48). Williams has turned the tables: those elite humanist educators who set themselves up as the last bastion of civilization within the British university are unveiled as the unwitting heirs of a violent and barbaric imperial history. The task will then be to construct a version of literacy that can extricate itself from this past and deploy its full democratic potential.

It is at this point that Williams turns to the centerpiece of the talk: his remarkable reading of Calgacus's speech in chapter 30 of Tacitus's *Agricola*. The speech denounces imperialism "in words," Williams writes, "of a concentrated power which I find without equal: indeed in what can be properly called a classical statement of human values" (*W* 49). In this sentence, Williams is consciously aligning the classical itself with the anti-imperial resistors of Roman supremacy. The most powerful passage of the speech, in Williams's eyes, refers to the Romans as *raptores orbis*: plunderers of the earth or *brigands du monde* (in the French translation Williams quotes). "They plunder, they butcher, they ravish, and call it by the lying name of 'empire,'" announces Calgacus, "They make a desert and call it 'peace.'"[28] To which Williams responds, "Here are the received conditions of civilisation, ordered government and peace, seen as covering, with false names, the real practices of theft, massacre and rape" (*W* 49). Unlike the distanced representation of the Britons in the *Annals*, Calgacus's speech consists of a "close, sinewy, classical statement of the virtues of civilisation—liberty, community, justice, a plain-living self-respect—and these brought to a climax within the terrible necessity of opposing their destroyers" (*W* 50). These values will form the substantial basis of Williams's alternative conception of universality.

Yet it is of the nature of universality to exceed any given instance. Calgacus's speech is inserted in the midst of what is, in effect, a eulogy to the Roman general Agricola, but what impresses Williams most is precisely its power to surpass its occasion. He notes the various expert interpretations of this impression—for example that Tacitus is merely flexing his oratorical muscles,[29] or perhaps trying to embody what were now seen to be the old senatorial virtues against the tyranny and corruption of the empire from which Agricola had suffered. Yet Williams claims that the actual speech ultimately surpasses these contextual determinants: it is a "universal statement against the whole project that was the reputed glory of Rome"; it has echoes in early Welsh poetry where "the sad sound of a different idea of humanity, including the experience of humanity in defeat," was registered (*W* 50). The question of universality is thus bound up with that of the word *humanitas*, which is usually translated as "civilization" or "culture."

Williams notes the cynically incisive observation in a different passage in the *Agricola* in which Tacitus describes the Romans' strategic use of soft power (or cultural imperialism) as a way of incorporating the Britons into Roman hegemony:

> The result was that those who just lately had been rejecting the Roman tongue now conceived a desire for eloquence. Thus even our style of dress came into favour and the toga was everywhere to be seen. Gradually, too, they went astray into the allurements of evil ways, colonnades and warm baths and elegant banquets. The Britons, who had had no experience of this, called it "civilization" [*humanitas*], although it was a part of their enslavement.[30]

Just as Williams had criticized nationalist essentialism as itself the hegemonic form of the British state, so he singles out Tacitus's matter-of-fact statement that *humanitas*, in the narrow sense of an imposed culture, was a tool of Roman imperial hegemony. Likewise, just as Williams in his earlier work had reconfigured "culture" as an ordinary, democratic phenomenon opposed to ruling class dominance, so here he makes a case for a "wider *humanitas*, against a powerful war-machine and a display of material wealth and skill, which we can at least temporarily extract" (*W* 51). *Humanitas* thus splits into three: the dominant Roman ego-ideal of "civilization," the cynical form of Roman colonial hegemony, and a set of universal values inseparable from anti-imperial resistance.

It is at this point that Williams turns specifically to questions of literary composition. As a way of articulating the singularity of Calgacus's speech, Williams draws on a little-explored but major aspect of his life's work: the relationship between speech and writing, not least in drama.[31] It is precisely the dramatic mode that holds the key to the ambiguous status of the speech within the context of the *Agricola* as a whole:

> For while it will not do to extract the speech as an absolute condemnation of imperialism, it will not do either to dissolve it into a eulogistic narration. What the dramatic mode made possible, in what has to be seen as a major cultural liberation, was what in fact we find here: a narration, a speech, of a number of voices; thus inherently, in its multivocal character, a way of presenting voices, which while they speak have their own and temporarily absolute power, but which because other voices will speak have to be gathered, finally, into a whole action. (*W* 52)

This is a key move because it suggests, without ever stating it, that the radical universality of *humanitas* is *formed*. Williams acknowledges the substantial universality of Calgacus's speech—the values of "liberty, community, justice, a plain-living self-respect"—but refuses to separate it from the forms and conventions through which it is articulated (*W* 50). This is a highly original argument because it suggests that it is high literacy that enables the identification and limitations of such forms and conventions, and, by extension, that *high literacy is internal to the construction of critical universality*. Consequently, rather than being seen as that which is *opposed* to demotic orality—as by elitists who write off the modern oral forms of radio, cinema, and television as so many barbarian instances of vulgar mass culture—true literacy should be seen as that which complements and comprehends it:

> It is high literacy which shows us the remarkable diversity—literally as wide as the world—of the meanings and values which these works carry . . . and one which is not to be reduced to plausible singularities of consideration or conclusion, or to the use of literature, in some highly selective tradition, to ratify the habits of some temporary or self-interested group. . . . It is high literacy, finally, which calls the bluffs of authority, since it is a condition of all its practical work that it questions sources, closely examines offered authenticities, reads contextually and comparatively, identifies conventions to deter-

mine meanings: habits of mind which are all against, or should be all against,
any and every pronunciation of a singular or assembled authority. (*W* 54–55)

Williams has pried high literacy from authority's grip and trained its guns
back on the citadels of British Rome. In doing so, he allies it with the
restoration of a "remarkable diversity" that resists the selective traditions of
empire and, later, the imperial nation-state.

FOR A DEMOCRATIC AND
DECOLONIZED HUMANITIES

To the minority cosmopolitanisms of modernism and liberalism, premised
upon an elite privatization of literacy, Williams opposes the democratic actualization of high literacy. To the abstract humanity of liberalism and empire,
he opposes a substantive, formally embodied universality embedded in democratic anti-imperialism. To the abstract legal identities of the British state he
opposes the lived, practical formation of new social identities combined with
new political geographies. What would it mean to inherit these ideas today?
High literacy, as Williams understands it, presupposes the democratization of
the skills of critical reading, writing and speaking—and, by extension, of the
university as such. While no historically existing university has even remote-
ly approached genuine democracy, the contemporary neoliberal university
offers a particularly egregious case of the privatization of high literacy, not
least in a period when "humanities" departments are often the prime target of
financial cuts and are classed—and priced—as a luxury for an elite minority
of middle-class students. The social distancing of higher education, then, has
been achieved in tandem with a severe reduction in that other meaning of
"distance": the distance of social autonomy. The university system is now so
"close" to the dominant social relations of capitalist society—in land ownership, financialization, and the precarity of labor contracts—as to be an almost
direct embodiment of it.

Yet Williams was also writing partly to convince those scholars who saw
themselves as the last bastion of civilization—the defenders of high literacy
against the incoming demotic hoards, intent on studying the vulgar arts of
TV, cinema, and popular culture—that such new scholarship was in fact an
extension of, rather than a threat to, high literacy. The same argument must
be made today in relation to popular calls for the "decolonization" of the
university. Decried by the dominant order as the latest invasion of the barbarians, these developments would have been wholeheartedly welcomed by
Williams for two reasons: First, they democratize critical literacy and extend
it into new areas that are central to the formation of new social identities:
curriculum formation, architecture, history, memorial culture—to name but a
few. Indeed, in terms of curriculum formation in particular, we are, in effect,

witnessing courageous attempts to reinstate the principle that Williams himself found so important in the Workers' Educational Association: democratic control over what is taught. Second, if schools and universities are key operators of the ideological suture between the individual-family unit and the abstraction of the nation-state, then decolonizing the university is a powerful way of dismantling the everyday hegemony and selective traditions of the state. The very process of decolonizing curricula and universities, if taken seriously, will thus almost inevitably entail a reevaluation and extension of "high literacy" itself; at every step, it will be faced by powerful opposition that will attempt either to crush it or, more likely, to incorporate those elements of the movements that extend its hegemony while maintaining its basic operations.

Yet these remarks only partially hint at the ambitious, socialist vision that lurks in Williams's late work. I shall conclude by spelling out what I take to be its true utopian potential, and in so doing will risk a more speculative language than Williams might have approved. The central idea implied by Williams's late work is that substantive universality, precisely because it is formed (i.e., is formalized in given genres and representational conventions), can only become substantive to the extent that high literacy is itself universalized and democratized. (The extent to which the previous sentence sounds suspiciously like an incipient idealism is a measure of our alienated, idealist conception of literacy.) Anti-imperial *humanitas* thus requires, for its substantive social realization, a supersession of the structural unevenness of literacy and learning associated by Williams with modernism and "theory," such that an expanded, anti-authoritarian literacy can become actualized in ordinary everyday life. To pose the problem in this way is to connect it to that broader historical process known as "cultural revolution." (One thinks, for instance, of Cuba's heroic literacy campaign, though compared to Williams's implicit vision this would constitute merely the zero degree of literacy in its true sense.) It would require the communalization of the "means of communication," to use a term developed earlier in Williams's career.[32] Given, however, that most cultural forms innate to class society also embody its alienations and class divisions, the universalization of true literacy as an institutional precondition of social universality would also require the invention of new forms to embody new social relations. As such, there is no guarantee that universality will not substantively alter as its material formalizations undergo further transformations. And at this point we have reached something like the "Absolute" of Williams's thought: a fully actual democracy, speaking, writing, thinking, and reading itself in all its true complexity.

NOTES

1. I am grateful to Natalya Bekhta and Gero Guttzeit for their comments on an earlier draft.

2. For Gilroy's critique, see Paul Gilroy, *There Ain't No Black in the Union Jack* (1987; repr., Abingdon, UK: Routledge, 2002), 50–53.

3. This can perhaps be seen as Williams's variation on Stuart Hall's "authoritarian populism." Cf. Stuart Hall, *The Hard Road to Renewal: Thatcherism and the Crisis of the Left* (London: Verso, 1988).

4. Arguably, the literary form of this mode would be realism. It is no coincidence that in the same period that "distance" becomes a central term of Williams's theoretical vocabulary, he engaged in several defenses of the continued importance and contemporaneity of realism. See, for example, the essays contained in (*W* 226–74).

5. These permutations are developed in finer detail in "The Politics of the Avant-Garde" and "The Language of the Avant-Garde" (*PM* 49–80).

6. Williams's general enthusiasm for the Open University was tempered by his perception of its conscious break with the principle of educational self-governance that had informed the Workers' Educational Association in which he had taught in the immediate postwar period. He held that it substituted a form of technocratic populism for genuine democratic "interchange and encounter between the people offering the intellectual disciplines and those using them" (*PM* 157).

7. See Raymond Williams, *Who Speaks for Wales?*, ed. Daniel Williams (Cardiff, UK: University of Wales Press, 2003); and Hywel Dix, *After Raymond Williams: Cultural Materialism and the Break-Up of Britain* (Cardiff, UK: University of Wales Press, 2008).

8. An exception is Christopher Prendergast, "Nation/*Natio*: Raymond Williams and 'The Culture of Nations,'" *Intermédialités/Intermediality* 1 (2003): 123–38, though he fails even once to mention Williams's reflections on Wales.

9. The often downright bizarre behavior of certain representatives of "Remainer" liberalism during the Brexit campaign demonstrates the powerful subjective defense mechanisms caused by clinging tenaciously to such abstractions in the face of concrete realities that reveal one's idealized self-conceptions to be founded on little more than alienated modes of sociality.

10. Gilroy, *There Ain't No Black*, 51.

11. Ibid., 52.

12. Ibid, 53.

13. Ibid.

14. Daniel Williams, introduction to *Who Speaks for Wales?*, xxxvi–xxxix.

15. Cf. Daniel Williams: "[Gilroy] never registers the fact that Williams was Welsh at all. Williams is forced to wear an English mask." Daniel Williams, *Wales Unchained: Literature, Politics and Identity in the American Century* (Cardiff UK: University of Wales Press, 2015), 98.

16. I have developed these ideas on Williams's social ontology at greater length in Daniel Hartley, "On Raymond Williams: Complexity, Immanence, and the Long Revolution." *Mediations* 30, no. 1 (Fall 2016): 39–60.

17. "Images of Society" is the title of chapter 4 of *The Long Revolution*.

18. "It is also only in very complex ways, and by moving confidently towards very complex societies, that we can begin that construction of many socialisms which will liberate and draw upon our real and now threatened energies" (*PL* 437).

19. See in particular *Towards 2000* (*T* 193–94) and *What I Came to Say* (*W* 64–67). The latter is a good example of Williams's total contempt for any conception of national identity premised upon ethnic homogeneity.

20. In *Politics and Letters* (1979), Williams claimed, "The most welcome single introduction into Marxist thought of the last decade has been the decisive re-entry of the problem of the capitalist state" (*PL* 120).

21. Williams mentions Hechter in *What I Came to Say* (*W* 73).

22. Cf. Hamza Alavi's description of the effect of British capitalist penetration into the Indian colonial economy: "The specific structural features of the colonial agrarian economy are formed precisely by virtue of the fact that Imperial capital disarticulates the internal economy

of the colony . . . and integrates the internally disarticulated segments of the colonial economy externally into the metropolitan economy." Hamza Alavi, "India and the Colonial Mode of Production," *Economic and Political Weekly* 10, no. 33/35 (1975): 1235–62.

23. See Chris Williams, "Problematizing Wales: An Exploration in Historiography and Postcoloniality," in *Postcolonial Wales*, ed. Jane Aaron and Chris Williams, 3–22 (Cardiff, UK: University of Wales Press, 2005).

24. Daniel Williams, introduction to *Who Speaks for Wales?*, xxx.

25. I have tried elsewhere to connect Schwarz's essays on stylistic discontinuity in the Brazilian novel to Williams's reflections on similar tensions in the history of English prose. See Daniel Hartley, "Combined and Uneven Styles in the Modern World-System: Stylistic Ideology in José de Alencar, Machado de Assis, and Thomas Hardy," *European Journal of English Studies* 20, no. 3 (2016): 222–35.

26. That said, I recognize the validity of Francis Mulhern's response to Williams's argument—that the nations produced through the expansion of capitalism are "more than flag-bedecked marketplaces . . . They are collective identifications with strong supports in economic, cultural and political histories; they are, as much as any competing formation, 'communities.'" Quoted in Daniel Williams, introduction to *Who Speaks for Wales?*, xxxvi (ellipse in original).

27. Ibid., 196.

28. Tacitus, *Agricola and Germany*, trans. Anthony R. Birley (Oxford: Oxford University Press, 1999), 22.

29. This is, in effect, Auerbach's reading of Percennius's speech in the *Annals*, which gives voice to the soldiers' grievances: "The grand style of historiography requires grandiloquent speeches, which as a rule are fictitious. Their function is graphic dramatization (*illustratio*) of a given occurrence, or at times the presentation of great political or moral ideas; in either case they are intended as the rhetorical bravura pieces of the presentation." Erich Auerbach, *Mimesis: The Representation of Reality in Western Literature*, trans. Willard R. Trask (1946; repr., Princeton, NJ: Princeton University Press, 2003), 39.

30. Tacitus, *Agricola and Germany*, 17.

31. The best-known texts are *Drama in Performance* (1954; repr., Milton Keynes: Open University Press, 1991); and *Drama from Ibsen to Brecht*, 2nd rev. ed. (1968; Harmondsworth: Penguin, 1973). In *Writing in Society*, Williams published "On Dramatic Dialogue and Monologue (Particularly in Shakespeare)," based on seminars he had been teaching at Cambridge from 1980 to 1983. He also deals in detail with the problem of the incorporation of working-class speech into the novel in "Notes on English Prose 1780–1950," first published in 1969 but reprinted in *Writing in Society*. I have written at length on Williams's theory of prose and his approach to speech in naturalist drama in *The Politics of Style: Towards a Marxist Poetics* (Chicago: Haymarket Books, 2017), chapters 4 and 5.

32. This vision is spelled out very clearly in Raymond Williams, "Means of Communication as Means of Production" (*CM* 57).

Chapter Six

Inexplicable Goodness

Raymond Williams, Charles Dickens, *and* The Ministry of Utmost Happiness

Paul Stasi

The teaching of love is fundamental but so also is the teaching of freedom.
—Raymond Williams, "The Future of Marxism" (1961)

KNOWABLE COMMUNITIES

Amitav Ghosh's 2016 text *The Great Derangement* tries to understand why climate change, perhaps the most important subject of the modern period, should have little to no presence in novels dating back, perhaps, to the industrial revolution, but certainly since the so-called "Great Acceleration" of the oil-fueled post–World War II era. "What is it about climate change," he asks "that the mention of it should lead to banishment from the preserves of serious fiction? And what does this tell us about culture writ large and its patterns of evasion?"[1] The answers, for Ghosh, are many, but they all have their origins in the self-legislating bourgeois subject. "What we need," Ghosh asserts, "is to find a way out of the individualizing imaginary in which we are trapped."[2] This imaginary is endemic to politics—understood "in terms of individual moral adventures" that, in the realm of climate change, leads to arguments about the number of light bulbs in Al Gore's house—but its roots are deep in Western culture, observable, in Ghosh's view, in a set of presuppositions inherent in the novel form.[3] "What is distinctive" about the novel, Ghosh argues, drawing on the work of Franco Moretti, "is precisely the concealment of those exceptional moments that serve as the motor of narrative."[4] "If novels were not built upon a scaffolding of exceptional moments,"

Ghosh continues, "writers would be faced with the Borgesian task of repro-ducing the world in its entirety. But the modern novel . . . has never been forced to confront the centrality of the improbable: the concealment of its scaffolding of events continues to be essential to its functioning."[5] The great "irony of the 'realist' novel" is that "the very gestures with which it conjures up reality are actually a concealment of the real."[6] Ignoring the "presence and proximity of non-human interlocutors," novels follow Western culture in understanding freedom "as a way of 'transcending' the constraints of materi-al life."[7] By separating itself from this material world, the individual rejects its conditioning power, locating agency squarely within the rational calcula-tions of its own transcendent reason.

In making this case, Ghosh joins the chorus of critics for whom the modern novel is a fundamentally individualistic enterprise. Indeed, its found-ing theorists—from Georg Lukács to Ian Watt to Nancy Armstrong—have outlined the ways in which the novel privileges a certain form of bourgeois subjectivity, often at the direct expense of the collective world from which these subjects emerge. It is striking then to find Raymond Williams arguing, in *The English Novel from Dickens to Lawrence* that "most novels are in some sense knowable communities" (*EN* 14). Looking back at a formative period in English fiction—"those twenty months, in 1847 and 1848, in which these novels were published: *Dombey and Son, Wuthering Heights, Vanity Fair, Jane Eyre, Mary Barton, Tancred, Town and Country, The Tenant of Wildfell Hall*"—Williams finds one central element: "the exploration of . . . the substance and meaning of community" (*EN* 9, 11). This meaning takes shape in relation to individual human lives in a process described perhaps most clearly in *The Long Revolution:*

> When I think of the realist tradition in fiction, I think of the kind of novel which creates and judges the quality of a whole way of life in terms of the qualities of persons. The balance involved in this achievement is perhaps the most important thing about it. . . . [T]he distinction of this kind is that it offers a valuing of a whole way of life, a society that is larger than any of the individuals composing it, and at the same time valuing creations of human beings who, while belonging to and affected by and helping define this way of life, are also, in their own terms, absolute ends in themselves. Neither element, neither the society nor the individual, is there as a priority. The society is not a background against which the personal relationships are studied, nor are the individuals merely illustrations of aspects of the way of life. (*LR* 321–22)

Many key motifs of Williams's thought are present in this passage. The famous definition of culture as a whole way of life is here the very thing the realist novel addresses, as it takes up the structural position characteristic of culture as a discourse, from which it can examine and critique the world out of which it emerges. We also observe the careful balance between the individual, understood as an end in itself, and the shaping power of a social order. The entire passage, then, turns on this relationship between individual instance and society, a relation that Williams refuses to reduce to one term or the other; the individual is simultaneously an end in itself *while also at the same time* being an instance of a larger social whole.

The distinctiveness of this account is best seen by comparing it to what might initially seem like similar discussions by Lukács and Moretti, each of whom sees the novel as fundamentally constituted by the relation between its individual characters and their social destinies. For the mature Lukács, the historical novel—his privileged instance of the genre—"portray[s] the struggles and antagonisms of history by means of characters who, in their psychology and destiny, always represent social trends and historical forces."[8] The novel humanizes history, but it does so through characters that are primarily vehicles for the historical structures they help to convey. Moretti, for his part, outlines in *The Way of the World*, a theory of the *bildungsroman*—called the "'symbolic form' of modernity"—as a perpetual struggle between freedom and determination.[9] If modernity's "essence" is youth, its "intrinsically boundless dynamism" needs to be harnessed for socially acceptable ends.[10] Two formal principles emerge that Moretti names "classification" and "transformation." The first emphasizes stability—in it "youth is subordinated to the idea of 'maturity'"; the second emphasizes transformation, where "youth cannot or does not want to give way to maturity."[11] In the first instance we have novels like *Jane Eyre*, which subordinates its heroine to the imperatives of a social order; in the latter are novels like *The Red and the Black*, where the hero chooses death over accommodation to the social order. What is important to see is that in each case society triumphs; the ideological function of the *bildungsroman* is to make this triumph palatable. If the *bildungsroman* is "the *most contradictory* of modern symbolic forms," that is because "in our world socialization itself consists first of all in the *interiorization of contradiction*."[12]

Despite his emphasis on contradiction, Moretti's notion of the ideological function of the *bildungsroman* is relatively prescriptive: sociality is, in these novels, the realm of unfreedom toward which the individual must bend. It will surprise no one, of course, to discover that where Moretti reads ideology, Williams finds agency. Indeed, the fundamental emphasis of Williams's interest in culture was always toward the creation of common meanings. From his partial recuperation of conservative thinkers in *Culture and Society* to his assertion that "Culture Is Ordinary" to his insistence on the effaced labor constitutive of the country house poems, Williams provided a lifelong lesson in the *interested* reading of cultural objects, one guided by his view that "the arts and learning . . . are in a real sense a national inheritance, which is, or should be, available to everyone" (*RH* 8). Culture, that is to say, was a field of struggle and if Williams's early rendering of it in *Culture and Society* seemed, as E. P. Thompson famously suggested, to leave out the conflict, it is easy enough to see his later readings of cultural objects in texts such as *The Country and The City* as putting it back in. Against Lukács, then, Williams offers a defense of the individual as something other than a social type; against Moretti he reads the social as something other than ideological inscription. Each side of the equation emerges as the site of both freedom *and* determination. Indeed, as in "Culture Is Ordinary," what is most striking about Williams's readings of novels is the ways in which their individualized seeing is returned to communal forms of understanding.

In what follows I would like to expand on these claims through a close reading of passages from *The English Novel* and, in particular, its understanding of realism, using Williams's ideas about the novel form to analyze Arundhati Roy's 2017 novel *The Ministry of Utmost Happiness*. A vast tapestry of Indian society, Roy's novel clearly presses against the individualistic focus of the novel as a form even as it, simultaneously, defends the dignity of a set of individual subjects in the grip of the cascading violence and inequality of contemporary India. Her novel, in other words, illustrates the same dialectical relationship between individual and society present in Williams's work. It does so, in part, by defending sentiment against a social order that militates against it, a society described with the kind of partisan outrage the later Williams would have strongly endorsed.

A CHANGE OF HEART

The English Novel begins by describing a literary movement that developed "a new kind of consciousness" around "the new and unprecedented civilization in which it took shape" (*EN* 9). "Customary ways broke down or receded" while an "important split" developed "between knowable relationships and an unknown, unknowable, overwhelming society" (*EN* 11, 15). "The men and women who were writing," Williams continues, "took from the disturbance of these years another impetus: a crisis of experience, often quite personally felt and endured, which when it emerged in novels was a creative working, a discovery . . . a transformation and innovation which composed a generation out of what seemed separate work and experience" (*EN* 11). Their central concern was an "exploration" of "the substance and meaning of community"; their structure, fundamentally creative, bringing "in new feelings, people, relationships; rhythms newly known, discovered, articulated; defining the society, rather than merely reflecting it" (*EN* 11). And their most important discovery was a formal one, best exemplified in an author whose "complicated ways of seeing"—manifest "in the form of his novels"—"are more important to his achievement than his separable attitudes to money, to poverty, to the family and to other known social questions" (*EN*

48). The author, here, is Charles Dickens; the text, his "radically innovating *Dombey and Son*." Williams is, in other words, describing the high period of British realism, but he does so in the terms typically reserved for modernism. Formal innovation emerging from a crisis of experience itself tied to a newly urban landscape, a personal crisis that takes generational form and is lodged in the aesthetic structures of the work of art: these are the hallmarks of a critical inheritance that takes as axiomatic the distinction between modernist innovation and the realism it is said to have left behind. Williams blurs these lines. Realism originates, in his account, in a personal experience that is generational, describing a new reality with a new form, one that is an active element of the social world it seeks to represent.

In this passage, Williams reimagines the Victorian inheritance through his characteristic refusal of what I would call "reification," though this is not a word Williams himself often uses. Instead he tends to refer to separation, as in his revision of the terms "base and superstructure" in *Marxism and Literature*. The problem with these terms, Williams suggests, is "in the relative enclosure of categories or areas expressed as 'the base', 'the superstructure'" (*ML* 78). He continues,

> It is then ironic to remember that the force of Marx's original criticism had been mainly directed against the *separation* of "areas" of thought and activity (as in the separation of consciousness from material production) and against the related evacuation of specific content—real human activities—by the imposition of abstract categories. The common abstraction of 'the base' and 'the superstructure' is thus a radical persistence of the modes of thought which he attacked. (*ML* 78)

Williams's recourse to "real human activities" here is telling, part of his persistent valorization of experience. Far from a synonym for immediacy— as he once famously put it "there is no natural seeing and therefore" no "direct and unmediated contact with reality" (*PL* 167)—the category of experience is, for Williams, a way of signaling the complexity of a social life that forever outstrips our attempts to conceptualize it. It is a way of understanding social reality as, first of all, social—which is to say, communal—as well as fundamentally in flux. Realism, then, is not a codified thing, but a living response to a changing social environment, as indeed are all cultural forms.

And while experience is a register of what stands outside our theories— theories that must be tested "in experience" since "there is nowhere else to test them"—it is also the place where individuality meets social determination (*RH* 13). "Culture Is Ordinary," for instance, begins with a personal journey, from the Black Mountains past the "line of grey Norman castles," through the "farming valleys," and past "the steel-rolling mill" and "the gasworks," which is one "that in one form or another we have all made" (*RH* 3). History is legible here in a landscape that is at one and the same time personal and collective, a history of civilization observed by a particular individual on a bus. In describing novels as knowable communities, Williams is, in similar fashion, reimagining novelistic subjectivity as the bearer of social truth.

If experience names those "real human activities" that resist the "imposition of abstract categories," it does not do so by rejecting mediation. Rather, experience functions as part of what I have called Williams's critique of reification in the name of process, a critique that is, in some measure, the central argument of *The English Novel*. Take, for instance, Williams's reading of Jane Austen. Williams starts with the idea of the rural community, taken as the "epitome of direct relationships" in contrast to the unknowability of urban spaces (*EN* 17). In Austen we find what seems a "single tradition: that of the cultivated rural gentry," living in a "simple 'traditional' setting," in fictions concerned with "purely personal relationships" divorced from "the decisive historical events of [Austen's] time" (*EN* 18). This view, however, is immediately overturned as Williams outlines the shifting fortunes of nearly every major character in Austen's novels. "It must be clear," Williams concludes, "that it is no single settled society. It is an active complicated sharply speculative process: of inherited and newly enclosing and engrossing estates; of fortunes from trade and colonial and military profit being converted into houses and property and social position" (*EN* 21). "The paradox of Jane Austen," then "is the achievement of a unity of tone, of a settled and remarkably confident way of seeing and judging, in this chronicle of confusion and change" (*EN* 21). This tone, Williams suggests, represents "the development of an everyday uncompromising morality which is in effect separable from its social basis" (*EN* 23). The force of Austen's carefully balanced appraisals—sense and sensibility, pride and prejudice—distracts us from the insecurity that is everywhere in her plots. Williams here deftly combines something very basic—a reading of plot detail that will be familiar to all readers of Austen and yet somehow, at the same time, striking, since never organized in quite that fashion before—with a reading not only of form (taking tone to be a formal element of fiction) but also of the way form separates itself out from plot, creating a kind of autonomous moral realm of evaluation that is intimately tied to Austen's class background and yet appears to be separable from these origins. It is, in other words, a description of the "evacuation of specific content," or the separation of consciousness from material activity characteristic of Austen's style, given in an analysis that refuses such separations. Thus, when Williams turns to the knowable community in Austen— those "face-to-face" relations supposedly characteristic of village life—we are not surprised to see that this world is itself confined to a particular class. "No other community, in physical presence or in social reality, is by any means knowable" than the class to which Austen belongs (*EN* 24).

There are two aspects of this reading worth highlighting here. The first is the way the social reality brought to bear on Austen's novel is intrinsic to the form itself. We find here none of that characteristic New Historical mode where the reading of social reality eclipses the text. Indeed, Williams barely refers to anything outside the text at all; social reality is here entirely immanent to the novel. This is why Williams manages to tell us a new point about Austen as if it were something we already knew. So aptly does it describe our basic experience of reading the text that description is immediately also analysis; there is no natural seeing. You can, for instance, share these pages with undergraduates and they will immediately see what he means. (I regularly teach *Emma* and it is always a moment of great interest when we learn, around page 250, that Emma has been accompanied all the time by a servant, summoned as if from thin air at the moment Emma needs her.) Social content is legible in the form, in the kinds of thing that are available to Austen's narrator, in what she is able to perceive.

My second point is related, for if Austen, on the one hand, betrays exactly the kind of class prejudices we might expect of her particular location in the social order, Williams does not take her to task for this. It would be easy enough, in other words, to rewrite this entire passage as unmasking: the construction of an autonomous aesthetic that ignores social conditions in service of a middle-class ethos that pretends to be universal. But Williams does not unmask Austen; his point is not a demystifying one. Rather, the particular insight Austen offers is the kind of insight available to a person of her social class at a particular moment in English social history. To ask anything other of Austen is to misunderstand fundamentally the determining power of social life. What else could Austen do but observe with precision the social world visible from her particular vantage point?[13] Williams reads sympathetically, and he does so in a way that transcends the facile opposition between surface and depth mobilized in post-critique or surface reading analyses of literature. One can read, Williams shows us, symptomatically and yet with sympathy. Williams does something here that is remarkably difficult: he historicizes an aesthetic form while simultaneously taking it seriously as a form of insight. He balances the limitations of social class with the insight that social class allows. The reading, then, is perspectival—another way in which it might be called modernist.

The same virtues are evident in his argument about Dickens, who is, clearly, along with Hardy, at the very core of Williams's literary affections. Williams's chapter operates as a strong defense of those elements of Dickens for which he was often criticized. Indeed, if Austen's class restrictions become the precise measure of her insight into a shifting social reality, here Dickens's flat characters and sentimental solutions to social problems become his defining strengths. The critique is laid out relatively early: "Almost every criterion of that other kind of novel," Williams writes, "characteristically, the fiction of an educated minority, works against him" (*EN* 31). It is easy enough to see, in what follows, a description of a particular form of modernist organicism—let's call it Henry James's—one that critiques the "arbitrary coincidences . . . sudden revelations and changes of heart" of Dickens's texts. "He offers not the details of psychological process," Williams concludes, "but the finished articles: the social and psychological products" (*EN* 31).

It might seem strange to find Williams describing Dickens as turning process into product—it is, after all, one of his central critiques of various forms of reified thinking, as I have already suggested—but Williams immediately shifts the blame to a reified society. For Dickens gives us "a way of seeing men and women that belongs to the street," the "decisive movement—is a hurrying seemingly random passing of men and women, each heard in some fixed phrase" (*EN* 32). If Dickens's characters "speak at or past each other," it is because each is "intent above all on defining through his words his own identity and reality," a desire that is created by the shifting social order in which they exist (*EN* 33). Here we come to the core of Dickens's vision, which Williams describes in a variety of ways, each of which tells us something central about the relationship between lived reality and determining social conditions. Dickens shows us how "a way of life takes on physical shape" (*EN* 34); he describes the city "as at once a social fact and a human landscape" (*EN* 37). "Dramatising a moral world in physical terms" he gives us "a social condition . . . seen at a level where it is also a human condition" (*EN* 40, 51). Note, here, how this is the exact inverse of what Austen accomplished. There morality removed itself from the social; here it is embedded in it.

This social condition can, once again, be described through the concept of reification, as in the description of Shares as agent from *Our Mutual Friend*, which Williams quotes at length. Shares, here, is "not so much an isolated economic technique or an isolated aspect of character. It is more a free-acting force, separated from man though of course created by him. That it then in turns creates behavior, principles, power: this is the whole point" (*EN* 56). What Dickens is able to show us—through his style, his form, or what Williams consistently calls his "ways of seeing"—is the autonomy of that second nature we have created that then acts as a force outside of our control, a force as destructive and creative as the railroad in *Dombey and Son*, seen first as an earthquake, whose "fiery eruptions" lead to "dire disorder," followed by "crowds of people and mountains of goods" producing "a fermentation in the place that was always in action" (*EN* 42, 43). The process is almost evolutionary—capitalism abhors a vacuum—and Williams nicely shows how "the pride of power . . . is felt in the language" (*EN* 43). Dickens sees, in other words, the dialectical nature of capitalist development, its creative destruction. He shows us this and he embodies it in his form, in those very stylistic ticks—caricature, exhortation, overstatement, and simplification—for which he was so often taken to task.

Williams's defense of Dickens begins with a discussion of popular culture and it is clear that part of Dickens's power is, for Williams, his attachment to this "central history and culture of our own people" that has been "excluded, set aside, by the rigidities of an old educated world" (*EN* 29). These lines remind us of the argument in "Culture Is Ordinary," where Williams critiqued two related forms of elitism: the first that would denigrate working-class culture as vulgar, the second that would denounce the elitism of high culture in the supposed name of working-class subjects. This is the context in which Williams described the "arts and learning" as a "national inheritance, which is, or should be, available to everyone" (*RH* 8). "A desire to know what is best, and to do what is good," Williams concludes, "is the whole positive nature of man" (*RH* 7). Williams's reading of Dickens operates, then, on at least two distinct registers. On the one hand, Dickens's link to popular culture is part of that forgotten history: the working-class values Williams observes in his family or in the anonymous acts of kindness performed by neighbors while his father lay dying. On the other hand, Dickens is part of Williams's polemical rereading of the national inheritance, one that reveals a distinct set of values often occluded and, in doing so, tries to actualize them in a present context.

And here we come to the core of his defense of Dickens, a revaluation of the sentimental, which is anathema to that "other kind of novel," preferred by the educated elite. Revaluing sentiment, for Williams, serves a class purpose in two specific ways: as a critique of educated elites and their distaste for what the people enjoy but, more importantly, as a critique of the capitalist class and its destruction of all human values. "To see a change of heart and a change of institutions as alternatives," Williams writes "is already to ratify an alienated society" (*EN* 49). Thus if Dickens too often seems to "produce virtue almost magically . . . from the same conditions which in others bred vice," we need not believe in the strict veracity of these moments to realize that they are, nevertheless, "the kind of miracle that happens: the flowering of love or energy which is inexplicable by the ways of describing people to which . . . we have got used" (*EN* 52). Williams continues,

> There is no reason, that is to say, for love or innocence, except that almost obliterated by this general condition there is humanity. The exclusion of the human, which we can see operating in a describable system, is not after all absolute, or it would make no sense to call what is alienated human; there would otherwise be nothing to alienate. The inexplicable quality of the indestructible innocence, of the miraculously intervening goodness, on which Dickens so much depends and which has been casually written off as sentimentality is genuine *because* it is inexplicable. What is explicable, after all, is the system, which consciously or unconsciously has been made. To believe

> that a human spirit exists, ultimately more powerful than even this system, is
> an act of faith but an act of faith in ourselves. (*EN* 53)

It is, of course, possible to dismiss these lines as themselves sentimental;
many have done so, and placed them alongside those invocations of
Williams's working-class family I described above, seeing both as nostalgic
or romantic. But I think this is wrong. These moments cut to the core of
Williams's entire enterprise, which is to rescue genuine human connection
from a system bent on destroying and commodifying it, reducing lived experience to a set of reified formal relations. Obviously at odds with the Althusserian currents in British Marxism—a conflict clearly on display in *Politics
and Letters*—Williams shows us the ways in which Marxism is, very much,
and directly in contrast to Althusser himself, always a form of humanism. As
Williams wrote, in what Daniel Hartley calls "one of the most emphatic
passages of Williams's oeuvre" (hence perhaps the italics), *"No mode of
production and therefore no dominant social order and therefore no dominant culture ever in reality includes or exhausts all human practice, human
energy, and human intention"* (*ML* 125; italics in the original).[14] Reification,
alienation, formalist readings stripped of content, human interactions absent
of connection or warmth, the relative enclosure of categories of thought, the
"extraordinary decision to call certain things culture and then separate them,
as with a park wall, from ordinary people and ordinary work"—these are all
habits of thought Williams spent a lifetime trying to overturn (*RH* 5). With
regard to what I have called reification, Williams was remarkably consistent
in a theoretically grounded yet necessarily and pointedly unsystematic way.[15]

  With this in mind, I'd like to turn to Arundhati Roy's novel *The Ministry
of Utmost Happiness*, for Roy's literary vision bears striking similarities to
Williams's discussion of the realist novel in general and Dickens in particular. Indeed, the most immediately obvious thing about *Ministry* is its polyph-
ony. The novel is far from Austen's "settled way of seeing," and despite the
fact that Roy's politics are eminently clear—one enters the book knowing
them—there are, among other elements, strikingly internalized, and to that
extent, sympathetic, portraits of characters with which she is, nevertheless, in
sharp disagreement. An unsettled social order leads, in Roy, to an unsettled
narrative. In doing so, she tries to fracture the individualist spine of the novel,
opening it up to more immediately communal—and therefore political—
forms of engagement.

AN ACCEPTABLE AMOUNT OF BLOOD

That Roy is doing something unique with the novel form is apparent from
Ministry's reviews. On the one hand, the novel was praised for its "kaleido-
scopic range . . . its enormity, its recounting of everything without sacrificing

the sheer honesty of" *The God of Small Things*, drawing favorable comparison to Dickens and George Eliot.[16] On the other hand, the novel was taken to task for having "too much going on."[17] A review in *The Atlantic* is particular telling, as Parul Sehgal wonders, "Is *novel* the right word?" Roy's book lacks "psychological shading," refusing "the conventional task (or power) of fiction to evoke the texture and drama of consciousness." The world it describes is "often brutal, but never confusing or even very complex." Displaying a "near-total confusion about point of view," the text creates "characters as stand-ins for causes" resulting in "formulaic depictions of the very people she is trying to humanize." Not surprisingly these problems are all tied to the novel's politics. "To so confidently believe oneself to be on the right side of history," Sehgal opines, "is risky—for a writer especially. In the balmy glow of self-regard, complacency can easily take root."[18] A review in *The Wire* makes a similar point: the novel's characters "follow a predetermined trajectory and consequently do not develop. . . . They are above reproach, modelling all that is morally good with those on the right side of history."[19]

It would be difficult to find a more succinct summary of the relationship between the assumptions of political liberalism and those of the novel form. Novels must not know which side of history they are on or which side of history is correct; they must be complex, particularly in the construction of interiority, which is the novel's true vocation; and they must be formally consistent. We encounter here the values of that "other kind of novel," which looked askance at Dickens, precisely for his failure to provide "the details of psychological process," values associated, as I have already suggested, with modernism, more generally, and with Henry James, in particular.

What makes these critiques even more transparently ideological, however, is that Roy's novel is nothing, if not complex. Faced with the "Borgesian task of reproducing the world in its entirety," *Ministry* weaves a vast national tapestry that quickly abandons what seems its central storyline for a complicated investigation of the conflict over Kashmir. Along the way it spends significant time in the voice of a landlord who is also a torturer for the Indian state, an individual clearly wrong at every step and yet painfully human, a depiction that surely speaks to psychological shading and moral complexity. On the one hand, then, the text works directly against the individualistic framework of the novel form; its polyvocal nature decenters individual characters, allowing a collectivity to speak, with all of its messy contradictions on display. On the other hand, as a novel with a purpose, Roy runs afoul of our culture's expectations that novels withhold judgment, that they show without telling, that they present as settled what is far from settled. In some sense, then, the process Williams observed in Austen has been simplified, universalized, and applied as a standard from which to judge Dickens, Roy, or any number of socially committed novelists whose works are then considered didactic—which is to say, un-novelistic.

Roy, of course, knows precisely the logic she is up against. Midway through the novel, we encounter the following short section:

NOTHING

> I would like to write one of those sophisticated stories in which even though nothing much happens there's lots to write about. That can't be done in Kashmir. It's not sophisticated, what happens here. There's too much blood for good literature.
>
> Q1: Why is it not sophisticated?
> Q2: What is the acceptable amount of blood for good literature? [20]

What Segal wants is a sophisticated book about "purely personal relationships," one in which "nothing much happens." But of course, in a divided subcontinent riven with extremist forms of violence of all sorts, there are no purely personal relationships. Everything that happens is political.

And yet what is perhaps most telling about the novel—and readers of *The God of Small Things* will recognize this characteristic—is its defense of the personal. *The God of Small Things* tells the story of two twins and the tragedy that befalls their family when their mother Ammu sleeps with a Dalit of the Paravan caste named Velutha, a transgression for which Velutha is brutally killed. But the novel ends with a lyrical recounting of Velutha and Ammu's love affair, an affair we know will end in tragedy. A very similar structure is in play in *Ministry*, where the story of the violence in Kashmir also revolves around a love affair between Musa Yeswi, a Kashmiri militant and S. Tilottama, a woman from Kerala he meets at college and who eventually finds him in Kashmir. The personal and the political, that is to say, are intimately intertwined in this novel, even as they are never reducible to one another.

Ministry begins with a lyrical passage I would like to quote in full, one that neatly announces the themes of the novel and its overt interest in how politics touches all aspects of Indian social life:

> *At magic hour, when the sun has gone but the light has not, armies of flying foxes unhinge themselves from the Banyan trees in the old graveyard and drift across the city like smoke. When the bats leave, the crows come home. Not all the din of their homecoming fills the silence left by sparrows that have gone missing, and the old white-backed vultures, custodians of the dead for more than a hundred million years, that have been wiped out. The vultures died of diclofenac poisoning. Diclofenac, cow aspirin, given to cattle as a muscle relaxant, to ease pain and increase the production of milk, works—worked— like nerve gas on white-backed vultures. Each chemically relaxed, milk-producing cow or buffalo that died became poisoned vulture bait. As cattle turned into better dairy machines, as the city ate more ice cream, butterscotch-*

crunch, nutty-buddy and chocolate-chip, as it drank more mango milkshake, vultures' necks began to droop as though they were tired and simply couldn't stay awake. Silver beards of saliva dripped from their beaks, and one by one they tumbled off their branches, dead.

Not many noticed the passing of the friendly old birds. There was so much else to look forward to. (*M* 5, italics in original)

We start in magic, in lyrical sentences describing a natural world that is haunted by what is missing: sparrows and vultures, whose demise is tied to a singularly unpoetic word that breaks the passage's spell telling us, in affectless prose, that "the vultures died of diclofenac poisoning." This poison, we immediately learn, is experienced as progress, a progress that is endemic to the Indian modernity the book will soon examine with "so much else to look forward to" that it fails to notice what is happening under its nose. That the poison is cow aspirin only underlines its relationship to the Hindutva fascism the book chronicles and castigates, cows elevated to a sacred symbol by Hindu nationalists and central to the violence visited on one of the novel's protagonists. The novel's main themes, in other words, are, here, neatly announced, as is its investment in something like social totality: the relationship between modern India and those it leaves behind.

We turn the page and encounter the story of Aftab, a young boy who will eventually become Anjum. Anjum is a Hijra, a South-Asian term for third-gender or intersex people, who have a precise, if liminal, space within Indian society, one that is thousands of years old. What seems at first to be an individual story is immediately revealed to be social as Anjum learns that she is not alone. But no sooner is this story developed than we are swept into a whirlwind of social protest and struggle that focuses, eventually, on Kashmir, but in doing so also takes up the Gujarat massacre, the rise of Modi and Hindutva fascism, along with the displacement of indigenous peoples and the nearly half-century struggle of Maoist insurgents over land rights in central India.

As Anjum develops, an older Hijra named Nimmo pulls her aside and tells her why Hijras are "incapable of happiness" (*M* 27). At first, Anjum is surprised; she has only recently found the Hijra community and, still prepubescent, is overjoyed to find others who feel as she does about their identity. "No one's happy here." Nimmo continues,

It's not possible. *Arre yaar,* think about it, what are the things normal people get unhappy about? I don't mean *you,* but grown-ups like you—what makes them unhappy? Price-rise, children's school-admissions, husbands' beatings, wives' cheatings, Hindu-Muslim riots, Indo-Pak war—*outside* things that settle down eventually. But for us the price-rise and school-admissions and beating-husbands and cheating-wives are all *inside* us. The riot is *inside* us. The war is *inside* us. Indo-Pak is *inside* us. It will never settle down. It *can't*. (*M* 27)

Nimmo's description of the internal conflict Hijras face is supported by Anjum's story: "Anjum lived in the Khwabgah [the Hijra commune] with her patched-together body and her partially realized dreams for more than thirty years" (*M* 33). Far from irreproachable, Anjum is complex, unhappy, by turns petulant and overly dramatic, and yet the subject of Roy's genuine sympathy. She is, in other words, a psychologically complex individual. At the same time, Anjum's liminal identity—one that steps across a seemingly fixed border—is, more or less obviously, a symbol for a more generalizable human condition, one that wishes to overcome the various boundaries of nation and religion, race and caste, that humans erect to separate one another, boundaries visible in the multiple injustices the novel depicts. But in becoming a symbol for all humanity, Anjum also sheds her existence as a type, as what might seem a contemporary story about the personal journey of an excluded identity explodes into a broader set of questions about community and inclusion—questions that gain added resonance by her particular circumstances, but also transcend them.

Indeed, if the Indo-Pakistani War is, in Nimmo's speech, a metaphor for internal conflict—in a move that seems to privatize what is more properly historical—Anjum soon finds herself caught up in a horrific instance of violence representing an actual Indo-Pakistani War: the 2002 Gujarat massacre. Beginning when a train was overturned, killing fifty-eight Hindu pilgrims, the riots took place over three days, killing an estimated two thousand people, with Muslims being explicitly targeted by Hindus for their supposed role in the initial deaths. The current (2021) Prime Minister of India—Narendra Modi—was the Chief Minister of Gujarat at the time and is widely considered responsible for escalating the violence. Anjum is understandably traumatized by her experiences, feeling a particular form of survivor's guilt. Since "killing Hijras brings bad luck" she is spared: "She alone. So that *they* might be blessed with good fortune. Butcher's luck" (*M* 67). Leaving the Khwabgah, Anjum takes up residence in a cemetery: "For months Anjum lived in the graveyard, a ravaged, feral specter, out-haunting every resident djinn and spirit, ambushing bereaved families who came to bury their dead with a grief so wild, so untethered, that it clean outstripped theirs" (*M* 67). Eventually Anjum transforms the graveyard into a guest house, which becomes the site of a community of misfits who represent the kind of bonds across difference Roy offers against the communal violence with which her book is littered. At this moment, however, what we see is the inextricable relationship between internal and external conflict. Psychological trauma and political trauma are nearly impossible to untangle. The privatization of historical conflict is not, then, something the book endorses, nor is it an overarching metaphor for all of its characters. It is, rather, one character's description of her experience, one the book simultaneously validates and challenges as it widens its narrative scope. [21]

If we think of *The Ministry of Utmost Happiness* as, in Williams's phrase, a "knowable community," then what it attempts in its next sections is nothing less than a panorama of Indian society at a moment of rising wealth, inequality, and violence. On the one hand, New Delhi (the capital of India) "was to become supercapital of the world's favorite new superpower" (*M* 100). India's modernity is heralded by the arrival of a range of transnational companies: "Kmart was coming. Walmart and Starbucks were coming" (*M* 101). On the other hand, Roy describes the arrival of these companies directly in relation to what they displace: "Skyscrapers and steel factories sprang up where forests used to be, rivers were bottled and sold in supermarkets, fish were tinned, mountains mined and turned into shining missiles. Massive dams lit up the cities like Christmas trees. Everyone was happy" (*M* 101–2). The degradation affects not just the natural world, but the people as well: "Away from the lights and advertisements, villages were being emptied. Cities too. Millions of people were being moved, but nobody knew where to. 'People who can't afford to live in cities shouldn't come here,' a Supreme Court Judge said" (*M* 102). As India is on the path to renewal and economic success under neoliberalism, it also produces vast misery and inequality. Peasants' homes are demolished, while wealthy urbanites, "people (who counted as people) said to one another, 'You don't have to go abroad for shopping any more. . . . It's like really like *saala* fantastic *yaar*.'" Meanwhile "Experts aired their expert opinions for a fee: *Somebody* has to pay the price for Progress, they said expertly" (*M* 103).

As interested as Roy is in condemning the complicity between a reactionary, religiously inflected government and the structure of global capital, she is also invested in showing the resistance to these forces, which takes many forms. Various characters are on hunger strikes; there are foreigners studying social movements, others making documentary films, people protesting their displacement by transnational corporations; survivors of the Bhopal disaster, where a pesticide plant exposed half a million people to a toxic gas leak that killed, conservatively, 5,000 people; and in the background of it all, Gujarat ka Lalla—Modi—accelerating his march on Delhi. "Where he looked, he would see only himself," Roy writes. "The new Emperor of Hindustan. He was an ocean. He was infinity. He was humanity itself" (*M* 109). We also get our first glimpse of Kashmir—which will dominate the rest of the novel. A banner is carried by the mothers of the Disappeared—people lost to the violence in Kashmir—and it tells of 68,000 dead, 10,000 disappeared. [22] The wealthy walk by them and comment on how lovely Kashmir is: "Apparently it's completely normal now, *ya*, safe for tourists. Let's go? It's supposed to be stunning" (*M* 120). It is here too that we first meet the orphan, Miss

Jebeen the Second, swept up by Tilo who eventually makes her way to Anjum's graveside guest house.

Alongside this panorama of Indian society are some vivid character sketches. Perhaps the most memorable is of Gulabiya, the security guard hired to watch over a Honda billboard on the side of a public toilet. Gulabiya works "seven days a week, twelve hours a day" and lives "under a small blue plastic sheet right next to the billboard" (*M* 116). Gulabiya falls asleep—he will lose his job as a result—and dreams of a time when his hometown wasn't destroyed by the production of a new dam, a dam that ruined his family's traditional way of life and then became the only job in town, perversely forcing the people it displaced to rely on it for their economic well-being. The section proceeds, then, by making clear the relationship between the individual stories it tells and the larger social forces that condition them. Once again, Roy is doing almost exactly what we might think a novelist should do: she is situating her subjects within a larger social world, and she is particularizing them in ways that humanize the political displacements her novel describes.

Having expanded to include elements of the entire social order, Roy's optic tightens again to give us the Kashmiri struggle as it plays out among a set of characters who met while in college: Musa, the revolutionary; Tilo, an architecture student; Biplab, the ironically named government minister and landlord (his name means revolution); and Naga, a journalist who has come to identify with the power structures he is meant to hold accountable. But even as the text centers itself around these particular characters, its form continues to shift. There is a first-person monologue from Biplab, the inclusion of a set of found documents, including a "Psycho-Social Evaluation" of the Indian government's most violent operative, police reports concerning his victims, coerced confessions and "*The Reader's Digest Book of English Grammar and Comprehension for Very Young Children*," written by Tilo and containing a set of unanswerable questions about the moral complexity of the Kashmiri situation (*M* 201, 275). "Who is the hero of the story?" Tilo repeatedly asks (*M* 279). The answers turn almost entirely on perspective.

Now we are always more or less sure where Roy's sympathies lie—with the oppressed and the downtrodden—but though her novel retains this most basic impulse of the realist novel, it also utilizes some of the formal techniques associated with modernism. In particular, its documentary poetics— the inclusion of texts from within the novel's diegetic world—produces a form of perspectivalism where the narratives of particular characters read off of one another to produce a truth larger than any individual perspective could attain by itself—another way in which the novel fractures the individualistic focus of a traditional novel.

Nevertheless, as I have already suggested, the novel is also a love story that, as with *The God of Small Things*, revolves around a tragedy: Musa's wife and daughter, Miss Jebeen the First, were both killed by a stray bullet fired by Indian security forces, which, in turn leads Musa to become a revolutionary. In what is perhaps the tenderest moment of the text, Tilo asks Musa to describe his wife and daughter: "It was possible for Tilo and Musa to have this strange conversation about a third loved one . . . because they trusted each other so peculiarly that they knew, even if they were hurt by it, that whoever it was that the other person loved had to be worth loving" (*M* 373–74). Tilo takes in his story without jealousy, recognizing that it is not really about her, that if she really cares for Musa she must allow him to be the protagonist of his own story, a story that might not revolve around her. Love, here, requires the decentering of the subject. As Musa tells Tilo his story, Roy describes the moment as one in which they "repudiate the world they lived in and call forth another one, just as real" (*M* 368). This line is crucial: the world they inhabit, here, is as real as the world of politics from which they seek refuge. It cannot obliterate the world they live in—indeed, they will soon be caught up more deeply in its violence and injustice—but it stands as a rebuke to it.

What makes the violence in Kashmir so destructive, Musa suggests, is its evacuation of the human, which is why he must hold on to the personal even as he must also transcend it. "You know what the hardest thing for us is?" he asks Tilo:

> The hardest thing to fight? Pity. It's so easy for us to pity ourselves . . . such terrible things have happened to our people. . . in every single household something terrible has happened [. . .] More than Azadi [freedom], now it's a fight for dignity. And the only way we can hold on to our dignity is to fight back. Even if we lose. Even if we die. But for that we as a people—as an ordinary people—have to become a fighting force . . . an army. To do that we have to simplify ourselves, standardize ourselves, reduce ourselves . . . everyone has to think the same way, want the same thing . . . we have to do away with our complexities, our differences, our absurdities, our nuances . . . we have to make ourselves as single-minded . . . as monolithic . . . as stupid. . . as the army we face. But they're professionals, and we are just people. This is the worst part of the Occupation . . . what it makes us do to ourselves. This reduction, this standardization, this *stupidification* . . . Is that a word? (*M* 377–76, unbracked ellipses in the original)

Musa understands, here, that in order to win the war, the people of Kashmir must harden themselves. This lesson is mirrored in Roy's description of the gradual transformation of Kashmiris militants, who proceed with a certainty born of religious fundamentalism. "What does freedom mean?" the new militants, ask and their answer is clear: "There is no God but Allah" (*M* 327). Thus, according to Roy, "The Strict Line plunged the Valley into a dilemma. People knew that the freedom they longed for would not come without a war, and they knew the Strict Ones were by far the better warriors" (*M* 327). They "loved the Less Strict Ones, but they feared and respected the Strict Ones" (*M* 328). This dynamic moves in only one direction: "The Strict Ones begot even Stricter Ones" (*M* 328). What is here understood as "being Strict" is akin to what Musa calls reduction: the turning of ordinary people, with all their messy complexity—Anjum, let's say, and her friends in the grave-yard—into warriors. Roy is clearly on the side of revolution, then, but she is equally attuned to its human costs. Musa's stupidification is, here, another version of the system against which Williams was writing.

Musa concludes his story by saying "I'll never take what happened to my family personally. But I'll never *not* take it personally. Because that is impor-tant too" (*M* 374). These lines could stand as an epigraph to the entire novel. What has happened to Musa is transpersonal, due to historical forces and structural inequities that sweep up individuals in the larger structures of history, a vision summarized by the repeated imagery of ants, carrying away Miss Jebeen the Second's cake, or instancing the relative lack of world interest in the struggle of Kashmir (*M* 217, 331–32). But the other part of the quotation is equally important: it was personal, it did matter. Every death that results from inequality or war or human greed or stupidity counts. If it didn't there would be no reason to care about those problems in the first place. Social conditions only become legible as human conditions. They are imper-sonal and personal at the same time.

We see the same combination of personal and impersonal in the story of Saddam Hussein, a Hindu man who took the name of the Iraqi dictator after watching a video in which he faced death with "courage and dignity" (*M* 94). Saddam's story is one of horrific violence; like Anjum, he suffers from survivor's guilt. "I was part of the mob that killed my father," he says, though this is not really true (*M* 93). A Dalit of the Chamar caste, Saddam and his father removed the dead cows upper-class Hindus refuse to touch. When his father and his father's friends, having just picked up a carcass, refuse to pay an exorbitant bribe to a police officer named Sehrawat, they are arrested for cow slaughter. Saddam is not and waits outside with the dead cow. Soon a crowd develops, into which Saddam, sensing trouble, sinks. The crowd then breaks down the police station and murders his father and his father's friends. Saddam hardens, vowing to kill Sehrawat and taking on the name of a vi-cious and autocratic dictator.

Two developments alter his story. The first is that he falls in love with Zainab, a woman who was adopted as a young girl by Anjum in the early part of the tale. The second is the "massive public protest in Gujarat" he sees on TV during one Independence Day: "Thousands of people, mainly Dalit, had gathered in a district called Una to protest the public flogging of five Dalits who had been stopped on the road because they had the carcass of a cow in their pickup truck. They hadn't killed the cow. They had only picked up the carcass like Saddam's father had, all those years ago" (*M* 409). Saddam "looked thrilled as speaker after speaker swore on oath that they would never again pick up cow carcasses for upper-caste Hindus" (*M* 409). Replacing the video of the original Saddam—and abandoning his plan for revenge—he now proudly displays a new video of "furious young Dalit men" hurling cow carcasses into the "office of a local District Collector" (*M* 412). "My people have risen up!" Saddam declares, "They are fighting! What is one Sehrawat for us now? Nothing" (*M* 412). Again, we find the intertwining of the private and the public, love and politics. Saddam is humanized as much by his newfound love as by the explosion of communal struggle; "Neither element, neither the society nor the individual, is there as a priority."

Ministry ends with its motley group of strangers—Tilo, Anjum, Saddam Hussein and his bride Zainab, and Miss Jebeen the Second—having just read the horrible tale of how the second Miss Jebeen's mother, an Adivasi and the member of a Maoist revolutionary group, was raped and brutalized by the Indian government:

> Each of the listeners recognized, in their own separate ways, something of themselves and their own stories, their own Indo-Pak, in the story of this unknown, faraway woman who was no longer alive. It made them close ranks around Miss Jebeen the Second like a formation of trees, or adult elephants—an impenetrable fortress in which she, unlike her biological mother, would grow up protected and loved. (*M* 432)

The novel here offers us a lesson in how to read it: if we can see something of ourselves in the stories of other's suffering, we can perhaps learn to care not only for our own children, but for others as well. Miss Jebeen—and the community that grows around her—is a potent symbol of what this can achieve. Indeed, if the novel seems to celebrate diversity in its proliferation of different axes of oppression and struggle—and in doing so court a kind of liberal, pluralist vision amenable to the capitalism Roy decries—it always returns to the idea of community. Personal sorrow here is transcended by connection, even as what is personal is shown to be always already social, part of a collective human experience. The ability to share that sorrow is itself a recognition of this fact. Perspectivalism, then, is returned to its ground in a concrete social world. In this way, *The Ministry of Utmost Happiness* shows us, in the manner of Williams's definition of realism, a "society that is larger than any of the individuals composing it," while simultaneously valuing those individuals as "absolute ends in themselves."

Roy has been taken to task for the positivity of this ending. For some, its valorization of the outcast courts precisely the kind of celebration of creative precarity on which neoliberalism thrives.[23] For others, the ending recalls the sins of an earlier sentimentalist. "After the tortures and the beheadings," Joan

Acocella wrote in *The New Yorker*, "This is a little too cozy. I expect someone to pop up, any minute, and say, 'God bless us, everyone!'"[24] We can
sneer at Dickens for his sentimentality, for his belief "that a human spirit
exists, ultimately more powerful than even this system," but to do so is to
align ourselves with alienation itself. What makes the ending work—what
saves it, ultimately, from being cheap universalizing sentiment—is the specificity of the social world within which it occurs, in Roy's clear-sighted
analysis of the social conditions that would seem to prevent such a flowering,
that make it seem inexplicable. And yet this is, against all odds, precisely the
kind of miracle that happens.

NOTES

1. Amitav Ghosh, *The Great Derangement: Climate Change and the Unthinkable* (New
York: Penguin Books, 2016), 14.
2. Ibid., 181.
3. Ibid., 172–73. The phrase "individual moral adventures" is John Updike's and comes in
his critical, more or less racist review of Abdul Rahman Munif's *Cities of Salt*, one of the few
novels that addresses oil culture directly. Ghosh discusses the review on pages 100–105,
though the phrase becomes a leitmotif throughout. Updike had also written, "It is unfortunate,
given the epic potential of his topic, that Mr. Munif . . . appears to be . . .insufficiently
Westernized to produce a narrative that feels like what we call a novel. His voice is that of a
campfire explainer" (qtd. in Ghosh 102–3).
4. Ibid., 22.
5. Ibid., 31.
6. Ibid.
7. Ibid., 40, 161.
8. Georg Lukács, *The Historical Novel*, trans. Hannah Mitchell and Stanley Mitchell (Middlesex: Penguin Books, 1961), 33.
9. Franco Moretti, *The Way of the World: The "Bildungsroman" in European Culture*,
trans. Albert Sbragia (New York: Verso, 1987), 5.
10. Ibid., 5, 6.
11. Ibid., 8.
12. Ibid., 10, emphasis in the original.
13. This method of reading, of course, is what gets Williams into trouble in *Culture and
Society*, where the discussion of conservative thinkers seems to ignore their most troubling
viewpoints in the name of a more sympathetic understanding of their views on culture, while
validating their thought through a less mediated notion of experience than the one I'm describing here. The questioners in *Politics and Letters* are characteristically forceful in making the
point, as Williams is—equally characteristically—as deferential as he is unyielding. See the
exchange at 100–109. The reading of Austen, seems to me, to balance critique and insight in
equal measure, in a way that is often lacking in the readings in *Culture and Society*, though the
inattention to reactionary views is more troubling in overtly political authors such as Burke
than in a reading devoted not really to Austen herself, but to her literary form.
14. Daniel Hartley, "On Raymond Williams: Complexity, Immanence, and the Long Revolution," *Mediations* 30, no. 1 (Fall 2016): 41.
15. We have already observed Williams's aversion to abstraction, which, in turn, led to a
resistance to theorization as such (this, despite such theoretical innovations as "structures of
feeling," about which Thomas Laughlin writes in chapter 4 above). Williams seemed to have
viewed the creation of intellectual systems as of a piece with the elimination of the human he
diagnosed in contemporary capitalism. At the same time, Williams genuinely considered his
work an ongoing project—one with guiding principles, that was nevertheless open to revision

as historical circumstances changed—a quality that emerges most clearly in the remarkable interviews in *Politics and Letters*. Evidently, he understood this openness as a counter to the rigidity of system building.

16. Anita Felicelli, "Outside Language and Power: The Mastery of Arundhati Roy's 'The Ministry of Utmost Happiness,'" *Los Angeles Review of Books*, June 21, 2017.

17. Oeendrila Lahiri, "'The Ministry of Utmost Happiness' Is Timely, but Not Deserving of the Booker," *The Wire*, September 1, 2017.

18. Parul Sehgal, "Arundhati Roy's Fascinating Mess," *The Atlantic*, July/August 2017.

19. Lahiri, "'The Ministry of Utmost Happiness.'"

20. Arundhati Roy, *The Ministry of Utmost Happiness* (New York: Vintage, 2017), 288, hereafter referred to parenthetically as M.

21. Similarly, though the violence of Partition—the Indo-Pakistani War—is, in some sense, the originary violence of the Indian state, the conflicts Roy outlines are not reducible to that one historical moment.

22. The phrase, of course, originates in Argentina, and so Roy, here, connects the violence in Kashmir to a transnational community of women protesting authoritarian rule.

23. This possibility is raised by Mendes and Lau, though ultimately they argue that "Roy's celebration of the agency of the precariat does not in the end overshadow the writer's consistent representation of an India rife with aggressive capitalism, uncaring neo-liberal forces, and oppressive social conformities." See Ana Cristina Mendes and Lisa Lau, "The Precarious Lives of India's Others: The Creativty of Precarity in Arundhati Roy's *The Ministry of Utmost Happiness*," *Journal of Postcolonial Writing* 56, no. 1 (2020): 73.

24. Joan Acocella, "Arundhati Roy Returns to Fiction, in Fury," *The New Yorker*, June 5 & 12, 2017.

Chapter Seven

Structures of Feeling, Late Capitalism, and the Making of African Literature in the Global Literary Marketplace

Madhu Krishnan

It was a stifling hot November day in Abeokuta, Nigeria, and, unaccustomed to the humidity and burning heat, I tried desperately to stay cool as I navigated the crowded auditorium of the city's cultural center, searching for an empty seat. Onstage, the premiere of Ogun State was in the middle of a long address to a packed audience otherwise occupied with taking selfies, catching up with friends and trying to catch a glimpse of the literary elite spread out across the hall. Groups of students decked out in matching shirts, some from as far away as Lagos and Abuja, peppered the hall, their excitement palpable at being here at the opening of the literary and cultural event of the year: the fourth annual Aké Arts and Book Festival. Over the course of the next several days, this scene would repeat itself time and again, with auditoriums, galleries, and performance spaces packed with audience members enjoying book chats, film screenings, live performances, and panel discussions. The brainchild of writer and literary activist Lola Shoneyin, the Aké festival has become a significant event in the African literary landscape, attracting thousands of visitors over its seven editions and surviving a move from Abeokuta to the economic capital of Lagos in 2018 (an eighth edition, due to take place in October 2020, was moved to a virtual format due to the COVID-19 pandemic). Hugely popular both with local audiences and international visitors, and boasting sponsorship as varied as the Miles Moreland Foundation, Government of Canada, French Embassy in Nigeria, African Women's Development Fund, Sterling Bank, Lipton Tea, and Budweiser, among many others, the festival operates as a particularly complex cultural object and event, whose external and internal relations display a multifaceted network of varying and sometimes competing interests, inclinations, and priorities that extend well beyond the boundaries of any simplistic notion of the arts or culture.

I begin this essay on the possibilities that a return to the work of Raymond Williams might offer world literary studies with this brief anecdote because the Aké festival, along with the literary ecology of which it forms a part, exemplifies the ways in which current models of understanding fail to fully account for the lived complexity of cultural production in the global South. Where, in the realm of African literary studies, it has become commonplace to view African literature as a fixed category, through a predetermined set of theoretical models inevitably oriented toward the global North as market and audience, a return to Williams, I argue, can enable a more nuanced picture of the dynamics of cultural production to emerge. To that end, I focus on the example of African literature, not as a microcosm of world literature, as such, but as one specific test case for understanding its functioning. While Aké is a particularly visible example of the complex vitality of literary cultures on the African continent, it is by no means alone. Over the last six years (since 2015) of intensive, field-based research in different African contexts, I have witnessed similar scenes whether in Kampala, Nairobi, Yaoundé, Cape Town or elsewhere, all of which demonstrate firsthand the way the expression of literary culture is entangled within a series of complex social, economic, and political relations that extend beyond neat categorizations of the literary field, global literary market, or world republic of letters. And yet, these varied formations remain far less visible in any world literary topography than the relatively small body of work that circulates as global African literature, despite the myriad connections between living literary cultures on the African continent and the set of commodities that represent African literature in the marketplace.

One of the central preoccupations of this essay, then, is to think about the mechanisms through which this cleaving occurs and how the methods for cultural study proposed by Williams might offer one path for reconnecting what seem to be disparate modes of literary production. Rather than rely on a priori models for understanding the constitution of world literatures, this essay therefore explores the ways in which the modes of cultural study outlined and revised across Williams's career can provide a critical grounding for analyzing the nature of a selective tradition of African writing as it appears in the global literary market today, as well as elucidate the more complex internal and external relations that connect the seemingly discrete spaces of the global literary market with the lived vitality of literary production as practiced and felt. My intention in so doing is not necessarily to echo now-common arguments about the perceived chasm between audience, market, and producer in African—and more broadly, world—literary studies, nor is it to engage in well-rehearsed debates around exoticism, strategic essentialism, and related areas of critique.[1] Rather, I am interested in thinking about how Williams's work, written more than half a century ago, might provide a method for adding nuance and complexity to the ways in which we conceive of categories such as African literature, world literature, or postcolonial literature, and by so doing, the mechanisms of literary and cultural production today.

Early in the pages of *The Long Revolution*, Williams, in a seemingly obvious statement, provides the reader with a diagnosis of the central challenge facing cultural study, writing that "it is only in our own time and place that we can expect to know, in any substantial way, the general organisation [of a society]. We can learn a great deal of the life of other places and times, but certain elements . . . will always be irrecoverable" (*LR* 67). This "further common element, which is neither the [social] character nor the pattern [of culture], but as it were the actual experience through which these were lived" may forever elude the critic (*LR* 68). At the same time, within the boundaries of culture, it leaves perceptible traces as part of a structure of feeling:

> It is as firm and definite as "structure" suggests, yet it operates in the most delicate and least tangible parts of our activity. In one sense, this structure of feeling is the culture of a period: it is the particular living result of all the elements in the general organisation. And it is in this respect that the arts of a period, taking these to include characteristic approaches and tones in argument, are of major importance. For here, if anywhere, this characteristic is likely to be expressed; often not consciously, but by the fact that here, in the only examples we have of recorded communication that outlives its bearers, the actual living sense, the deep community that makes the communication possible, is naturally drawn upon. (*LR* 69)

Emphasized in this passage, a structure of feeling is not something that can be easily defined or ascertained; both "delicate" and solid, unevenly distributed and felt, perceivable only in its traces, a structure of feeling captures something of that intangible sense of the vitality of lived experience, in all of its complex fullness, which is most evident in what feels like immediacy. Returning to the anecdote with which I started this essay, then, we might begin to identify the relations from which structures of feeling—their lack of visibility and the difficulty inherent in excavating their full sense—are produced as one of the primary drivers of the seeming incompatibility of African literary critical scholarship, on the one hand, and African literary cultural production as experienced, on the other.

Much of the recent scholarship on African literature in the global literary marketplace has followed the models of world literary production and consecration outlined in Bourdieu's notion of the field of cultural production and its extension into the world republic of letters by Casanova.[2] Significant in this work is the notion of the field of cultural production as "a field of struggles" defined by "position-takings" and "literary or artistic positions."[3] Where, for Bourdieu, the field of cultural production operates largely as a series of discrete national traditions that shift over time, Casanova's formulation of world literary space as "a relatively unified space characterized by the opposition between great national literary spaces, which are also the oldest— and accordingly the best endowed—and those literary spaces that have more recently appeared and that are poor by comparison" offers a model for conceptualizing the larger iterative processes through which literary works move across locations endowed with differing levels of prestige and influence.[4] It is through this process that it becomes "possible to evaluate and recognize the quality of a work or, to the contrary, to dismiss a work as an anachronism or to label it 'provincial,'" with the ultimate effect of creating "a universal artistic clock by which writers must regulate their work if they wish to attain legitimacy."[5] In the context of African literature, a relatively small selection of texts and authors have been identified as attaining this mode of legitimacy, entering the literary markets and fields of the global North and acquiring world literary prestige.

My interest in this detour through world literary systems is less to assess the validity of these claims than it is to consider what they leave out and what placing Williams's own work in dialogue with these models might enable to emerge. Williams writes,

> We tend to underestimate the extent to which the cultural tradition is not only a selection but also an interpretation. We see most past work through our own experience, without even making the effort to see it in something like its original terms. What analysis can do is not so much to reverse this, returning a work to its period, as to make the interpretation conscious, by showing historical alternatives, to relate the interpretation to the particular contemporary values on which it rests; and, by exploring the real patterns of the work, confront us with the real nature of the choices we are making. (*LR* 74)

Taken not simply as a given but as an interpretative act, the dominant tradition—what I am here loosely consolidating under the category of global African literature—is simply one subset among others, whose own position in terms of its visibility might itself efface the larger, complex totality from which it is selected. In the context of world literary production, it takes its most obvious contemporary guise, as Williams observes, as "the fantastic projection of a few centres"; in all of its force, the monolith of the selective tradition presents itself as a given, to the detriment of our ability to perceive its internal relations, as well as its external relations to the larger ecology from which it is derived and the alternative visions encoded therein (*T* 142). Once we perceive the selection of a cultural tradition as itself an interpretative act, fundamentally entangled with the larger values, preoccupations, and elements of a society, the so-called autonomy of the literary field or world republic of letters is called into question. Rather, that is, than view literature, or culture more broadly, as operating as a homology to the economic and social fields, it becomes directly intertwined through a multifaceted network of relations, some more obvious than others, which together produce the mechanisms of selection through which a tradition is formed.

In what follows, I take Williams's guidance in viewing this analysis through patterns, heeding his caution that "it is with the discovery of patterns of a characteristic kind that any useful cultural analysis begins, and it is with the relationships between these patterns, which sometimes reveal unexpected identities and correspondences in hitherto separately considered activities, sometimes again reveal discontinuities of an unexpected kind, that general cultural analysis is concerned" (*LR* 67). Recent novels such as Chimamanda Ngozi Adichie's *Americanah* (2013), Yaa Gyasi's *Homegoing* (2016), Imbolo Mbue's *Behold the Dreamers* (2016), Taiye Selasi's *Ghana Must Go* (2013), Teju Cole's *Open City* (2011), and Ayọbámi Adébáyọ̀'s *Stay with Me* (2017), for instance, have dominated both critical and popular attention in the United States and United Kingdom, functioning as exemplars of success in commercial and critical terms, on the one hand, and, on the other, as key texts participating in the dominant tradition of the global African novel or African literary renaissance of the twenty-first century. Examining these texts together, we can observe a number of tendencies that offer evidence of a deeper structure of feeling underlying their selection and status as world literary texts consecrated by the world republic of letters. Chief among these are patterns of form, theme, and narrative style, including a notable preference for texts that follow a broadly realist tradition. Recalling, with Williams, that cultural works appear within a "much wider and more general social formation," my interest here is to consider the ways in which these dominant tendencies and patterns speak to the relationship between contemporary social formations and the development of a specific subset of African literary production as global African literature, a particular cultural form that has emerged in the centers and markets of the global North (*SC* 75).

The most striking feature that emerges across these novels is their emphasis on the individual and affective rather than the overtly collective and political. Adichie's *Half of a Yellow Sun*, for instance, has been commended for "the strong light that shines on the book's principal players, rather than on the politics and strategies that shaped the war,"[6] while Doreen Strauhs, in her study of contemporary African literary NGOs, asserts that contemporary writers, unlike their predecessors in the 1960s and 1970s, reject an overtly political or social orientation in their writing.[7] Across these texts, the figure of the detached and alienated individual repeats itself time and again: in Adichie's *Americanah*, protagonist Ifemelu, a woman of middle-class origins who finds herself becoming a feted blogger in the United States, is repeatedly described in terms that evoke emptiness and disconnection from those around her, with few realized personality characteristics developed beyond her physical appearance. As I have written elsewhere, the narrative's evacuation of politics belies the true extent of relations that motivates its plot.[8] The fact of Ifemelu's migration to the United States, for instance, motivated by the closure of her university due to ongoing lecturer strikes, attests to the centrality of structural adjustment policies on the erosion of the public sector in Nigeria, with devastating impact on the provision of basic social services. Yet, within the context of the novel, this deeper context remains unspoken, submerged by a greater preoccupation with the single, remarkable individual and her unlikely rise to prosperity and success in the United States, deploying prestige markers, affect, and tokens of material success as a substitute for a substantiated and developed personality intricately connected to deep structures.

The same might be said for Julius, the protagonist of Teju Cole's *Open City*, whose meandering nightly walks through Manhattan's sprawling cityscapes are characterized by deep ruminations on the city's multilayered history as a veneer to cover the malignant narcissism at the character's core and his total inability to connect with the others he encounters. Even where the focus of the narrative remains on a family or familial line, as is the case in *Behold the Dreamers*, *Homegoing*, and *Ghana Must Go*, the larger structures of relation that tie these individuals to society remain tenuous and largely superficial, overshadowed by an emphasis on singularity and discrete notions of autonomous personhood.[9] More broadly, these narratives are ones whose very structures and forms prevent the reader from discerning what Williams refers to as the "the general organisation" of a society registered in a text or set of texts, on the one hand, and mimic or reproduce the fragmentary workings of neoliberalism, on the other, masking the connectedness of things under a bland and limited individuality. In this sense, we might perceive in contemporary, global African literature a reproduction at the narrative and formal level of the twinned precepts of the hustle and the neoliberal self, predicated on the privatization of everyday life and the ascendancy of entrepreneurialism as the locus of daily life.[10]

A common element in these novels is their treatment of what can be loosely termed the narrative of return. In *Americanah*, Ifemelu decides, despite her success, to leave her lucrative career as a blogger in the United States and return to a changed Nigeria; in *Ghana Must Go*, the family converges in their ancestral home in Ghana at the novel's conclusion in a moment of reconciliation and catharsis; in *Homegoing*, the novel ends with two distant cousins, unaware of their relationship, returning to the coastal landscapes where the family line had been fractured centuries before; in *Behold the Dreamers*, the novel ends with the family's return to Cameroon, now economically secure, following protagonist Jende's dismissal from his job and failure to obtain asylum. In each case, return is a mode of narrative resolution, functioning alternatively as a moment of necessary psychic heal-ing, completed quest for selfhood, or attainment of material status. At the same time, return offers an outlet for each narrative at a moment when its plot has exceeded its own capacities, jumping scales to move from the local and the domestic to the transnational without intermediary engagement.[11] The resulting narrative forms remain paradoxically insular, punctuated by the repeated appearance of stock characters who function largely as underdevel-oped foils for the main characters alongside movements into transnational and paranational space that nonetheless fail to articulate a fully developed vision of scalar entanglements. More broadly, while each of these texts them-selves appears at a superficial level to encompass a transnational scale in their narrative forms, plot, and structure, these fail to engage with deeper mediations regarding the constitution of these very scales and their implica-tion in a broader, neoliberal vision of globality. This superficial engagement with scale, then, is precisely what makes them amenable to—and so easily assimilable by—a world literary discourse that similarly obscures the mediat-ing links between local and metropolitan centers.

At a formal level, this is emphasized by a reliance on fragmentary narra-tive forms that feature multiple, shifting perspectives and move across time and space in a largely episodic manner. These are particularly notable for driving, to a large extent, each text's own version of scale jumping, on the one hand, and, on the other, by complicating their straightforwardly realist forms through a gesture toward a kind of modernist experimentalism. Yet, as Williams reminds us in *Towards 2000*, "the originally precarious and often desperate images" of modernism, when transposed to these market-oriented and more popular forms, "have been transformed . . . to become, at an effective surface, a 'modernist' and 'post-modernist' establishment." As he continues, "these forms which still claim the status of minority art have become the routine diversions and confirmations of a paranational commod-ity exchange, with which indeed they have many structural identities" (*T* 141). In *Homegoing*, for instance, chapters stand as connected, though large-ly self-contained, short stories that alternate between the United States and Ghana, following a family line fractured by kidnapping and enslavement. The ultimate effect of this structure is a narrative in which characters remain only partially developed, the various strands of their individual stories abruptly cut off as the text jumps between space and time. While *Homegoing* remains broadly chronological in its movements, in *Ghana Must Go*, the narrative shifts between present and past, alternately focalized by the various members of the central Sai family across continents. In *Americanah*, mean-while, sections shift between Ifemelu's story and the considerably less devel-oped narrative of her former love, Obinze, who undertakes undocumented migration to the United Kingdom and is eventually deported back to Nigeria. This tendency toward fragmentary and multivocal narratives is itself a rela-

tively new development, emerging in contrast to earlier novels such as Adichie's *Purple Hibiscus* (2003), Chris Abani's *GraceLand* (2004), or Helen
Oyeyemi's *The Icarus Girl* (2005), which function more broadly as bildungs-
romans, preoccupied with the figure of the child.

In more recent novels, however, frequent shifts in temporal and spatial
orientation, as well as character focalization, function to simultaneously ac-
celerate the narrative pace while diluting any sustained sense of momentum
in favor of an aesthetics seemingly rooted in the precepts of a dispersed
vision of subjectivity that cannot be decoupled from the larger changes in
modes of social interaction and engagement in the twenty-first century. This
instantiation of space-time compression [12] —in which places and events that
appear to be distant and discrete are placed into close proximity, not through
the development of robust relations or connections, but through modes of
juxtaposition and the manipulation of scalar effects—fabricates within these
narratives what Williams once referred to as a "heuristic utopia" whose "versions of desire, and of new feelings and relationships, are not only often
vague but in their most subjective and private versions . . . are [also] subject
to capture by the existing social order" (*T* 13–14). Rather than serve as a
mode of resistance against the strictures of late capitalism, which delimit the
ability of these plots to develop a sense of fullness or lived capacity, these
modes of space-time manipulation betray a closely entangled relation with
the uneasy fluidity of liquid modernity and the extension of neoliberalism as
an ontological ordering of reality. [13] In *The Sociology of Culture*, Williams
notes how "formal innovation is a true and integral element of the changes
[in a social formation] themselves: an articulation, by technical discovery, of
changes in consciousness that are themselves forms of consciousness of
change" (*SC* 142). Within the category of global African literature, what
appears is a specifically constituted cultural form, the "new African novel,"
whose own structural assimilation of the precepts of neoliberalization stands
as neither cause nor effect, but one particular manifestation of their entangled
amplification in the twenty-first century.

In *The Long Revolution* Williams also asserts,

> The history of a culture, slowly built up from such particular work, can only be
> written when the active relations are restored, and the activities seen in a
> genuine parity. Cultural history must be more than the sum of the particular
> histories, for it is with the relations between them, the particular forms of the
> whole organisation, that it is especially concerned. I would then define the
> theory of culture as the study of relationships between elements in a whole
> way of life. (*LR* 66–67)

It is my assertion in this essay that the patterns discernible in the contemporary global African novel, as I am loosely referring to these examples, are
most usefully analyzed when placed in dialogue with the material conditions

through which it has emerged such that the active relations across these seemingly disparate areas can be discerned. Rather than view these works as part of an autonomous field of cultural production whose relations with the political, economic, and social fields are only ever homologies, these texts—both individually and as a category—must be seen in Williams's terms as part of a complex totality. A few key areas of active relation that require attention, then, can be described: the ramifications of structural adjustment and Bretton Woods management systems not merely on the cultural landscape in Africa but, more keenly, on the felt determinations of the individual and society under late capitalism; the material conditions under which increased migration of Africans to the global North (particularly the United States) have occurred; the ongoing and accelerated expropriation of resources from the continent under the "new scramble for Africa"; the entrenchment of neoliberal modes of governance and economic development under developmentalist narratives and "Africa rising"; the erasure of structural accountability in favor of individual responsibility more broadly under the auspices of liquid modernity; the increased but radically asymmetrical and uneven connectivity offered by contemporary information technologies, including social media.[14]

One immediate way in which these forces are felt is in the ways in which African literary production remains constrained by its absorption into a global literary market whose center remains elsewhere, a consequence in large part of structural adjustment policies and their legacies on the African continent. Commenting on the preference, by foreign publishers, for work by a small coterie of "hit" authors from the global South, Akin Adesokan remarks that "if this phenomenon advances literary cultures in postcolonial contexts, it does so through a process of 'reversed extraversion'—the centripetal dispersal of influence of a novel first published outside of its author's primary sphere of interest. This institutional development represents a noteworthy move for the transformation of an audience into a market."[15] For Adesokan, the transformation of an audience into a market lies at the root of the aesthetic and formal patterns that mark global African literature, particularly its turn toward a mode of otherness that aligns with the desires and inclinations of that market and its social formations. It is certainly the case that the material inequities in publishing, both at the local and global levels, have contributed to the consolidation of certain modes of writing as particularly "marketable" and replicable. In her 2017 essay "On the African Literary Hustle," for instance, Sarah Brouillette notes how, in the African context,

> the post-independence quest to develop literary readerships and publishing and printing trades faced massive hurdles; it was nearly stopped by IMF & World Bank structural adjustment and trade liberalization in the 1990s, and has now been all but abandoned. The field of contemporary Anglophone African litera-

ture relies instead on private donors, mainly but not exclusively American, supporting a transnational coterie of editors, writers, prize judges, event organizers, and workshop instructors. The literary works that arise from this milieu of course tend to be targeted at British and American markets.[16]

For Brouillette, the "NGOization" of African literary production has produced a situation in which all that is able to be created is a minority culture oriented toward an elite and often foreign audience, on the one hand, and market, on the other. Taking Adesokan's and Brouillette's comments together, what appears is a critical view in which the production of African literature has become subject to the so-called logic of the market—corporatized, professionalized, driven by "modern patronal" relations (*SC* 55), and put in the service of "narrower and more evidently residual interests," on the one hand, and "paranational commodity exchange," on the other (*T* 139, 141). In particular, Brouillette's formulation highlights the extent to which political and economic forces directly impact the shaping of the cultural landscape and the place of the African writer and African literary work within it. Where Williams, writing in the 1960s, highlighted the difficulty in the British landscape of determining new institutions and actors that might change the "preexisting standard patterns" expressed in literature, in the post-structural adjustment context described here, what emerges is a situation in which "the real experience of mobility" is determined, not by a shift toward liberation and autonomy, but, rather, by a restriction of the same (*LR* 284–85). It is moreover the case that, where we might perceive the success of individual writers as a sign of the opening of the literary landscape to those individuals previously denied access to its core, a change of scale or perspective to examine the ways in which the whole society is changing presents a picture that is far less positive and far more determined by the seemingly impenetrable grind of late capitalism, international finance, and the erosion of the public good in favor of private interest.

At the same time, the very notion of a "new" African novel, the dominant form of global African literature, whose emergence signals a literary renaissance is itself only a partial view, obscuring its wider relations. For proponents of this view, the late twentieth century and first years of the new millennium were marked by a dearth of literary production circulating in the global literary marketplace from the continent and its diasporas, following an earlier surge of literary production from the 1950s to early 1980s, characterized by figures such as Chinua Achebe, Wole Soyinka, Ngũgĩ wa Thiong'o, Buchi Emecheta, and Ama Ata Aidoo. This "literary renaissance" can be traced to a number of factors, including but not limited to these: the return to democracy in Nigeria, the end of dictatorships in countries such as Kenya and Uganda, the end of apartheid and transition to democracy in South Africa, the liberalization and financialization of African economies and markets, and the aforementioned domination of the "Africa rising" narrative to which this gives rise. At the same time, and despite the emphasis on the handful of contemporary writers associated with it, the African literary renaissance did not arise out of a vacuum. Instead, a deeper look at its internal relations demonstrates how closely its emergence is tied to a larger and more varied African literary ecology, characterized by the rise of Africa-centered literary collectives and outlets, such as Nigeria's Farafina, South Africa's Chimurenga, Ugandan FEMRITE, and, later, institutions such as Cassava Republic Press (Nigeria and the United Kingdom), the African Writers Trust (Uganda), Storymoja (Kenya and Ghana), Bakwa (Cameroon), Huza Press (Rwanda), Jalada (Kenya), and Writivism (Uganda). While, compared to their more visible counterparts in the global literary market, these formations are relatively less known or visible outside of the continent, key lines of interconnection remain, indicating a far more complex picture of cultural production and literary expression than the standard narrative allows.[17]

In a 2018 keynote address titled "African Writing and the Forms of Publicness," Moradewun Adejunmobi makes a powerful argument against the domination of models for understanding cultural production that focus solely on that subset of work most visible in the global North.[18] In a sprit aligned with Williams's reminder "that even in a very simple society it is hardly ever one single 'social character' or 'culture pattern' that the individual encounters," Adejunmobi instead calls for a cultural criticism that is attuned to the dynamics of visibility that mediate perceptions of cultural activity (*LR* 107). Central to Adejunmobi's argument is a distinction between the fact of being in public and the fact of visibility that is intimately tied to a conception of publicness as a *way* of being in public—or society—operating through a plurality of relations. Once this distinction is recognized, it becomes vital to develop a social analysis that foregrounds the systems of mediation that render a cultural form public and have the potential, alternately, to significantly extend the degree of publicness associated with objects and subjects already in the public view or to render these subjects and objects more or less visible. In the case of African literary production, what is rendered less visible and sometimes imperceptible are the great bodies of writing by African and African diasporic writers that are, in the most basic sense, public, but that remain barely, if at all, visible to the multiple extended publics that dominate the global literary marketplace: those publics endowed, for multiple reasons and via multiple relations, with greater authority and greater visibility as publics.

Though delivered in a different context, Adejunmobi's comments present a number of connections with Williams's own conception of culture. In particular, her analysis of the dynamics of visibility make clear the urgency of a more complicated envisioning of the patterns and mappings of literary production that Williams proposes. First, the distinction drawn between the

state of being in public and the state of being visible indicates a new emphasis on the concept of a structure of feeling as something possessed in different ways by different individuals and groups, which then becomes an important site through which to attempt to recuperate these different modes of
possession that are themselves more or less visible. By so doing, we can
uncover traces, remnants, or patterns that might enable us to make visible—
or more visible—those social characters, patterns of society, and intellectual-
creative discourses that remain public but effaced by the dominant strands of
the selective tradition. Equally, Adejunmobi's formulation of publicness as a
way of being mediated by structures of power and authority places a renewed
emphasis on the need to perceive and take seriously those attempts—including, or possibly especially, those that have failed—to challenge dominant
modes and institutions, even where their visibility and publicness varies
across time and space.

Central to this discussion of the dynamics of visibility and invisibility is,
of course, the extent to which these are mediated by economic forces—
particularly, but not exclusively, those that pertain to cultural production.
Writing in 1961, Williams observed, "In the case of books, we already have a
good range of independent publishers, though the pressures on them to sur-
render independent policies are severe. A rapid process of amalgamation
(often retaining apparently independent imprints) is already under way, and
new kinds of owners, often little concerned with literature, are becoming
more common" (*LR* 390). Reams have been written on the dynamics of the
global literary market, its topographies, its vectors of power and domination,
and I do not wish to recount these arguments in detail here. Rather, it suffices
to note how, in the present-day situation with a saturated global literary
market dominated by the big five publishers—all of whom operate multiple
imprints with specific modes of branding and target audience—this process
of amalgamation seems all but complete.

Along with the consolidation of the publishing industry, moreover, has
appeared a concomitant constriction of the bookselling industry, characterized, for example, by the closure of independent bookshops, the rise of
Amazon, and, more recently, the 2019 acquisition of Foyles by high street
competitor Waterstones. While independent publishers remain active, their
future and potential for sustainability remains questionable. More broadly,
there is also a sense in which the labor of independent and small publishers,
particularly those located outside of the metropolitan centers of the global
literary market, is continually appropriated, assimilated, and obfuscated. To
illustrate this point, consider the example of Kwani Trust. A Nairobi-based
"literary NGO,"[19] Kwani Trust began from a series of meetings and discussions among writers, literary producers, and creatives based in Nairobi held
in 2002. Kate Wallis lucidly outlines the origins of Kwani Trust:

Self-defining as a "Kenyan based literary network," the organization evolved out of an expanding email conversation between a group of writers, artists, and those passionate about literature, moderated by filmmaker Wanjiru Kinyanjui, about why new writers weren't being published in Kenya (Kwani Trust, "About Us"). Out of these discussions, which moved to a series of physical conversations in Nairobi (many of which took place in the garden of *The East African* editor Ali Zaidi and sculptor Irene Wanjiru), came the idea to set up a new publishing house (Kwani Trust, "Our History"). This gained momentum in the immediate aftermath of Binyavanga Wainaina winning the UK-based Caine Prize for African Writing in 2002. By early the following year the literary journal *Kwani?* had been launched online with Wainaina as its first editor and a grant had been obtained from the US-based NGO Ford Foundation enabling the magazine to be published in print.[20]

As an entity, Kwani Trust was shaped by a series of complex relations, notably the extent to which its emergence was enabled by the end, in 2002, of the decades-long dictatorship of Daniel Arap Moi and the subsequent flourishing of creative expression and critical inquiry as key facets of public discourse; its entanglement in larger networks of NGO-driven North-South funding under the auspices of development, democracy, and leadership; and its relationship to the circulation of cultural and literary capital in the global literary market through association with metropolitan prize culture. To date, its activities have spanned publishing, including full-length fiction, a flagship journal, and short-form Kwanini booklets; open mic and live literature nights; workshops and mentorship; a biennial literary festival; and numerous collaborative projects with literary collectives from across the African continent.

In 2013, in honor of its tenth anniversary, the trust administered the Kwani Manuscript Project, a one-off prize for the most promising book-length, unpublished manuscript by an Africa-based author, with the publication of short-listed works by Kwani itself. The Kwani Manuscript Project provides an important and vivid illustration of the ways in which a locally conceived act of cultural production becomes enmeshed in global forces. Among the short-listed titles, two novels in particular have garnered significant critical acclaim in the global literary market: Ayọ̀bámi Adébáyọ̀'s *Stay with Me* and Jennifer Nansubuga Makumbi's *Kintu*. In both cases, however, each novel's success has operated largely through mechanisms, structures, and institutions located in the metropolitan centers of the American and British publishing industry, minimizing—and in some cases erasing—Kwani's own involvement in their development and editorial practices. *Stay with Me*, for instance, despite having been initially edited and revised under the auspices of the Manuscript Project and through the labor of its editorial team, was nonetheless first published in 2017 by Canongate in the United Kingdom and Penguin Random House in the United States. Though published in an

Africa edition by Kwani Trust later that year, the novel, which went on to join the short list of prestigious literary prizes including the (then) Baileys Women's Prize for Fiction, the Wellcome Book Prize, and the 9mobile Prize for Literature, has been marked by a general and critical reception that has continued to locate it based upon its earlier American and British editions, with few explicit mentions of its gestation or origins on the African continent. Instead, the novel has been incorporated into a larger narrative around the African literary renaissance, positioned as a characteristic exemplar of "new" Nigerian fiction (called, for instance, "a big-hearted Nigerian debut" by the *Guardian* and "a portrait of a Nigerian marriage in a heartbreaking debut novel" in the *New York Times*), packaged and circulated as an exotic artefact oriented toward a largely Euro-American marketplace and audience.[21]

Kintu, by contrast, was first published by Kwani Trust in 2014, becoming something of a cult sensation among a small readership, primarily located either on the African continent (particularly East Africa), due largely to the unavailability of the novel elsewhere, save a few select literary festivals, because of international rights and distribution difficulties. For a larger audience, however, *Kintu* only came into being in 2017 when it was published by the independent press Transit Books in the United States, with a subsequent British edition published in 2018 by Oneworld Publications. Unlike *Stay with Me*, the East African origins of the novel have been given more recognition, likely due to the gap between its original publication by Kwani and subsequent publication in the United States. At the same time, the critical acclaim that accompanied the novel's Transit Books edition, as well as its positioning as a new work, indicate something of the same mechanisms at play. The very fact of the novel's American publication is itself indicative of the asymmetrical distribution of cultural capital across literary fields, markets, and contexts, as well as their relative visibility. *Kintu* eventually found an American publisher due largely to the intervention of American blogger and critic, Aaron Bady, who had read the book after its Kenyan publication. It is no coincidence that prior to this, the novel had been rejected by numerous publishers in America and Britain, who complained that its lack of attention to the postcolonial period and its unapologetic centering of its story on a distinctively Ugandan (indeed, Bugandan) epistemic and cultural framework would make it unattractive to metropolitan markets. In both the cases of *Stay with Me* and *Kintu*, then, what comes to the fore is the extent to which each work's eventual absorption into a global literary market, with acclaim, renders less visible the more complex transnational, paranational, and regional ecologies of relation that mediated its appearance. The precise workings of these relations, which I have only described in outline here, function beyond any sort of tightly enclosed conception of an autonomous zone of cultural production or literary field, mediated by material, infrastructural, market, financial, and cultural elements.

Williams notes the ways in which the dominant institutions of culture create a paralysis so that attempts to shift their parameters can only become ever more entrenched in the already-existing hierarchy of domination:

> There is a continuing sense of deadlock, and much of the experience generated within it seems sterile. This is because the terms of mobility, thus conceived, are hopelessly limited. The combination of individual mobility with the stability of institutions and ways of thinking leads to this deadlock inevitably. And the experience of artists and intellectuals is then particularly misleading, for while such experience records particular local tensions, much of the real experience of mobility, in our own time, is that that of whole social groups moving into new ways of life: not only the individual rising, but the society changing. This latter experience is, however, very difficult to negotiate while the institutions towards which writers and thinkers are attracted retain their limited social reference, and while new groups have been relatively unsuccessful in creating their own cultural institutions. There is an obvious danger of the advantage of individual writers drawn from more varied social origins being limited or nullified by their absorption into pre-existing standard patterns (as obviously now in the pattern of higher education) or by their concentration on fighting these patterns, rather than finding or helping to create new patterns. (*LR* 284–85)

Inevitably, this fossilization of the institutional landscape is inseparable from larger changes in the conception of the individual and society, both of which, as Williams reminds us, remain "descriptions which embody particular interpretations of the experience to which they refer: interpretations which gained currency at a particular point in history, yet which have now virtually established themselves in our minds as absolutes" (*LR* 95). Under capitalism, our "version of society can only be the market, for its purpose is profit in particular activities rather than any general conception of social use, and its concentration of ownership in sections of the community makes most common decisions, beyond those of the market, limited or impossible," necessitating an apparent radical decoupling of the individual from society (in contrast to their actual interconnectedness) and leading to "the stupid comparison" of the two as adversarial and oppositional entities (*LR* 345, 343). In the sixty years since the time of Williams's writing, this situation has only accelerated, developing into a conception of the individual not even as consumer so much as an entrepreneur of the self under late capitalism, whose life is now solely understood through the logic of the market—which appears, at the time of this writing, in the midst of the COVID-19 pandemic, less and less stable and secure than ever before. Under these conditions, "the challenge to create new meanings and to substantiate them" appears more daunting than ever, with the interiorization, personalization, and individualization of everything (*LR* 350).

And yet, it is apparent that the larger relations through which the idea of African literature has emerged as part of a complicated, holistic, and internally variable ecology are far more complex than what is often obtained through extant models of understanding, themselves characterized by the quest to create new meanings, patterns, and forms. By returning to concepts such as structures of feeling, we begin to see a more complicated picture emerge in which social, political, and economic determinations have effaced the visibility of the larger networks of production through which the African literary ecology functions. In particular, this is an ecology in which the relations between the lived literary cultures that persist, albeit under pressure and often against great odds, on the African continent and those more visible, consecrated works published in the markets of the global North remain complex and changing. Apparent in this less visible work, exemplified in the operations of literary collectives such as Kwani Trust, is a mode of literary production that functions through varying models of collective labor, based on a commitment to avant-garde aesthetics, formal experimentation and the levelling of generic barriers toward a shared, radical vision of an Africa-centered internationalism that does not replicate the topographies of the global literary marketplace or world republic of letters.

Scrupulously committed to a remapping of the world through a systemic insistence on its utopian horizons—a remapping articulated within the literary works these collectives produce by their self-conscious positioning via editorial and paratextual material and through their own larger collaborative processes—this work is marked by its deliberate distancing from the market as locus of meaning making and valuation. At the same time, these collectives remained deeply entangled with the very institutions toward which they appear in opposition, whether through avenues of funding reliant on sponsorship and donor money from NGOs based in the global North or their relations with global African literature through the participation of individual celebrity writers in these collectives (for instance, Binyavanga Wainaina, founder of Kwani, won the Caine Prize; Adichie ran the Farafina Trust workshop, now the Purple Hibiscus workshop, for the Lagos-based literary collective of the same name; Jalada's most visible and widely circulated project to date is its Translation project, centered on a story by Ngũgĩ wa Thiong'o), reprinting arrangements that enable independent African presses to publish continental editions of globally circulating novels, or shared participation in workshops, festivals, and events. Recuperating these relations internal to the larger African literary ecology enables a reinvigoration of the way in which we receive the structures of feeling registered within global African literature. This, in turn, allows us to begin to perceive the ways in which different, and sometimes conflictual, structures of feeling bear their traces within the body of work that is more visible in the literary centers of the global North. That is, the submerged relations that connect global African literature with the wider literary ecologies with which they interact, including those centered on the African continent, begins to become apparent, enabling a mode of reading that goes against the grain of neoliberal appropriation and functions, at least to a certain degree, as a mode of critique.

In a novel such as Cole's *Open City*, for instance, reinvigorating the relations that obtain between the text and the author's own work as a literary activist, notably through Twitter and involvement in Nigeria-based publishing projects and literary initiatives, allows us to measure the critical distance between the text's narrative structure and its subtle critique of the discourses of late capitalism. With a work like Adichie's *Americanah*, moreover, making visible these wider relations might provide one way of foregrounding the text's submerged political commentary on structural adjustment and education in Nigeria, while considering Adichie's own role as facilitator of the Purple Hibiscus Writing Workshop, originally run cooperatively with Farafina Trust. In both cases, what comes to the fore are the ways in which each text can be seen to encode a distinct set of relations to the world market depending upon which of its wider relations are most visible in our reading practices. The positioning of a selection of texts as global African literature, then, says more about the interests of the dominant centers of the literary market that attempt to drive that act of selection than it does about the works themselves, which can be read against the grain as participating in something entirely different, if not entirely separate.

What a return to Williams might bring to world literary studies, then, is an approach that accounts for the full complexity of cultural production as it is lived and experienced, one that enables us to understand the mechanisms through which certain subsets of literature become more highly visible through their selection by a dominant tradition whose centers are elsewhere, while also allowing us to locate and identify the larger network of relations that span wider and sometimes multiple literary ecologies. Returning to the Aké festival example with which I began this essay, what a conception of culture and cultural studies inspired by Williams offers is a way of looking at such an event as a whole and as it really is, including those aspects that function through a seeming disjuncture: lines of relation and movement linking the students so eager in their attendance with the headlining celebrity writers capturing their attention, the small collectives and local literary clubs driving this labor, the politicians in attendance, corporate sponsors, and more. Only a view of African literature that can encompass all of these elements can attempt to engage with its fullness, as a cultural category. It is through the models of cultural study proposed and worked through in Williams's work that we can find tools for how to create it.

NOTES

1. Considerable work has been done in this area. See, for instance, the chapter "African Literature and the Anthropological Exotic" in Graham Huggan, *The Postcolonial Exotic: Marketing the Margins* (London: Routledge, 2001); or Sarah Brouillette, *Postcolonial Writers in the Global Literary Marketplace* (Basingstoke, UK: Palgrave Macmillan, 2007).

2. See, for instance, Doseline Kiguru, "Prizing African Literature: Creating a Literary Taste," *Social Dynamics* 42, no. 1 (2016): 161–74; Doseline Kiguru: "Literary Prizes, Writers' Organisations and Canon Formation in Africa," *African Studies* 75, no. 2 (2016): 202–14; Jarad Zimbler, Ben Etherington, and Rachel Bower, "Crafts of World Literature: Field, Material and Translation," *The Journal of Commonwealth Literature* 49, no. 3 (2014): 273–78; Kate Wallis, "Exchanges in Nairobi and Lagos: Mapping Literary Networks and World Literary Space," *Research in African Literatures* 49, no. 1 (2018): 163–86.

3. Pierre Bourdieu, *The Field of Cultural Production* (Cambridge, UK: Polity Press, 1993), 30.

4. Pascale Casanova, *The World Republic of Letters* (Cambridge, MA: Harvard University Press, 2004), 83.

5. Ibid., 90.

6. John C. Hawley, "Biafra as Heritage and Symbol: Adichie, Mbachu, and Iweala," *Research in African Literatures* 39, no. 2 (2008): 20.

7. Doreen Strauhs, *African Literary NGOs: Power, Politics, and Participation* (Basingstoke, UK: Palgrave Macmillan, 2013), 104.

8. See Madhu Krishnan, *Contingent Canons: African Literature and the Politics of Location* (Cambridge: Cambridge University Press), 52–58.

9. In the case of *Behold the Dreamers*, a novel that follows the fortunes of the Jonga family as they become entangled with the upper-class Edwards in New York City, the narrative climax occurs when patriarch Jende loses his job as a driver for Lehman Brothers executive Clark Edwards following the 2008 financial crash. While it is possible to read this as an example of a deliberate engagement with external structures, the novel nonetheless remains centered on the individual dynamics of the Jonga family with little development of broader interpersonal or social relations.

10. Lester K. Spence, *Knocking the Hustle: Against the Neoliberal Turn in Black Politics* (New York: Punctum Books, 2015).

11. It is important to note that for Neil Smith, jumping scales is viewed as a strategy deployed by activist groups such that they are able "to dissolve spatial boundaries that are largely imposed from above and that contain rather than facilitate their production and reproduction of everyday life." In these novels, however, jumping scales offers no such radical potential, instead effacing the deep structures of political and economic relation between discrete locations. See Neil Smith, "Homeless/Global: Scaling places," in *Mapping the Futures: Local Cultures, Global Change*, ed. John Bird, Barry Curtis, Tim Putnam, and Lisa Tickner (London: Routledge, 1993), 90.

12. See "A Global Sense of Place," in Doreen Massey, *Space, Place and Gender* (Cambridge, UK: Polity Press, 1994).

13. Zygmunt Bauman, *Liquid Modernity* (Cambridge, UK: Polity Press, 2000); Mitchum Huehls and Rachel Greenwald Smith, "Four Phases of Neoliberalism and Literature: An Introduction," in *Neoliberalism and Contemporary Literary Culture*, ed. by Mitchum Huehls and Rachel Greenwald Smith (Baltimore: Johns Hopkins University Press, 2017), 3.

14. See, for instance, Pádraig Carmody, *The New Scramble for Africa*, 2nd ed. (Cambridge, UK: Polity Press, 2016).

15. Akin Adesokan, "New African Writing and the Question of Audience," *Research in African Literatures* 43, no. 3 (2012): 16.

16. Sarah Brouillette, "On the African Literary Hustle," *Blindfield Journal*, August 14, 2017, accessed May 31, 2020, https://blindfieldjournal.com/2017/08/14/on-the-african-literary-hustle/.

17. I use the term "formations" following Williams's definition and history outlined in chapter 3 of *The Sociology of Culture* (*SC* 57–86).

18. Moradewun Adejunmobi, "African Writing and the Forms of Publicness," keynote lecture at the Small Magazines, Literary Networks and Self-Fashioning in Africa and its Diasporas conference, January 19, 2018, Bristol, United Kingdom.

19. The phrase comes from Strauhs's *African Literary NGOs*.

20. Wallis, "Exchanges in Nairobi and Lagos," 166.

21. These are the titles, respectively, of reviews by Diana Evans and Michiko Kakutani. See Diana Evans, "Stay with Me by Ayọ̀bámi Adébáyọ̀ Review—a Big-Hearted Nigerian Debut," *The Guardian*, March 9, 2017, https://www.theguardian.com/books/2017/mar/09/stay-with-me-by-ayobami-adebayo-review; and Michiko Kakutani, "Portrait of a Nigerian Marriage in a Heartbreaking Debut Novel," *New York Times*. July 24, 2017, https://www.nytimes.com/2017/07/24/books/review-ayobami-adebayo-stay-with-me.html.

Chapter Eight

Television and Other Popular Media from the 1960s to Now

Daniel Worden

In Raymond Williams's *Keywords*, the entries for "communication" and "media" both undergo transformations emblematic of capitalism's historical arc. "Communication," in Williams's etymological account, shifts from describing an "object thus made common" in the fifteenth century, to "the abstract general term for [the] physical facilities" of "roads, canals, and railways" in the seventeenth century (*K* 72). In the twentieth century, he writes, "communication" develops further "to refer to such media as the press and broadcasting" (*K* 72). The term "communication" morphs from a "noun of action" that describes "making common," through a period in which it referred to material infrastructures, the physical "lines of communication" established by roads and routes, to signifying "information and ideas" (*K* 72). This transition moves from what we might think of as a feudal understanding of the term, with its focus on the commons, to a capitalist sense of communication as both a material and immaterial object that can be captured as monetary value. The concept of communication "melts into air," to use a phrase familiar in Marxist theory, as the "commons" transforms into commodities such as transmission cables and information.[1]

A term similar in scope to "communication," "media" is first a process-oriented concept, "an intervening or intermediate agency or substance" (*K* 203). Dating from the eighteenth century, "media" comes to describe particular print forms like the newspaper, and later "the specialized capitalist sense in which a newspaper or broadcasting service—something that already exists or can be planned—is seen as a medium for something else, such as advertising" (*K* 203). Media, in Williams's account, initially refers to a concept, but then is tethered to the economic concerns of advertising and audience. In other words, media moves from a generalized intermediary to a specifically monetized conception of circulation. Similar to, but even more so than "communication," "media" involves us in the market-based logic not just of commodity culture but corporatization as well. On the surface, the trajectories of "communication" and "media" seem intuitive—even obvious. Yet, as made apparent in Williams's work on cultural forms, the imbrication of the terms "communication" and "media" in economic conditions is central both to a materialist critique of culture and to the political possibility of equitable cultural institutions. The different etymologies, connotations, and referents of "communication," and "media" are drawn out in Williams's *Keywords*, creating a web of connections and associations whose complexity Williams tied to socialism. In *Politics and Letters*, Williams remarks that "the break towards socialism can only be towards an unimaginably greater complexity," an increasing complexity that Williams documents in volumes like *Keywords*, and that can be seen in the terms "communication" and "media," each of which connotes overlapping structures and practices (*PL* 129). Tracing the complex imbrications of communication and media in capitalist modes of production and networks of information is, then, one way of producing a socialist analysis of culture.

Today, the concept of media is often accompanied by the concept of the platform, which expands monetary exchange through not just television broadcasting and its transmission of advertising, but also through daily interactions mediated by apps and interfaces. As Marc Steinberg argues, the emergence of platforms as a way of structuring activity transforms mediated economic transactions into a nearly unavoidable fact of everyday life. For if the platform is "an intermediary that facilitates third-party transactions," then platforms ranging from "Uber to Amazon to YouTube" have made media not only entertainment, but also integral to even basic economic activities like grocery shopping and commuting.[2] Just as "media" differs from "communication" in Williams's *Keywords*, our contemporary term "platform" differs from its predecessor "network," a term often used to describe digital media as well. As Steinberg notes, "platform" and "network" differ in a key way that resembles closely the difference between "media," with its inclusion of advertising and corporate structure, and "communication," with emphasis on the commons: "Unlike the earlier keyword *network*, which offered a sense of openness, freedom, and rhizomatic extensivity that preempts efforts to control the network, the platform concept is generally applied to the definitive closure of the network, the reigning in of a moment of perceived freedom that the open web was to offer."[3] Just as the shifts in "communication" and "media" entail the normalization of monetization and commodification, the shift in terminology from "network" to "platform" connotes the restructuring of virtual public space by monetized formats.

Given its etymological roots in the commons and egalitarian information exchange, it is no surprise that the term "communication" would be so central to Williams's work on media forms—from newspapers and novels, to cinema and television. As Williams states in *Communications*, his "emphasis on communications asserts, as a matter of experience, that men and societies are not confined to relationships of power, property, and production" (*C* 18). Media becomes instrumentalized by capitalism, and indeed its related term, "mediation," raises for Williams "inevitable and important difficulties" about whether form can resist or challenge ideology. "Communication" is both etymologically grounded in the notion of the commons and emblematic of how capitalism has remade the world and our own thinking about it, through the reworking of residual concepts such as the commons into functional concepts within a capitalist system. While media pushes us into thorny debates about ideology and the possibility of an "outside" to capitalist totality, communication leaves us with a commitment to communal life and an awareness of how ideas connect to material realities.

This distinction between "media" and "communication" also maps onto the late twentieth- and early twenty-first-century history of cultural studies, insofar as work under the heading of "media studies" tends to connote content-focused or formal analysis, while research under the heading of "communication" connotes quantitative analysis, especially in the context of the United States academy. While, for example, Fredric Jameson's cultural Marxism or Laura Mulvey's psychoanalytic formalism might neglect the quantitative analysis of elements like circulation, audience reception, corporate ownership, and regulatory frameworks of media forms, they nonetheless resemble Williams's account of communication as a cultural force that is historically grounded in not just institutions, but also infrastructures.[4] When Jameson and Mulvey investigate forms like Hollywood cinema through the totalizing frameworks of late capitalism or patriarchy, these totalities connote material conditions even if they are broader and less grounded in institutional specifics than Williams's accounts of, for example, the workings of the BBC or the British press. It is this historical materialism that makes Williams's work all the more relevant today, as a method for understanding disparate cultural artifacts in relation to the structures that make them available to us. As Williams phrased it in "Base and Superstructure in Marxist Cultural Theory," "What we are actively seeking is the true practice which has been alienated to an object, and the true conditions of practice—whether as literary conventions or as social relationships—which have been alienated to components or mere background" (*CM* 49). The dual emphasis here on "practice" and "conditions of practice" pushes us to understand not just a particular object as one instance of a broader social field, but also the social field itself as structured by material forces that inflect or even determine cultural activity. The overlapping keywords we use to describe cultural systems—"communication," "media," "network," "platform"—alert us to the complexities of grounding cultural analysis in material conditions, as the language we use to describe these systems has been inflected by them already.

Williams's dialectical and historically attentive framework for analyzing popular media as an aesthetic, economic, and technological structure is evident in postmodern accounts of media that found in DIY and, later, digital technologies, modes of resistance and subversion. Indeed, in *Communications*, Williams makes a case for the broader public ownership and management of television, envisioning a cultural institution "with a real sense of responsibility and with as many people as possible taking part" (*C* 161). First published in 1962, *Communications* coincides with the increase of DIY possibility that would come with technological change in the late twentieth and early twenty-first centuries. In it, Williams advocates for individual expression via an understanding of media forms and, crucially, public and democratic participation in the management of new media institutions. In a particularly interesting section about education, a topic central to Williams's work both in adult learning environments and the more traditional Oxbridge academic system, Williams outlines how television and other popular media forms should be taught. This instruction should include not only "their history and current social organization," but also "the ways in which they actually work" (*C* 132). By introducing students to the nature of these media forms, he argues, the public could learn about the "tension between the glamour and the reality" of the cultural industries (*C* 133). Williams's vision here of a widespread demystification of media would not only transform viewers' understanding of what they view on a television screen and how it came to be, but would also give viewers the tools to become producers themselves. Indeed, the diversification of broadcasting platforms was becoming technologically and economically possible when Williams was writing about television, possibilities that have increased dramatically in our time.

Despite this prescience about DIY possibilities that would increase with digital technologies, Williams, nevertheless, analyzed a moment in television history that has now passed. While state-funded networks like the BBC and PBS continue to broadcast, first cable television and now streaming services have transformed what Williams thought of as a truly popular medium into a vast landscape of consumer options, with specialty cable channels and platforms that cater to particular niche interests. Yet, as Williams points out in *Communications*, historical materialism entails not just a sober accounting of how the ownership of cultural institutions is consolidated, but also an awareness that these historical processes were never inevitable: "It is difficult to see that things might have been otherwise, can still be otherwise" (*C* 33).

As the moment of broadcasting and mass media has given way to cable television and streaming platforms, it seems unclear what the possibilities for alternatives to popular image cultures are, when multinational media corporations focus less on broadcast audiences than on niche markets and "influencers." The field is far more fragmented now than when the addition of a single new television channel, like BBC 2 in 1964, seemed to open up political possibilities for socialist politics. Indeed, while the Internet was the occasion for the celebration of a new digital commons in earlier decades, the rise of the "platform economy" or "platform capitalism," in which the Internet is cordoned off through apps and mobile devices into monetized information flows, makes much of that thinking seem quaint, if not downright naïve.[5] As capitalism has intensified the commodification of data, it seems as if media itself is at the center of capitalist organization, rather than a mere mechanism for its advertisement. This shift began to occur in the 1980s, after William's work on television, as technology companies realized that "the future . . . lay not in hardware per se but rather in the Microsoft model of selling software, or cultural contents."[6] McKenzie Wark, for example, has taken this trajectory as an occasion to declare that we are in a new era beyond capitalism: "This is not capitalism anymore; it is something worse. The dominant ruling class of our time no longer maintains its rule through the ownership of the means of production as capitalists do. Nor through the ownership of land as landlords do. The dominant ruling class of our time owns and controls information."[7] This shift means, for Wark, that our critical framework needs an overhaul, to understand and critique these economic structures that push beyond the terms developed in Marxism to analyze capitalism. Yet, as much of Williams's work reminds us, emergent technologies and modes of production do not wholly replace previous modes of social organization. The "necessary complexity" that Williams links to his contemporary historical moment and to any truly socialist future is flattened out by claims of a postcapitalist, technological transition (*PL* 437).[8] Indeed, it is apparent that the processes tethered to the sense of postcapitalist technological possibility, such as automation, are not new but, instead, persistent features of capitalist production.[9] The data and information flows that are often taken as emblematic of a structural shift by thinkers like Wark still require hardware to be visible. Transmission cables and factory-assembled commodities, along with all of the capital infrastructure that contributes to their functioning, remains necessary for "immaterial labor" to even be possible. Perhaps the most important lesson to be learned from Williams, then, is that historical materialism should be both attentive to the complex entanglements of residual, persistent, and emergent structures, while also being wary of claims that posit an abrupt transition from one economic regime to another, thus dismissing the persistence of exploitative structures across modes of production.

Indeed, the emergence of "platform capitalism," whether conceived as a mere extension of capitalist modes of production or as a more substantial shift that rewrites the terms of accumulation and exploitation, entails precisely the kind of analytical work that Williams undertook to understand the transition to modernity in his famed books *The Country and the City* and *The Long Revolution*. Historical analysis informs our understanding of the present as an unfolding struggle, and Williams's work provides a method and example of how to do cultural theory in a historical materialist mode that can recognize both limits and possibilities:

> I find increasingly that the values and meanings I need are all in the process of change. If it is pointed out, in traditional terms, that democracy, industry, and extended communication are all means rather than ends, I reply that this, precisely, is their revolutionary character, and that to realise and accept this requires new ways of thinking and feeling, new conceptions of relationships, which we must try to explore. (*LR* 14)

This attunement to possibility, though, coexists with a recognition that "the intensity with which the old patterns have been learned is itself a barrier to the communication of new patterns" (*LR* 400). With this in mind, it is clear how Wark's focus on the transformations occasioned by technology obscures the persistence of the "old economy" amidst the new. A factory job in the logistics industry is not necessarily an abrupt shift from a factory job in the manufacturing industry, but an adjustment in the technological apparatus in which human labor operates.

This change in technological apparatus has forced some—on both the left and right—to imagine that automation would give us a world without work, in which a "Universal Basic Income" could provide a baseline of human welfare. Automation and an accompanying "Universal Basic Income" would render labor itself a matter of choice rather than a matter of necessity, yet this remains a distant possibility given the realities of our "gig" economy. As Aaron Benanav has demonstrated, theories of automation and Universal Basic Income are structured around utopian thinking, often explicitly modelled on science fiction ideas like *Star Trek: The Next Generation*'s "replicator," a robust 3-d printer technology that "brings about the end of economic scarcity," and those utopian visions occlude the ways in which contemporary labor struggles have been produced not by automation—the replacement of workers by technology—but instead by overproduction, which has led to underemployment and the growth of contingent, underpaid jobs in the service sector.[10] Indeed, as Lane Relyea has argued, the apparently subversive politics of the DIY aesthetic mesh with the flexible labor structures touted by the "gig economy" and finance capitalism:

> DIY serves as the honorific term for the kind of subject required by the constant just-in-time turmoil of our networked world. It has come to stand for a potent mix of entrepreneurial agency and networked sociality, proclaiming itself heir to both punk autonomy, the notion of living by your wits as an

outsider, and to a subcultural basis for authentic artistic production, the assumption that truly creative individuals exist in spontaneously formed social undergrounds.[11]

This "shift from production to project" reworks what it means not just to labor, but also to participate in a society organized around corporate platforms.[12] A discreet television program is the product of many laborers working within the language of this entrepreneurial system, even if their gig economy backers are multinational corporations, but also one instance of data within a monetized media system, wherein the content of any one television show is largely irrelevant. It is this double focus that Williams equips us to have, through his attention to the material conditions as well as the cultural projections of media.

Williams's method remains vital, then, even if the technological landscape he was writing about has shifted substantially. In the 1960s, Williams was critical of how advertising amounted to "an intrinsic setting of priorities" for television around commercial interests (*TV* 66). Today, advertising has become both more complex and more streamlined as platforms such as Facebook and Netflix target advertisements to individual consumers. In the case of the Netflix series *House of Cards*, one of the first original television series that Netflix produced outright, Michael D. Smith and Rahul Telang have outlined how the platform created trailers for the series that catered to different viewers' preferences:

> Customer data, and the ability to personalize the Netflix experience for its subscribers also gave Netflix new options to promote its shows. . . . It could see what each subscriber had viewed, when, how long, and on what device, and could target individual subscribers on the basis of their actual viewing habits. Netflix even created multiple "trailers" for the show. One featured Kevin Spacey (for subscribers who had liked Spacey's movies); another featured the show's female characters (for subscribers who liked movies with strong female leads); yet another focused on the cinematic nuances of the show (for subscribers who had liked [director David] Fincher's movies).[13]

This individualized form of advertising is, on the one hand, more complex than the broadcast advertising that Williams wrote about, reflective of new media platforms and neoliberal capitalism in its focus on individuals and niche demographics rather than the older notion of the "masses" or the "public." Yet, on the other hand, it is also simpler in its relation to consumer culture. Netflix advertises itself on its own platform, in an attempt to persuade subscribers to keep watching. It is a closed system, wanting consumers to keep consuming the very thing they are already consuming. Even by merely describing the shape of advertising on Netflix here, per Williams's methodology, the "intrinsic priority" of the streaming platform becomes apparent.

Indeed, one of the ideas that surfaces in Williams's writings about popular media forms like television and newspapers is that the content of any particular line of communication can only be understood if that content is analyzed in relation to its material structures. That is, the advertisements in a newspaper are equally important as its news items, and the types of programming available on television are as relevant to an understanding of its role in society as the ownership of the broadcasters. Williams's approach has been generative in the way it synthesizes production, circulation, audience reception, and experimentation. Indeed, Williams encouraged us to consider the unique serial nature of television, so as to avoid conflating a media form like television with older forms like film: "To break this experience [of watching television] back into units, and to write about the units for which there are readily available procedures, is understandable but often misleading, even when we defend it by the gesture that we are discriminating and experienced viewers who don't just sit there hour after hour goggling at the box" (*TV* 96). In the spirit of this critical imperative to treat television in terms of its own medium, Linda Williams's book-length analysis of the HBO television show *The Wire* emphasizes how the television show's serial form and its refusal to provide any particular character with a redemptive narrative arc result in a new kind of melodrama:

> [*The Wire*] does not betray its principles by granting a happy ending to a particular individual. Most important to the new type of melodrama that *The Wire* forges are the opportunities offered by the serial's multiplication of worlds and their interaction over time. The sensibility of both "world and time" is what cannot be achieved even in a long movie, for it only happens with repetition over time, when the rhythm of certain situations is felt again and again.[14]

The Wire, in Williams's account, uses the form of melodrama to evoke the emotional range of life in postindustrial Baltimore, and other television forms prominent in the same period also relay similar "structures of feeling."

The Wire is one among many prestige television dramas, many associated with HBO but increasingly produced by other cable channels and streaming services as well. It has been commonplace to place these shows, including *The Wire*, as well as others like *Breaking Bad*, *The Good Wife*, *Mad Men*, *The Marvelous Mrs. Maisel*, and *The Sopranos*, in the tradition of the novel. Just as Charles Dickens once articulated the world of nineteenth-century Britain, so now does prestige drama feed us stylized versions of our own realities. Yet, this analogy may conceal more than it reveals about media in our contemporary moment.[15] While a show like *The Wire* offers a long-form, multifaceted exploration of social systems, from life in public housing to work at a struggling newspaper, an unmistakable component of its appeal is its specificity. The particular contours of Baltimore, from its neighborhoods to its accents and food, shape the show, and those details give viewers access to a place that they otherwise may never have. This situatedness allows for a dialectical movement from the site specificity of Baltimore to the structural totality of the postindustrial United States. Baltimore becomes emblematic of a larger reality in which the viewers of *The Wire* also exist, even if they experience the show as voyeurs, peering in to the imagined lives of others. That is typically what the "television-as-realist-novel" argument hinges upon, and it is understandable why viewers of *The Wire* would find such a structure compelling. Indeed, it is a hallmark of realist narrative within capitalism, a televisual adaptation of what Williams identified in Dickens's novels.

After quoting a passage from *Dombey and Son*, Williams distills the moral imperative of the novel: "That potent and benignant hand, which takes off housetops and shows the shapes and phantoms which arise from neglect and indifference; which clears the air so that people can see and acknowledge each other, overcoming that contraction of sympathy which is against nature; that hand is the hand of the novelist; it is Dickens seeing himself" (*CC* 156).[16] Extending this reading to *The Wire*'s use of surveillance, the "potent and benignant hand" has been replaced by a more complicated sense of the medium's morality and even politics. While Dickens's writing, in Williams's reading above, is ultimately about Dickens's moral vision, *The Wire* expresses not a singular authorial perspective, but the collaborative and inherently commodified structure of television production. It then is also imperative to consider the means by which *The Wire* is produced and viewed—through a paid subscription cable network and, now, streaming service.

If part of *The Wire*'s appeal is its representation of Baltimore as a social totality, with something like a series of nested communities that, in keeping with gangster films, connote older modes of social organization like the village, the clan, or the trade union (represented in *The Wire* through the Baltimore projects, the drug organization, the police, public school teachers, dockworkers, and newspaper reporters), then that nostalgia for social organization is made all the more distant from our reality by the privatized nature of the television show's broadcasting structure. Indeed, the layers of privatization that lead to *The Wire* being viewed on a home television penetrate much deeper into social organization than the print culture that allowed for the flourishing of the realist novel. This is perhaps most evident in *The Wire*'s metatextual references. The world of *The Wire* does not often invoke television as a fundamental arbiter of its social world, yet it is constructed around the idea of police surveillance. While the realist novel is bound up in print culture both at the formal and the content levels, with its steady invocations of letter writing, diary entries, publishing houses, newspaper coverage, and even novels themselves as benchmarks of the social reality the form is contributing to, *The Wire* is concerned not with public communications but with spying on private communications. That is, the voyeuristic pleasure afforded by reading a private letter in an epistolary novel is compounded in *The Wire* as a plot device, rendering the erosion of private communication not only a formal issue of storytelling but also a priority of our social system's power structure. *The Wire* is a work in privatized television about the erosion of privacy in late capitalism, and its prescient theme of wiretapping resonates with the surveillance and monitoring, of our own behaviors as viewers, ubiquitous to any television streaming service today. When Williams considers how "in the modern trend towards limited ownership [of communications firms], the cultural conditions of democracy are in fact being denied: sometimes, ironically, in the name of freedom," the implication for a reading of *The Wire* bears on the moral politics of realism (*C* 33). As noted earlier, if the promise of Dickensian realism is that through a voyeuristic journey into the lives of the poor, the reader gains sympathy for their suffering, then *The Wire*'s promise of moral redemption—that in viewing *The Wire*, its viewers gain a heightened moral sensibility—is central to its critical acclaim. The self-righteousness of *The Wire*'s viewers was so common that it was parodied when the blog *Stuff White People Like* noted in 2008, "For the past three years, whenever you say 'The Wire,' white people are required to respond by saying 'it's the best show on television.' Try it next time you see a white person!"[17] The moral promise of *The Wire* results in enthusiastic fandom and pretenses of "insider" knowledge about how the criminal class operates, sentiments that are notably unrelated to the real streets of Baltimore to which the television show is supposed to grant proximity.

An iconic scene in *The Wire* stages the show's social realism as aspirational, seeking a vision of liberal equality that is undercut by the material conditions in which the show's characters live. In the opening scene of the fourth season, a female criminal enforcer named Snoop walks the aisles of a hardware store, carrying a used nail gun. Snoop stops to look at other nail guns, and then talks with a hardware store clerk:

Clerk: Ah, I see you got the DeWalt cordless. Your nail gun—DeWalt 410.

Snoop: Yeah. The trouble is, you leave it in a truck for a while, need to step up and use the bitch, the battery don't hold up, you know?

Clerk: Yeah, cordless'll do that. You might want to consider the powder-actuated tool. The Hilti DX 460 MX or the Simpson PTP—these two are my Cadillacs. Everything else on this board is second-best, sorry to say. Are you contracting, or just doing some work around the house?

Snoop: No, we work all over.

Clerk: Full time?

Snoop: No, we had about five jobs last month.

Clerk: Ah. With that rate, the cost of the powder-actuated guns justifies itself.

Snoop: You say "power"?

Clerk: Powder.

Snoop: Like gunpowder?

Clerk: Yeah. The DX 460 is fully automatic, with a.27-caliber charge. Wood, concrete, steel to steel—she'll throw a fastener into anything. And for my money, she handles recoil better than the Simpson or the P3500. Now, you understand what I mean by recoil?

Snoop: Yeah, the kickback. I'm with you.

Clerk: That's right.

Snoop: .27 caliber, huh?

Clerk: Yeah, not large ballistically, but for driving nails, it's enough. Any more than that, you'd add to the recoil.

Snoop: Man, shit. I seen a tiny-ass .22 round-nose drop a nigga plenty of days, man. Motherfuckers get up in you like a pinball, rip your ass up. Big joints, though—big joints, man, just break your bones, you say, "Fuck it." I'm gonna go with this right here, man. How much I owe you?

Clerk: $669 plus tax. [Snoop counts and hands the clerk money.] No no, you just pay at the register.

Snoop: Nah, man, you go ahead and handle that for me, man. And keep the rest for your time.

Clerk: This is 800 dollars.

Snoop: You earned that buck like a motherfucker. Keep that shit. [18]

In this exchange, Snoop and the clerk speak as knowledgeable, experienced laborers, though the kind of labor they perform is obviously different. As the season moves forward, Snoop and her colleague Chris kill people at the bidding of drug dealer Marlo Stanfield, and they use the nail gun to board dead bodies up into abandoned Baltimore houses. While Snoop's sense of a "job" differs from the clerk's, they nonetheless have a moment of clear exchange, so much so that Snoop tips the clerk, who "earned that buck like a motherfucker." In a television show that is focused on failing institutions— the police, public housing, labor unions, public schools, newspapers—this scene presents us with a comforting interaction, even if Snoop is buying a nail gun for criminal activity.

This moment of parity, though, happens in the "Hardware Barn." The ultimately transactional relationship between Snoop and the clerk, as well as Snoop's role as a "contractor" for a drug dealer rather than a construction firm, undercuts the working-class connection between the two characters, even as the scene itself displays that connection as an unrealized possibility. The service worker and the criminal enforcer operate with complementary appreciations of craft. Yet, as Snoop's payment in $100 bills directly to the clerk demonstrates, the criminal economy in which Snoop operates can be glimpsed by those in "normal" society only in fleeting, consumer transactions. The clerk's confusion, as Snoop walks away with a new nail gun, both acknowledges social complexity—Snoop represents an alternate mode of capitalist organization than that of "normal" consumer society—and serves as an identification point for the viewers of *The Wire*, tuning in to the beginning of the series' fourth season, to peer into a part of society to which they largely do not have access. [19]

The place where Snoop experiences something like wider social belonging in the working class is also a place of individual consumption. Through the hardware store scene, the viewer is asked to both appreciate the pleasantries of Snoop and the clerk's conversation, and also experience a jolt of nihilistic pleasure as Snoop leaves the store and gets into a car, telling her accomplice Chris that the clerk "said if you want to shoot nails, this here is the Cadillac, man. He mean Lexus, but he ain't know it . . . . This here is gunpowder-activated, .27 caliber, full auto, no kickback, nail-throwing mayhem, man. Shit right here is tight. Fuck just nailing up boards. We could kill a couple motherfuckers with this right here. You laughing. I've been schooled, dog. I'm trying to tell you." [20] The Hardware Barn scene provides a glimpse of communication across economic and racial difference that is often figured in the series as a worthy aspiration. In *The Wire*, the viewer gets to both view a criminal underclass from a distance, like the hardware store clerk, and experience being an "insider," as the scene transitions from the hardware store to the parked car, thus leading the viewer from a familiar place to life "way down in the hole," as *The Wire*'s theme song emphasizes.[21]

The Wire's dramatization of social belonging as individual consumption, infused with egalitarian aspirations and extralegal labor, is both a part of its social realism and a distinctive tension in the medium of television itself. In *Television*, Williams positions the form as a uniquely individualized one, characterized contradictorily as a type of "mass communication" even as television technologies "were developed for transmission to *individual* homes" (*TV* 17). The ability of broadcasting to communicate directly into the private home gave the medium of television unprecedented possibility and power in the late twentieth century, and now it is hard to imagine everyday life without television and its extensions into digital platforms. Reality television routinely invokes television as a structuring principle, through tropes like the confessional booth, the isolation chamber, and the contest, all of which serve as signposts for the constructedness of the reality experience.[22] Yet, in an environment where, as Williams remarked in *Television*, "most people spend more time watching various kinds of drama than in preparing and eating food," the trappings of television reality connote less a disruption of an otherwise seamless façade and more the structuring of everyday life through televisual conceits. This kind of general theoretical leap is warranted in Williams's analysis, as television in its fully monetized and privatized form comes to be a way for capitalist logic to penetrate the individual home, bypassing any community structures that might offer alternatives. Indeed, in his discussion of news programs in *Television*, Williams summarizes the determining relationship that the privatization of television creates: "To see international news brought by courtesy of a toothpaste is not to see separable elements, but the shape of a dominant cultural form" (*TV* 66). *The Wire*, that is to say, is a critique of contemporary capitalism facilitated by the structures of contemporary capitalism.

For all of his awareness of capitalism's control over television, Williams nonetheless held out hope that television could serve as a progressive line of communication. In the 1979 documentary program *The Country and the City*, based on Williams's 1973 book of the same name, Williams offers his account of the morphing meanings and economics of the British country estate in a television format. Directed by Michael Dibb, who also directed the 1972 *Ways of Seeing* programs featuring John Berger, the television special engages in visual juxtapositions that seek to make use of the visual capacities of the medium in a unique way. Williams remarked, in *Television*, that although much of what is on television merely recycles older forms, there remains something uniquely possible within the medium:

> There are moments in many kinds of programme when we can find ourselves looking in what seem quite new ways. To get this kind of attention it is often necessary to turn off the sound, which is usually directing us to prepared transmissible content or other kinds of response. What can then happen, in some surprising ways, is an experience of visual mobility, of contrast of angle, of variation of focus, which is often very beautiful. (*TV* 75)

In *The Country and the City* program, this kind of visual beauty is not merely aesthetic, but purposefully illustrative of Williams's argument about the interconnectedness of Romantic fantasy and industrialization. That is, the increasing division of the country and the city, accompanied by aestheticized representations of country life as perpetually pre-industrial, both masks and inflects the industrialization of urban and rural space.

In the television show, during a segment wherein Williams discusses the "different and selective ways" that literature addressed changes to rural life, he describes William Wordsworth's "embrace of nature."[23] A sequence of nature scenes unfold as Wordsworth's "Lines Composed a Few Miles above Tintern Abbey" is read. The program then transitions to the tourist attraction of Wordsworth's cottage, reinforcing the way in which the poet's Romantic vision of nature has become "very general" among the public (see figure 1). The tourist attraction, with its visible signage and crowd of backpacked visitors, is in stark contrast to the vision of nature connoted by the poetry. While this juxtaposition in and of itself reinforces Williams's argument about how the Romantic vision of nature coextends with the process of industrialization, it is further reinforced later in the program. As a passage from Dickens's *Hard Times* is read describing the polluted, industrialized Coketown, a shot of large factory equipment pans downward. The piece of factory equipment has "Taylor, Wordsworth & Co. Linseeds" stamped on it (see figure 2). While this repetition of the name "Wordsworth" is not commented upon in the program's narration, it nonetheless visually recalls the Romantic poet discussed in the program ten minutes previously. An intentionally framed coincidence, then—the Romantic poet Wordsworth's conception of nature and the industrial manufacturing that would extract commodities from nature—provides a conceptual linkage between nature and culture, reinforcing and even elaborating on Williams's argument in *The Country and the City*.

Wordsworth's doubled appearance in *The Country and the City* program as both industrial reality and Romantic poetry recalls Snoop's nail gun purchase discussed earlier. In both of these instances, material conditions (industry and organized crime in *The Country and the City* and *The Wire*, respectively) are juxtaposed with visions of the natural world (Wordsworth's poetry) and communal belonging (Snoop's conversation with the Hardware Barn clerk). Both television shows present this tension as structuring our relationships and feelings within capitalism. The complex contradictions embedded

Figure 8.1.   Wordsworth as poetic tourism in *The Country and the City*, directed by Michael Dibb, 1979.

within our inclinations, our desires for fellow feeling, and our despondency at irreparably broken and exploitative structures are made manifest on the screen—not to be flattened out by a simplified argument or solution, but to stand unresolved.

While Williams found in television some possibilities for opening up new ways of thinking, his materialist analysis kept those utopian impulses in check, mitigating the possibilities of the new medium with the realities of its implementation and the often reactionary quality of its content. Less interested in technological utopias than his media studies contemporary Marshall McLuhan, who found in new media a power that is "separate from their uses,"[24] Williams posits that technological determinism disregards history in general: "For if the medium—whether print or television—is the cause, all other causes, all that men ordinarily see as history, are at once reduced to effects" (*TV* 130). Contrary to McLuhan's formalism, Williams occupies something of a pragmatic space, attuned to the possibilities of emergent technologies but also cognizant of how social organization and advocacy within the state is needed to steer cultural formations toward radical democracy, rather than corporate control.

Figure 8.2.   Wordsworth as industrial machinery in *The Country and the City*, directed by Michael Dibb, 1979.

Today, television entertainment provided via online streaming services is just one form delivered to individual viewers through Internet media. As Wendy Hui Kyong Chun argues, the blending of news media with entertainment, advertising, and political opinion, all tailored to an individual's browsing histories is central to how digital culture has become habitual to us: "This combination of gossip with politics is not an unfortunate aspect of new media and digital culture, but the point. New media blur these distinctions because they are part of the postindustrial/neoliberal economy."[25] As is evident in Williams's writings about the force of advertising on television and the threat, to democratic governance of television, posed by privatized, corporate control, this blurring is an extension of, and the triumph of, the privatization of television broadcasting. Yet how streaming and digital media organize subjects is notably different from the way television allowed broadcasters to conceive of their publics: "If mass media produced consistent forms to create a consistent, coherent audiences, new media thrive on differences to create predictable individuals."[26] While other Marxist frameworks stemming from Adorno or Althusser might take this as an occasion for negative dialectics or ideology critique, Williams cautions us to find ways to work for equality within our compromised conditions. As he said in *Politics and Letters*, the closures and failures that unfold within the Marxist project are not definitive: "Once you have decided for revolutionary socialism, not because it is quicker or more exciting, but because no other way is possible, then you can even experience defeat, total defeat, such as a socialist of my generation has known, without any loss of commitment" (*PL* 411).

Like many critics today, I am prone to nihilistic speculation when confronted with the realities of climate violence, neoliberal privatization, structural oppression, and other capitalist modes of organization. In Williams's resolve and commitment, I find the intellectual optimism that I need to carry on with others.

NOTES

1. The phrase "all that is solid melts into air" appears, of course, in chapter 1 of Marx and Engels's *Manifesto of the Communist Party* to describe the drastic changes wrought by the bourgeois to everyday life and social structures. The phrase is the title, as well, of Marshall Berman's classic book about modernization and cultural transformation.

2. Marc Steinberg, *The Platform Economy: How Japan Transformed the Consumer Internet*. (Minneapolis: University of Minnesota Press, 2019), 5.

3. Ibid., 22.

4. I refer here to Jameson and Mulvey as influential yet representative of theoretically informed approaches to popular culture. This is not meant to be exhaustive of such approaches, but only to gesture toward a comparison between Marxist cultural studies in the UK tradition, articulated by figures like Raymond Williams and Stuart Hall, and cultural studies in the US tradition. Those connections and differences are, of course, varied.

5. For accounts of platform economic organization, see Nick Srnicek, *Platform Capitalism*. (Malden, MA: Polity, 2017); and Steinberg, *Platform Economy*.

6. Steinberg, *Platform Economy*, 15.

7. McKenzie Wark, *Capital Is Dead: Is This Something Worse?* (New York: Verso, 2019), 5.

8. While mentioned earlier in the volume as well, Williams's emphasis on the "necessary complexity" of socialist organization concludes *Politics and Letters*, thus reinforcing its importance in Williams's politics, as well as his methodology.

9. For an account of the ways in which automation is a "spontaneous discourse of capitalist societies, which, for a mixture of structural and contingent reasons, reappears in those societies time and again as a way of thinking through their limits," see Aaron Benanav, "Automation and the Future of Work—1." *New Left Review* 119 (September/October 2019): 11–12. Thanks to Paul Stasi for this reference.

10. See Aaron Benanav, "Automation and the Future of Work—2." *New Left Review* 120 (November/December 2019): 136.

11. Lane Relyea, *Your Everyday Art World*. (Cambridge, MA: MIT Press, 2013), 5.

12. Ibid., 10.

13. Michael D. Smith, and Rahul Telang, *Streaming, Sharing, Stealing: Big Data and the Future of Entertainment* (Cambridge, MA: MIT Press, 2016), 8.

14. Linda Williams, *On "The Wire,"* (Durham, NC: Duke University Press, 2014), 133.

15. For versions of the argument about *The Wire* and other TV dramas as realist fiction, see Noah Berlatsky, "'The Wire' Was Really a Victorian Novel," *The Atlantic*, September 10, 2012,https://www.theatlantic.com/entertainment/archive/2012/09/the-wire-was-really-a-victorian-novel/261164/; Walter Benn Michaels, "The Un-usable Past," *The Baffler*, no. 18 (January 2010),https://thebaffler.com/salvos/the-un-usable-past; Julian Murphet, *"The Wire*

and Realism," *Sydney Studies in English* 36 (2010): 52–76. For especially attuned readings of *The Wire* and realism in relation to contemporary capitalism, see Anmol Chadda and William Julius Wilson, "'Way Down in the Hole': Systemic Urban Inequality and *The Wire*," *Critical Inquiry* 38, no. 1 (Autumn 2011): 164–88; and Leigh Clare La Berge, "Capitalist Realism and Serial Form: The Fifth Season of *The Wire*," *Criticism* 52, no. 3/4 (Summer/Fall 2010): 547–67. I owe thanks to Paul Stasi for making this connection and referring me to this passage.

17. Christian Lander, "#85 The Wire," *Stuff White People Like*, March 9, 2008,https://stuffwhitepeoplelike.com/2008/03/09/85-the-wire/.

18. "The Boys of Summer," *The Wire*, season 4, episode 1, HBO, September 4, 2006,https://www.hbo.com/. Transcript adapted from "The Wire (2002–2008): Season 4, Episode 1—Boys of Summer—Full Transcript," https://subslikescript.com/series/The_Wire-306414/season-4/episode-1-Boys_of_Summer. Snoop is played by Felicia Pearson, and the clerk is played by Paul L. Nolan.

19. Indeed, *The Wire*'s authenticity was trumpeted in news reports that profiled actors like Felicia Pearson, who plays Snoop. As the *New York Times* reported, "The 26-year-old Ms. Pearson has lived the kind of hard life embodied by her character," thus cementing the connection between *The Wire* and the actually existing communities that the television show represents. See Walter Dawkins, "An Actress's Hard Life Feeds 'Wire' Character," *New York Times*, October 21, 2006,https://www.nytimes.com/2006/10/21/arts/television/21wire.html.

20. "The Boys of Summer."

21. Each season of *The Wire* uses a different version of the song "Way Down in the Hole," written by Tom Waits. For a reading of how this song and the series' use of multiple versions evoke traditions of Black spiritualism, see James Braxton Peterson, *The Hip-Hop Underground and African-American Culture: Beneath the Surface* (New York: Palgrave Macmillan, 2014).

22. For accounts of reality television's imbrication in late capitalism, see Anna McCarthy, "Reality Television: A Neoliberal Theater of Suffering," *Social Text* 25, no. 4 (Winter 2007): 17–42; and Laurie Ouellette and James Hay, *Better Living through Reality TV: Television and Post-Welfare Citizenship* (Malden, MA: Blackwell, 2008).

23. Michael Dibb, dir., *The Country and the City*, BBC, 1979,https://www.mikesouthon.biz/portfolio/the-country-and-the-city01title1. For a discussion of this documentary program with Edward Said, whose *Orientalism* was also the subject of a documentary titled *The Shadow of the West*, see "Media, Margins, and Modernity" (*PM* 177–97).

24. Marshall McLuhan, *Understanding Media: The Extensions of Man* (New York: McGraw Hill, 1964), 25.

25. Wendy Hui Kyong Chun, *Updating to Remain the Same: Habitual New Media* (Cambridge, MA: MIT Press, 2016), 13.

26. Ibid., 18.

Bibliography

Acocella, Joan. "Arundhati Roy Returns to Fiction, in Fury." *The New Yorker*, June 5 & 12, 2017.

Adejunmobi, Moradewun. "African Writing and the Forms of Publicness." Keynote lecture at the Small Magazines, Literary Networks and Self-Fashioning in Africa and Its Diasporas conference, January 19, 2018. Bristol, United Kingdom.

Adesokan, Akin. "New African Writing and the Question of Audience." *Research in African Literatures* 43, no. 3 (2012): 1–20.

Alavi, Hamza. "India and the Colonial Mode of Production." *Economic and Political Weekly* 10, no. 33/35 (1975): 1235–62.

Allison, Mark. "Politics." *Victorian Literature and Culture* 46, no. 3/4 (2018): 806–9.

Althusser, Louis. *Lenin and Philosophy and Other Essays.* Translated by Ben Brewster. New York: Monthly Review, 2001.

Anderson, Perry. *Considerations on Western Marxism.* London: Verso, 1976.

———. "The Missing Text: Introduction to 'The Future of Marxism.'" *New Left Review* 1, no. 114 (2018): 33–51.

———. "Socialism and Pseudo-Empiricism." *New Left Review* 1, no. 35 (1966): 2–42.

Auerbach, Erich. *Mimesis: The Representation of Reality in Western Literature.* Translated by Willard R. Trask. 1946. Reprint, Princeton, NJ: Princeton University Press, 2003.

Bahro, Rudolf. *The Alternative in Eastern Europe.* Translated by David Fernbach. London: Verso, 1981.

Baldick, Chris. *The Social Mission of English Criticism, 1848–1932.* Oxford: Oxford University Press, 1983.

Barron, Alex. "William Gibson on the End of the Future." *The New Yorker Radio Hour*, March 6, 2020. https://www.wnycstudios.org/podcasts/tnyradiohour/segments/william-gibson-end-future.

Bauman, Zygmunt, *Liquid Modernity*. Cambridge, UK: Polity Press, 2000.

Benanav, Aaron. "Automation and the Future of Work—1." *New Left Review* 119 (September/October 2019): 5–38.

———. "Automation and the Future of Work—2." *New Left Review* 120 (November/December 2019): 117–46.

Berlant, Lauren. *Cruel Optimism.* Durham, NC: Duke University Press, 2011.

Berlatsky, Noah. "'The Wire' Was Really a Victorian Novel." *The Atlantic*, September 10, 2012. https://www.theatlantic.com/entertainment/archive/2012/09/the-wire-was-really-a-victorian-novel/261164/

Berman, Marshall. *All That Is Solid Melts into Air: The Experience of Modernity.* New York: Penguin, 1988.

Blackledge, Paul. "Practical Materialism: Engels's *Anti-Dühring* as Marxist Philosophy." *Critique* 45, no. 4 (2017): 483–99.

Bloch, Ernst. *The Principle of Hope*. Vol. 1. Translated by Neville Plaice, Stephen Plaice, and Paul Knight. Cambridge, MA: MIT Press, 1986.

Bottomore, Tom, ed. *A Dictionary of Marxist Thought*. 2nd ed. Oxford: Blackwell, 1991.

Bourdieu, Pierre, *The Field of Cultural Production*. Cambridge, UK: Polity Press, 1993.

"The Boys of Summer." *The Wire*, season 4, episode 1, HBO, September 4, 2006. https://www.hbo.com/.

Brantlinger, Patrick. *Crusoe's Footprints: Cultural Studies in Britain and America*. New York: Routledge, 1990.

Brouillette, Sarah. "On the African Literary Hustle." *Blindfield Journal*, August 14, 2017. Accessed May 31, 2020. https://blindfieldjournal.com/2017/08/14/on-the-african-literary-hustle/.

———. *Postcolonial Writers in the Global Literary Marketplace*. Houndsmills, Basingstoke, UK: Palgrave Macmillan, 2007.

Carmody, Pádraig. *The New Scramble for Africa*. 2nd ed. Cambridge, UK: Polity Press, 2016.

Casanova, Pascale. *The World Republic of Letters*. Cambridge, MA: Harvard University Press, 2004.

Chadda, Anmol, and William Julius Wilson. "'Way Down in the Hole': Systemic Urban Inequality and *The Wire*." *Critical Inquiry* 38, no. 1 (Autumn 2011): 164–88.

Chun, Wendy Hui Kyong. *Updating to Remain the Same: Habitual New Media*. Cambridge, MA: MIT Press, 2016.

Clark, T. J. "For a Left with No Future." *New Left Review* 74 (March/April 2012): 53–75.

Coleridge, Samuel Taylor. *Biographia Literaria : Or, Biographical Sketches of My Literary Life and Opinions*. Edited by James Engell and W. Jackson Bate. Princeton, NJ: Princeton University Press, 1983.

Collini, Stefan. "From 'Non-Fiction Prose' to 'Cultural Criticism': Genre and Disciplinarity in Victorian Studies." In *Rethinking Victorian Culture*, edited by Juliet John and Alice Jenkins, 13–28. Houndsmills, Basingstoke, UK: MacMillan, 2000.

Connor, Steven. "Raymond Williams's Time." In *Raymond Williams Now: Knowledge, Limits and the Future*, edited by Jeff Wallace, Rod Jones, and Sophie Nield, 164–80. Houndsmills, Basingstoke, UK: Palgrave Macmillan, 1997.

Dawkins, Walter. "An Actress's Hard Life Feeds 'Wire' Character." *New York Times*, October 21, 2006. https://www.nytimes.com/2006/10/21/arts/television/21wire.html.

Dibb, Michael, dir. *The Country and the City*. BBC, 1979. https://www.mikesouthon.biz/portfolio/the-country-and-the-city01title1.

Dix, Hywel. *After Raymond Williams: Cultural Materialism and the Break-Up of Britain*. Cardiff, UK: University of Wales Press, 2008.

Eagleton, Terry. "Criticism and Politics: The Work of Raymond Williams." *New Left Review* 1, no. 95 (January/February 1976): 3–23.

Edgley, Roy. "Dialectical Materialism." In *A Dictionary of Marxist Thought*, 2nd ed., edited by Tom Bottomore, 142–43. Oxford: Blackwell, 1991.

Eliot, T. S. *Selected Essays*. London: Faber, 1932.

Engels, Frederick. *Anti-Dühring: Herr Eugen Dühring's Revolution in Science*. Translated by Emile Burns. In *Karl Marx and Fredrick Engels Collected Works*, vol. 25, 1–309. New York: International Publishers, 1987.

———. *Dialectics of Nature*. Translated by Clemens Dutt. In *Karl Marx and Frederick Engels Collected Works*, vol. 25, 311–588. New York: International Publishers, 1987.

Evans, Diana. "Stay with Me by Ayòbámi Adébáyò Review—a Big-Hearted Nigerian Debut." *The Guardian*, March 9, 2017. https://www.theguardian.com/books/2017/mar/09/stay-with-me-by-ayobami-adebayo-review.

Felicelli, Anita. "Outside Language and Power: The Mastery of Arundhati Roy's 'The Ministry of Utmost Happiness.'" *Los Angeles Review of Books*, June 21, 2017.

Foster, John Bellamy. "The Dialectics of Nature and Marxist Ecology." In *The Ecological Rift: Capitalism's War on the Earth*, by John Bellamy Foster, Brett Clark, and Richard York, 215–48. New York: Monthly Review Press, 2010.

———. *Marx's Ecology: Materialism and Nature*. New York: Monthly Review, 2000.

———. "Marx's Open-Ended Critique." *Monthly Review* 70, no.1 (2018): 1–16.

———. *The Return of Nature: Socialism and Ecology*. New York: Monthly Review, 2020.

Foster, John Bellamy, and Paul Burkett. *Marx and the Earth: An Anti-Critique*. Chicago: Haymarket Books, 2017.

Gallagher, Catherine, and Stephen Greenblatt. *Practicing New Historicism*. Chicago: University of Chicago Press, 2000.

Galloway, Alexander R., Eugene Thacker, and McKenzie Wark. "Introduction: Execrable Media." In *Excommunication: Three Inquiries in Media and Mediation*, 1–24. Chicago: University of Chicago Press, 2014.

Ghosh, Amitav. *The Great Derangement: Climate Change and the Unthinkable*. New York: Penguin Books, 2016.

Gibson, William. @greatdismal. January 14, 2020, 7:06 p.m. https://twitter.com/GreatDismal/status/1217221448038637568.

Gilroy, Paul. *There Ain't No Black in the Union Jack*. 1987. Reprint, Abingdon, UK: Routledge, 2002.

Gramsci, Antonio. *Selections from the Prison Notebooks*. Edited and translated by Quintin Hoare and Geoffrey Nowell Smith. New York: International Publishers, 1971.

Grossberg, Lawrence. "Raymond Williams and the Absent Modernity." In *About Raymond Williams*, edited by Monika Seidl, Roman Horak, and Lawrence Grossberg, 18–33. London: Routledge, 2010.

Grusin, Richard. "Radical Mediation." *Critical Inquiry* 42, no. 1 (Autumn 2015): 124–48.

Guillory, John. "Genesis of the Media Concept." *Critical Inquiry* 36, no. 2 (Winter 2010): 321–62.

Hall, Stuart. *The Hard Road to Renewal: Thatcherism and the Crisis of the Left*. London: Verso, 1988.

Hartley, Daniel. "Combined and Uneven Styles in the Modern World-System: Stylistic Ideology in José de Alencar, Machado de Assis, and Thomas Hardy." *European Journal of English Studies* 20, no. 3 (2016): 222–35.

———. "On Raymond Williams: Complexity, Immanence, and the Long Revolution." *Mediations* 30, no. 1 (Fall 2016): 39–60.

———. *The Politics of Style: Towards a Marxist Poetics*. Chicago: Haymarket Books, 2017.

Hawley, John C. "Biafra as Heritage and Symbol: Adichie, Mbachu, and Iweala." *Research in African Literatures* 39, no. 2 (2008): 15–26.

Hechter, Michael. *Internal Colonialism: The Celtic Fringe in British National Development, 1536–1960*. London: Routledge, 1998.

Higgins, John. *Raymond Williams: Literature, Marxism and Cultural Materialism*. London: Routledge, 1999.

Hilliard, Christopher. *English as a Vocation: The "Scrutiny" Movement*. Oxford: Oxford University Press, 2012.

Huehls, Mitchum, and Rachel Greenwald Smith. "Four Phases of Neoliberalism and Literature: An Introduction." In *Neoliberalism and Contemporary Literary Culture*, edited by Mitchum Huehls and Rachel Greenwald Smith, 1–20. Baltimore: Johns Hopkins University Press, 2017.

Huggan, Graham. *The Postcolonial Exotic: Marketing the Margins*. London: Routledge, 2001.

Jacoby, Russell. "Western Marxism." In *A Dictionary of Marxist Thought*, 2nd ed., edited by Tom Bottomore, 581–84. Oxford: Blackwell, 1991.

Jameson, Fredric. *Signatures of the Visible*. New York: Routledge, 1990.

Jones, Paul. *Raymond Williams's Sociology of Culture: A Critical Reconstruction*. Houndsmills, Basingstoke, UK: Palgrave Macmillan, 2004.

Kakutani, Michiko. "Portrait of a Nigerian Marriage in a Heartbreaking Debut Novel." *New York Times*. July 24, 2017. https://www.nytimes.com/2017/07/24/books/review-ayobami-adebayo-stay-with-me.html.

Kiguru, Doseline. "Prizing African Literature: Creating a Literary Taste." *Social Dynamics* 42, no. 1 (2016): 161–74.

———. "Literary Prizes, Writers' Organisations and Canon Formation in Africa." *African Studies* 75, no. 2 (2016): 202–14.

Krishnan, Madhu. *Contingent Canons: African Literature and the Politics of Location.* Cambridge: Cambridge University Press, 2018.

La Berge, Leigh Clare. "Capitalist Realism and Serial Form: The Fifth Season of *The Wire*." *Criticism* 52, no. 3/4 (Summer/Fall 2010): 547–67.

Lahiri, Oeendrila. "'The Ministry of Utmost Happiness' Is Timely, but Not Deserving of the Booker." *The Wire*, September 1, 2017.

Lakatos, Imre. *The Methodology of Scientific Research Programmes.* Vol. 1. Edited by John Worrall and Gregory Currie. Cambridge: Cambridge University Press, 1978.

Lander, Christian. "#85 The Wire." *Stuff White People Like*, March 9, 2008. https://stuffwhitepeoplelike.com/2008/03/09/85-the-wire/.

Leavis, Frank Raymond. *The Great Tradition: George Eliot, Henry James, Joseph Conrad.* London: Chatto & Windus, 1948.

Leys, Ruth. *Utopia as Method: The Imaginary Reconstitution of Society.* Houndsmills, Basingstoke, UK: Palgrave Macmillan, 2013.

Lukács, Georg. *The Historical Novel.* Translated by Hannah Mitchell and Stanley Mitchell. Middlesex: Penguin Books, 1961.

Marx, Karl. *A Contribution to the Critique of Political Economy.* Translated by S. W. Ryazanskaya. Marxists.org.

———. *Grundrisse.* Translated by Martin Nicolaus. New York: Penguin Books, 1973.

Marx, Karl, and Friedrich Engels. *The German Ideology.* Amherst, NY: Prometheus Books, 1998.

———. *Manifesto of the Communist Party.* 1848. *Marxists Internet Archive.* https://www.marxists.org/archive/marx/works/1848/communist-manifesto/index.htm.

Massey, Doreen, *Space, Place and Gender.* Cambridge, UK: Polity Press, 1994.

McCarthy, Anna. "Reality Television: A Neoliberal Theater of Suffering." *Social Text* 25, no. 4 (Winter 2007): 17–42.

McLuhan, Marshall. *Understanding Media: The Extensions of Man.* New York: McGraw Hill, 1964.

Medvedev, Roy A. "Stalin and Linguistics: An Episode from the History of Soviet Science." In *The Unknown Stalin*, by Zhores A. Medvedev and Roy A. Medvedev, translated by Ellen Dahrendorf, 200–209. London: I. B. Tauris, 2003.

Mendes, Ana Cristina, and Lisa Lau. "The Precarious Lives of India's Others: The Creativity of Precarity in Arundhati Roy's *The Ministry of Utmost Happiness*." *Journal of Postcolonial Writing* 56, no. 1 (2020): 70–82.

Michaels, Walter Benn. "The Un-usable Past." *The Baffler*, no. 18 (January 2010). https://thebaffler.com/salvos/the-un-usable-past.

Milner, Andrew, ed. *Re-Imagining Cultural Studies: The Promise of Cultural Materialism.* London, SAGE, 2002.

———. *Tenses of Imagination: Raymond Williams on Science Fiction, Utopia and Dystopia.* Oxford: Peter Lang, 2010.

Moretti, Franco. *The Way of the World: The "Bildungsroman" in European Culture.* Translated by Albert Sbragia. New York: Verso, 1987.

Mulhern, Francis. "Critical Revolutions." *New Left Review*, no. 110 (2018): 39–54.

———. *The Moment of "Scrutiny."* London: New Left Books, 1979.

———. "Towards 2000, or News from You-Know-Where." In *Raymond Williams: Critical Perspectives*, edited by Terry Eagleton, 67–94. Boston: Northeastern University Press, 1989.

Mulvey, Laura. *Visual and Other Pleasures.* Bloomington: Indiana University Press, 1989.

Murphet, Julian. "*The Wire* and Realism." *Sydney Studies in English* 36 (2010): 52–76.

Ngai, Sianne. *Ugly Feelings.* Cambridge, MA: Harvard University Press, 2005.

Nilges, Mathias. *How to Read a Moment: The American Novel and the Crisis of the Present.* Evanston, IL: Northwestern University Press, 2021.

———. *Right-Wing Culture in Contemporary Capitalism: Regression and Hope in a Time without Future.* London: Bloomsbury, 2019.

North, Joseph. *Literary Criticism: A Concise Political History.* Cambridge, MA: Harvard University Press, 2017.

———. "Two Paragraphs in Raymond Williams: A Reply to Francis Mulhern." *New Left Review*, no. 116/117 (2019): 161–87.

Ouellette, Laurie, and James Hay. *Better Living through Reality TV: Television and Post-Welfare Citizenship.* Malden, MA: Blackwell, 2008.

Parrinder, Patrick. "*Culture and Society* in the 1980s." In Patrick Parrinder. *The Failure of Theory*, 58–71. Brighton, Sussex, UK: Harvester Press, 1987.

———. *The Failure of Theory: Essays on Criticism and Contemporary Fiction.* Brighton, Sussex, UK: Harvester Press, 1987.

———. "On Disagreement and the Public Domain." In *The Failure of Theory*, 39–57. Brighton, Sussex, UK: Harvester Press, 1987.

———. "Utopia and Negativity in Raymond Williams." In *The Failure of Theory*, 72–84. Brighton, Sussex, UK: Harvester Press, 1987.

Peterson, James Braxton. *The Hip-Hop Underground and African-American Culture: Beneath the Surface.* New York: Palgrave Macmillan, 2014.

Pinkney, Tom. "Raymond Williams." In *A Dictionary of Marxist Thought*, 2nd ed., edited by Tom Bottomore, 584–85. Oxford: Blackwell, 1991.

Prendergast, Christopher. "Nation/*Natio*: Raymond Williams and 'The Culture of Nations.'" *Intermédialités/Intermediality* 1 (2003): 123–38.

Reed, Touré. *Toward Freedom: The Case against Race Reductionism.* London: Verso, 2020.

Relyea, Lane. *Your Everyday Art World.* Cambridge, MA: MIT Press, 2013.

Roy, Arundhati. *The Ministry of Utmost Happiness* (*M*). New York: Vintage, 2017.

Ryan, Dermot. "Review of Joseph North's *Literary Criticism: A Concise Political History*." *boundary 2*, January 29, 2018.

Sacristán, Manuel. *The Marxism of Manuel Sacristán: From Communism to the New Social Movements.* Translated and edited by Renzo Llorente. Chicago: Haymarket Books, 2015.

Samuelson, Robert J. "Losing Faith in the Future?" *RealClear Politics.* September 18, 2018. https://www.realclearpolitics.com/articles/2018/09/18/losing_faith_in_the_future_138105.html.

Seaton, Lola. "Ends of Criticism." *New Left Review*, no. 119 (2019): 105–32.

Sehgal, Parul. "Arundhati Roy's Fascinating Mess." *The Atlantic*, July/August, 2017.

Simpson, David. "Raymond Williams: Feeling for Structures, Voicing 'History.'" *Social Text*, no. 30 (1992): 9–26.

Smith, Michael D., and Rahul Telang, *Streaming, Sharing, Stealing: Big Data and the Future of Entertainment.* Cambridge, MA: MIT Press, 2016.

Smith, Neil. "Homeless/Global: Scaling Places." In *Mapping the Futures: Local Cultures, Global Change*, edited by John Bird, Barry Curtis, Tim Putnam, and Lisa Tickner, 87–120. London: Routledge, 1993.

Spence, Lester K. *Knocking the Hustle: Against the Neoliberal Turn in Black Politics.* New York: Punctum Books, 2015.

Srnicek, Nick. *Platform Capitalism.* Malden, MA: Polity, 2017.

Stalin, J. V. *Marxism and the Problem of Linguistics.* Marxists.org. https://www.marxists.org/reference/archive/stalin/works/1950/jun/20.htm.

Steinberg, Marc. *The Platform Economy: How Japan Transformed the Consumer Internet.* Minneapolis: University of Minnesota Press, 2019.

Strauhs, Doreen. *African Literary NGOs: Power, Politics, and Participation.* Houndsmills, Basingstoke, UK: Palgrave Macmillan, 2013.

Tacitus, *Agricola and Germany.* Translated by Anthony R. Birley. Oxford: Oxford University Press, 1999.

Thompson, E. P. "The Long Revolution I." *New Left Review* 1, no. 9 (1961): 24–33.

———. "The Long Revolution II." *New Left Review* 1, no. 10 (1961): 34–39.

———. "Romanticism, Moralism, and Utopianism: The Case of William Morris," *New Left Review* 1/99 (1976): 83–111.

Timpanaro, Sebastiano. *On Materialism.* Translated by Lawrence Garner. London: Verso, 1980.

Wallace, Jeff, Rod Jones, and Sophie Nield, eds. *Raymond Williams Now: Knowledge, Limits and the Future*. Houndsmills, Basingstoke, UK: Palgrave Macmillan, 1997.

Wallis, Kate, "Exchanges in Nairobi and Lagos: Mapping Literary Networks and World Literary Space." *Research in African Literatures* 49, no. 1 (2018): 163–86.

Wark, McKenzie. *Capital Is Dead: Is This Something Worse?* New York: Verso, 2019.

Williams, Chris. "Problematizing Wales: An Exploration in Historiography and Postcoloniality." In *Postcolonial Wales*, edited by Jane Aaron and Chris Williams, 3–22. Cardiff, UK: University of Wales Press, 2005.

Williams, Daniel. Introduction to *Who Speaks for Wales?* by Raymond Williams, xv–liii. Edited by Daniel Williams. Cardiff, UK: University of Wales Press, 2003.

———. *Wales Unchained: Literature, Politics and Identity in the American Century*. Cardiff, UK: University of Wales Press, 2015.

Williams, Linda. *On "The Wire."* Durham, NC: Duke University Press, 2014.

Williams, Raymond. "Base and Superstructure in Marxist Cultural Theory" ("BSS") *New Left Review* 1, no. 82 (November/December 1973): 3–16.

———. *Border Country (BC)*. Cardigan, Wales, UK: Parthian Books, 2006.

———. *Communications (C)*. Rev. ed. London: Penguin, 1970.

———. *The Country and the City (CC)*. Oxford: Oxford University Press, 1985.

———. *Culture and Materialism: Selected Essays (CM)*. London: Verso, 2005.

———. *Culture and Society: 1780–1950 (CS)*. New York: Columbia University Press, 1983.

———. *Drama from Ibsen to Brecht (D)*. 2nd rev. ed. 1968. Harmondsworth, UK: Penguin Books, 1973.

———. *Drama in Performance*. 1954. Reprint, Milton Keynes, UK: Open University Press, 1991.

———. *The English Novel from Dickens to Lawrence (EN)*. London: Chatto & Windus, 1973.

———. "The Future of Marxism" ("FM"). *New Left Review* 114 (November/December 2018): 53–61.

———. "The Idea of Culture" ("IC"). In *Border Country: Raymond Williams in Adult Education*, edited by John McIlroy and Sallie Westwood, 57–88. Leicester, UK: National Institute of Adult Continuing Education, 1993.

———. *Keywords: A Vocabulary of Culture and Society (K)*. Oxford: Oxford University Press, 1985.

———. "A Lecture on Realism" ("LR"). *Screen* 18, no. 1 (Spring 1977): 61–74.

———. *The Long Revolution (LR)*. Cardigan, Wales, UK: Parthian Books, 2013.

———. *Marxism and Literature (ML)*. Oxford: Oxford University Press, 1977.

———. *Modern Tragedy (MT)*. Rev. ed. London: Verso, 1979.

———. *Politics and Letters: Interviews with "New Left Review" (PL)*. London: Verso, 2015.

———. *The Politics of Modernism: Against the New Conformists (PM)*. London: Verso, 2007.

———. Postscript in *Culture and Society: 1780–1950*, 325–26. Harmondsworth, UK: Penguin, 1963.

———. Preface in *The Year 2000*, ix-xiii. New York: Pantheon Books, 1983.

———. *Preface to Film (PF)*. With Michael Orrom. London: Film Drama Limited, 1954.

———. *Problems in Materialism and Culture (PMC)*. London: Verso, 1980.

———. *Raymond Williams on Television: Selected Writings (RWT)*. New York: Routledge Classics, 1989.

———. "Realism and the Contemporary Novel," *Universities & Left Review* 1, no. 4 (1958): 22–25.

———. *Resources of Hope: Culture, Democracy, Socialism (RH)*. Edited by Robin Gable. London: Verso 1989.

———. *The Sociology of Culture (SC)*. Chicago: University of Chicago Press, 1995.

———. *Television: Technology and Cultural Form (TV)*. New York: Routledge Classics, 2003.

———. *Tenses of the Imagination: Raymond Williams on Science Fiction, Utopia, and Dystopia*, edited by Andrew Milner. New York: Peter Lang, 2010

———. *Towards 2000 (T)*. 1983. Reprint, Harmondsworth, UK: Penguin, 1985).

———. *What I Came to Say (W)*. London: Hutchinson Radius, 1989.

———. *Who Speaks for Wales?* Edited by Daniel Williams. Cardiff, UK: University of Wales Press, 2003.

———. *Writing in Society* (*WS*). London: Verso, 1991.

Wordsworth, William. *Selected Poems*. Edited by John O. Hayden. London: Penguin, 1994.

Zimbler, Jarad, Ben Etherington, and Rachel Bower. "Crafts of World Literature: Field, Material and Translation." *The Journal of Commonwealth Literature* 49, no. 3 (2014): 273–78.

Index

About the Contributors

Mark Allison is an associate professor and chair of the Department of English at Ohio Wesleyan University. He has published essays on Matthew Arnold, Thomas Carlyle, George Eliot, and the neglected Chartist poet Capel Lofft, among others. He contributed the entry on "Politics" to *Victorian Literature and Culture*'s special "Keywords" issue. His monograph, *Imagining Socialism: Aesthetics, Anti-Politics, and Literature in Britain, 1817–1918*, is forthcoming.

Daniel Hartley is an assistant professor in world literatures in English at Durham University. He is the author of *The Politics of Style: Towards a Marxist Poetics* (2017) and has published widely on Marxist theory and contemporary literature.

Anna Kornbluh is a professor of English at the University of Illinois at Chicago, where her research and teaching center on the novel and theory, especially formalism, Marxism, and psychoanalysis. She is the author of *The Order of Forms: Realism, Formalism, and Social Space* (2019), *Marxist Film Theory and Fight Club* (2019), and *Realizing Capital* (2014), and the founding facilitator for the V21 Collective (Victorian studies for the twenty-first century) and InterCcECT (The Inter Chicago Circle for Experimental Critical Theory).

Madhu Krishnan is a professor of African, world and comparative literatures at the University of Bristol. She is the author of *Contemporary African Literature in English: Global Locations, Postcolonial Identifications* (2014), *Writing Spatiality in West Africa: Colonial Legacies in the Anglophone/Francophone Novel* (2018), and *Contingent Canons: African Literature and* *the Politics of Location* (2018). She is currently working on a project around literary activism in twenty-first century Africa.

Thomas A. Laughlin has a PhD in English literature from the University of Toronto. He currently works as a contract instructor at multiple university campuses in southern Ontario.

Mathias Nilges is a professor of English at St. Francis Xavier University, Canada. He is the author of *Right-Wing Culture in Contemporary Capitalism: Regression and Hope in a Time without Future* (2019) and *How to Read a Moment: The American Novel and the Crisis of the Present* (2021). He has co-edited the books *Literary Materialisms* (2013), *Marxism and the Critique of Value* (2014), *The Contemporaneity of Modernism* (2016), *Literature and the Global Contemporary* (2017), and *William Gibson and the Futures of Contemporary Culture* (2021).

Paul Stasi teaches twentieth-century Anglophone literature at the University at Albany where he is an associate professor. He is the author of *Modernism, Imperialism, and the Historical Sense* (2012), the co-editor (with Jennifer Greiman) of *The Last Western: "Deadwood" and the End of American Empire* (2013), and the co-editor (with Josephine Park) of *Ezra Pound in the Present: New Essays on Pound's Contemporaneity* (2016).

Daniel Worden is associate professor in the School of Individualized Study and the Department of English at the Rochester Institute of Technology. He is the author of *Masculine Style: The American West and Literary Modernism* and *Neoliberal Nonfictions: The Documentary Aesthetic of Our Age* and the editor or co-editor of *The Comics of Joe Sacco: Journalism in a Visual World*, *Oil Culture*, and *Postmodern/Postwar & After: Rethinking American Literature*.

www.ingramcontent.com/pod-product-compliance
Lightning Source LLC
Chambersburg PA
CBHW070242290326
41929CB00046B/2336